The Evolution of Shakespeare's Comedy

The Evolution of Shakespeare's Comedy

A Study in Dramatic Perspective

Larry S. Champion

Harvard University Press   Cambridge, Massachusetts

Portions of this study in somewhat different form have appeared previously
in *Genre* ("The Perspective of Comedy: Shakespeare's Pointers in *Twelfth
Night*," I [1968], 269-289), and *Papers on Language and Literature* ("A
Midsummer-Night's Dream: The Problem of Source," IV [1968], 13-19).
Permission to reprint this material is gratefully acknowledged.

For My Parents

And for Nancy, Katherine, and Becky

Contents

The Evolution of Shakespeare's Comedy

"The poet's pen turns them to shapes"

1 Introduction

In his study of Shakespearean comedy, John Russell Brown observes that an Elizabethan dramatist "could choose between two basic comic forms, intrigue comedy and narrative comedy. In the broadest terms, the former may be said to have aimed at making a certain number of characters look ridiculous, the latter to have aimed at telling a story."[1] *The Comedy of Errors, The Taming of the Shrew,* and *The Merry Wives of Windsor* he describes as intrigue comedies and the remaining fourteen as experiments "to find a comic form which would present several characters or groups of characters in relation and contrast with each other and which would conclude in a scene which brought these various elements into some stable relationship."[2] The comments are significant in their typicality. For, although there may be disagreement concerning the classification of an individual play, there is no question of the general nature of Shakespeare's comic work. Both Muriel C. Bradbrook[3] and Alfred Harbage,[4] for example, describe Shakespeare's involvement in the romantic-narrative tradition of Renaissance English comedy as opposed to the satiric tradition. Neville Coghill[5] speaks specifically of a Donatan-Jonsonian type of comedy as opposed to a Shakespearean-Medieval type, and O. J. Campbell[6] concentrates on what he admits to be Shakespeare's occasional venture into satire and the private stage tradition.

Understandably, then, much critical concern has focused on the narrative or the theme of Shakespeare's work. H. B. Charlton describes the popular tradition of Elizabethan comedy as an "attempt to gratify a world-old sense of the comic or ludicrous at the same time as a new sensibility for the romantic. [In Shakespeare, love] takes its place . . . as the recognised presiding genius. It was the touchstone by which fine spirits were struck to their finest issues. It was also, of course, a test by which weaker mortals revealed their weaknesses, grosser ones their grossness, and foolish ones their folly."[7] The observation is not unlike those of other recent studies of Shakespearean comedy. Thomas M. Parrott, E. C. Pettet, S. K. Sen Gupta, John Vyvyan, and P. G. Phialas are interested, if not in precisely the same way, in Shakespeare's attempts to adapt the "world of romance to the service of comedy" through the "interplay of attitudes toward love [leading to] . . . a judicious or sensible attitude."[8] E. M. W. Tillyard, J. Dover Wilson, G. Wilson Knight, and Robert G. Hunter, among others, describe the growing problems of love in the dark and late comedies, which set forth the themes of mercy and justice, repentance and forgiveness.

To be sure, several studies have analyzed structural aspects of Shakespeare's comedies, usually from a specific point of view. Janet Spens[9] and Northrop Frye[10] connect Shakespeare's comedy with the mythos of Spring; insight into the structure is gained by recalling the ritual forms preceding drama—the period of preparation, the period of license and confusion, and the period of festivity itself. By analogy, comic structure normally begins with an anticomic society, a social organization blocking and opposed to the comic drive, which the action of the comedy evades or overcomes.[11] Perhaps the most exhaustive interpretation of structure through folk festival is that of C. L. Barber, who describes the manner in which Shakespeare "shapes the narrative through events to put its persons in the position of festive holiday celebrants."[12] From a different perspective, T. W. Baldwin has stressed the academic pattern of Shakespeare's early comedies and their close structural similarities with John Lyly's works.[13] Bertrand Evans deals convincingly with one aspect of comic structure—dramatic irony or levels of discrepant awareness, the way in which Shakespeare keeps the audience informed of what is hidden from some or all the characters on the stage.[14] And, of course, various individual plays have been effectively examined at length.

The best of these studies make it clear that the creative milieu for the professional playwright of the period was in every sense a popular one, not an academic, intellectualized product of a mythical English Academy. The English popular drama of Shakespeare's day, in other words, reflects the diversity of dramatic motifs and devices which time and custom had proved to be effective in provoking a successful response from the spectators. Consequently, we observe the romantic reunion of the aged parents Aegeon and Aemilia in

The Comedy of Errors alongside the Menandrine exploits of mistaken identity and clever servants. And, as Barber comments, "*Twelfth Night* puts together a tale from romance, Plautine farce, festivity, and the sort of merry sport or 'practice' which Shakespeare customarily added from his own invention."[15]

The essential flavor of Shakespearean comedy can thus be variously described. One observer might speak of the maneuvering of a young man toward a young woman which concludes with the bliss of matrimony and of a story in which the characters exist only to serve the predetermined narrative ends. To another, the emphasis appears to be on the release of characters who are in some kind of mental bondage, slaves to a self-imposed pattern of behavior. Still another will note Shakespeare's primary reflection through comedy of "the triumph of life over the waste land, the death and revival of the year impersonated by figures still human, and once again divine as well."[16] In short, it is helpful indeed to proclaim that Shakespeare was faced with "the alternatives of the Italian tradition, with all its prestige and its ready models, or the shapeless native popular play, in which material designed for narrative was struggling to accommodate itself to dramatic form."[17] But it is misleading to assume that for Shakespeare the avenues were mutually exclusive.

The more significant point is that from these diverse strains Shakespeare gradually was to develop a comic perspective in which the characters—who for the most part had been flat and one-dimensional (that is, bound to and by the narrative) whether in the ancient writers or in the University Wits—could find credible growth through their interaction upon one another. The characters of Attic comedy caricature particular Athenians whom Aristophanes considered to be undesirable for reasons moral, philosophical, or political. Socrates, for instance, is depicted as a symbol of the sophistic thought so destructive to traditional religion and morality. Euripides, Alcibiades, and Cleon, among many others, parade across the stage to draw the derisive laughter of the spectators, as Aristophanes sketches his characters broadly to reflect particular qualities or concepts of a recognizable individual or group. Obviously, then, character is the means to an end—the end of distorted personal representation. So also, character in New Comedy is a means to an end. In both Plautus and Terence, a specific narrational pattern emerges with characters significant only in the typicality of their roles: the Menaechmi, who are embroiled in the confusions of mistaken identity; Thraso and Pyrgopolynices, braggart warriors who lack the wit and courage to retain even a courtesan; the unruly Philolachas, who, while using his father's house to gain his physical pleasure, dupes his sire into believing the place haunted; Clinia, who outwits his father for much the same purpose, aided like Philolachas by his witty servant. The characters of the early English romantic comedies are only slightly less typical; their primary significance is again in the roles to be filled. Young lovers (lovesick swains such as Colin, Edward Lacy, and Mucedorus and admirably faithful and adorable lasses such as Bettris, Margaret of Fressing-field, and Ida) may expect, whether aristocratic or not, to confront irate fathers or guardians, who are more concerned with matters material and social than with those of love, and rival wooers, who are frequently willing to resort to dastardly devices to gain their pleasure. As Virgil K. Whitaker has observed in his discussion of the predominance of comedy over tragedy in English drama to 1613, "If one reads too many of Shakespeare's contemporaries, one becomes tired of credulous and patient wives, grasping fathers, scheming gallants, and hardhearted whores, just as one becomes weary of the virtuous slave girls, young men in love, and clever slaves of Roman comedy."[18] In effect, whether it be the Attic character or the stock character of Plautine and Terentian intrigue, the typical comic creature of the miracles, the late moralities, and the Heywood farces or the swains, lasses, and villains of the early romantic comedy—such comic roles for the most part confine and limit the character to a partial, frequently consciously distorted, reflection of the human personality. The comic perspective in these plays normally results from the spectator's acceptance of the convention of a stylized or static character either manipulated into humorous situations or involved in plots with predictable and anticipated crises and resolutions. The kinds of comedy, in effect, may vary, but the essential nature of the characterization does not.

This generalization is patently inaccurate, however, when applied to Shakespeare's work. Granted, it is commonplace to speak of the *different kinds* of Shakespearean comedy. The "happy" or "joyous" comedies, for instance, are contrasted with the "enigmatic" or "problem" comedies on the one hand and the "philosophic" or "divine" comedies on the other. And, among the first group, *The Two Gentlemen of Verona* is sometimes said to be a less successful "romantic" comedy than *Much Ado about Nothing*, and *Twelfth Night* is purported to be pure comedy whereas *As You Like It* incorporates potentially tragic motifs. In a broad sense, it is certainly true that the attitudes toward life expressed by comedy can range from the satiric to the sentimental, the farcical to the melodramatic—distinctions invariably based upon the nature of the plot and readily illustrated in the varied comic fare of Shakespeare's day. Shakespeare's comic artistry, however, is most significantly observed through an investigation of the comic perspective of the plays—in part, at least, the nature of the characterizations and the devices by which the characters are rendered humorous. Such an analysis suggests that Shakespeare's concern was not with different kinds of comedy but rather with plots involving an increasingly complex depth of characterization. Certainly Shakespeare began with plot, not character;[19] but just as certainly the kind of characterization demanded by the plots he selected reveals both his changing interests and his increasing abilities.

An examination of the comedies from this point of view demonstrates the consistency of Shakespeare's determination to maintain an effective perspective for comedy even while dramatizing different kinds of narratives and varying levels of the human personality. "The treatment makes or mars the subject," as one critic has observed; "Shakespeare's plays are no exception; we recognize the comedy dream-world, accept its conventions, and enjoy what he intended us to enjoy."[20] More specifically, Shakespeare throughout the comedies demonstrably works to achieve for the spectator the detached view so vital to the comic experience—not a Jonsonian detachment which presumes an attitude of derisive hostility, but a detachment of tolerance resulting from a position of knowledgeable security. The fullest enjoyment depends, not on the laughter arising from the shock of surprise or incongruity, but on this superior level of perception which permits the spectator to observe the plot without a total emotional commitment to it.

More precisely, Shakespeare will depict character at the level appropriate to his narrative. His comedy at times avoids credible characterization altogether by focusing entirely on the humor of physical action; at times it stresses the disparity between appearance and reality—what in his society a character sets himself out to be as opposed to what in reality he is behind the social mask; at times it portrays an experience involving a spiritual catharsis which transforms a personality or reconstitutes an entire society. (1) The character who is delineated only on the level of "physical action" never invites our response to him as an individual. Our detachment complete, the comedy is that of manipulation, and the humor is drawn not from character involvement or character incongruity but rather from our observation of puppet-like characters maneuvered into ludicrous situations. (2) The character who inhabits a stage-world in which there is no fundamental evil faces no decisions, of course, which reveal his spiritual or philosophic values. Yet, when, on the social plane, he pretends to be something which he is not, the gap between appearance and reality becomes material for comedy. In this situation the comic experience for the character is one of self-revelation; portrayed on the level of "identity," he is humorously forced to recognize or to acknowledge his true nature. Northrop Frye is speaking primarily of such drama when he remarks that comedy "is designed not to condemn evil, but to ridicule a lack of self-knowledge."[21] (3) The character who inhabits a stage-world in which evil is a reality and who is involved in ethical and moral decisions through which the spectators see into the foundations of his personality is completely human; portrayed on the level of "transformation," he undergoes an experience—like those of the great tragic figures—which effects a basic alteration of values.

Shakespeare, then, whose development as a comic playwright is consistently in the direction of complexity or depth of characterization, deals with each of these levels of characterization. His earliest works, like those of his contemporaries, are essentially situation comedies: the humor arises from action rather than character. There is no significant development of the main characters; instead, they are manipulated into situations which are humorous as a result, for example, of mistaken identity or slapstick confusion. Thus, the characters are revealed only in terms of what they do, outer action. The Antipholuses and the Dromios of *The Comedy of Errors* are cases in point, manipulated as they are amidst a confused wife, courtesan, kitchen wench, sea captain, and goldsmith. So also the princess with her ladies in *Love's Labour's Lost* are played puppet-like against Ferdinand and his lords who have renounced sex for Academe. In *A Midsummer-Night's Dream* the Athenian lovers— Hermia, Helena, Lysander, and Demetrius—are puppets manipulated into ridiculous self-contradiction by Oberon and Puck.

The ensuing phase of Shakespeare's comedy sets forth plots in which the emphasis is on identity rather than physical action, a revelation of character which occurs in one of two forms. Either a hypocrite is exposed for what he actually is or a character who has assumed an unnatural or abnormal pose is forced to realize and admit the ridiculousness of his position. Of the first type Malvolio and Don John are prime illustrations, their true nature hidden from at least some of the other characters for much of the play by their moral hypocrisy. Of the second type, Benedick and Beatrice in *Much Ado about Nothing* and Orsino and Olivia in *Twelfth Night* are characters whose experiences reveal to themselves as well as to others their true personalities. Benedick's and Beatrice's mockery of love is transformed into veneration; Olivia's pursuit of Cesario-Sebastian mocks her self-proclaimed forebearance of masculine company; Orsino's choice of Viola belies his sworn passion for a disdainful Olivia. While Orsino and Olivia may not, like Benedick and Beatrice, articulate their newly acquired knowledge, their behavior just as clearly reflects a normality not in evidence at the outset of the play. With either the hypocrites or the self-deluded, actions are a facade to conceal their true personalities; and, to the extent that the spectator is aware of this incongruity, the hypocrisy on the one hand and the lack of self-knowledge on the other are ridiculous and the ultimate exposure humorous. Admittedly there is no fundamental spiritual transformation of character; yet the false pride which blinds one to fully knowing himself is purged. In any case, the emphasis in these comedies is on the ridiculousness of the character, not his danger to society; he is comic, not evil, because in these stage-worlds the perspective is such that we are forced to assume that normality will ultimately prevail and that he will never be allowed to engage in activities of permanent consequence either to himself or to others. In the final comedies involving sin and sacrificial forgiveness, however, character development is concerned with a transformation of values.[22] In these stage-worlds the power of evil is not harmlessly contained within a circle of wit; and the characters, struggling on the fringe of comedy, must cope with the actual consequences of sin moral and political. The "comic" transformation of, for instance, Leontes in *The Winter's Tale* or Alonso in *The Tempest* is the result of a character's conversion to belief in a universe controlled by a principle of love most fully realized in its redemptive powers.

The fully developed character obviously creates problems for the dramatist who desires to maintain a comic perspective for the spectator rather than see his narrative turn to melodrama or tragicomedy. Since the spectator's involvement with physical action does not extend beyond the superficial laughter that a humorous situation arouses, the playwright—to the extent that he can maintain such a perspective—has no difficulty in achieving a comic tone for "flat" characters who make no ethical decisions. On the other hand, with greater character complexity, the spectator is easily provoked into emotional identification with character and situation, and his comic perspective is blurred. Whether the Renaissance comic form took shape primarily from "Saturnalian release" or from "Terentian intrigue," the dramatic experience which is to divert rather than distress is possible only so long as the spectator is either emotionally detached from the characters or, if emotionally involved with them, in possession of such knowledge or provoked into such a mood throughout the play as to be assured of a happy end accomplished by means which only temporarily appear unpleasant. Consequently, as Shakespeare's conception of character expanded, so also did his problem of maintaining a proper perspective for the spectator.[23] His success results from experimentation with the use of subordinate material to mirror the main action by mockery, parody, or caricature and with a kind of comic pointer or comic controller (a device at least as old as the *Dyskolos* of Menander, in which the god Pan overtly motivates and controls the action) who is himself involved in the action and yet whose relationships with other characters or whose actions and comments provide a sufficiently omniscient view —whether he himself possesses this view or not—for the spectator to rest secure that an impenetrable circle of wit has exorcised any dangers of permanent consequence.

The investigation of comedies drawn from each phase of Shakespeare's work will, in the following chapters, explore the various stages in the evolution of his comic vision. Although each of the comedies will be discussed at least briefly, the study will concentrate on nine: *The Comedy of Errors, The Two Gentlemen of Verona, A Midsummer-Night's Dream, Much Ado about Nothing, Twelfth Night, All's Well That Ends Well, Measure for Measure, The Winter's Tale,* and *The Tempest.* Mindful of Professor Charlton's comment that "in the interpretation of Shakespeare, novelty is its own condemnation,"[24] even the boldest critic must surely pause before claiming any novel insights into the playwright's artistry. And certainly I make no such claim. Through a discussion of the consistent dramatic aims in what has on occasion been described as a variegated comic canon, however, I hope to provoke a fresh appreciation for Shakespeare's comic artistry.

"Here we wander in illusions"

2 The Comedies of Action

Shakespeare's early comedies defy a single label, as J. Dover Wilson has observed.[1] It is possible on the one hand to point to a dominant Roman influence in *The Comedy of Errors*. On the other hand, the native romance tradition appears equally strong in *The Two Gentlemen of Verona*. If academic disputation is in evidence in *Love's Labour's Lost*, so also is popular folklore in *A Midsummer-Night's Dream*. These plays cannot be categorized for the simple reason that Shakespeare himself was in a developmental state as a comic playwright. Writing at a time when several dramatic traditions retained recognizable identity, he perhaps quite unconsciously worked under a diversity of artistic constraints which in the initial stages revealed the dominance of one or the other but ultimately was to result in a uniquely Shakespearean comic form capable of involving the spectator emotionally and at the same time maintaining a truly comic perspective.

The one major consistency in Shakespeare's early comedies, which are quite literally plot-filled, is the superficial level of characterization. That is, whether the narrative revolves around mistaken identity or disputation concerning the relative desirability of academic and female companionship, the characterization is one-dimensional. The comic experience arises primarily from the situation itself, not from either a revelation of hypocrisy or a transformation in the characters who are manipulated in the scene.

More specifically, in *The Comedy of Errors* neither Antipholus of Ephesus nor Antipholus of Syracuse and neither of the Dromio servants undergoes a revelation of character or exposure of some comic flaw or hypocrisy, and none is in any way transformed in personality. The humor results from the improbable possibilities that occur when identical twin brothers with identical twin servants separated for twenty-three years are cast unwittingly into a single society.[2] Basically, the comic situation involves both the public and private lives of Antipholus of Ephesus and, to some degree at least, the private life of Dromio of Ephesus. Privately, Antipholus resides with a wife whose salient point is her badgering tongue and a sister-in-law who is mildly passive to domestic friction until she becomes the flustered, albeit complimented, object of romantic intent from her supposed brother-in-law. With an even more delicate privacy Antipholus enjoys the occasional companionship of a courtesan. In similar fashion, his male-servant Dromio has cultivated the acquaintance of Nell, a greasy kitchen wench who bluntly lays claim to his person. Publicly, Antipholus of Ephesus enjoys a reputation for integrity and common sense; his life is without the least stain of improper commercial or moral report. Of immediate significance to the play is his commissioning Angelo, a goldsmith, to make a carcanet for his wife.

These issues provide the situation from which the comedy arises.[3] Dromio of Ephesus, mistaking Antipholus of Syracuse for his master, urges him to come home to dinner with his impatient wife while Antipholus is incensed that Dromio will not acknowledge the coin entrusted to him by his master. Shortly thereafter, Adriana and Luciana confront Antipholus of Syracuse personally, and the wife, following a histrionic display of spleen and heart, carts off the bemused "husband" to her home. The stage is now set for the central scenes of merriment involving the private lives of the Ephesus master and servant: (1) the husband's return to his home, the locked door, and the recalcitrant porter (Dromio of Syracuse); (2) the amorous pursuit of Luciana by her "brother-in-law"; and (3) the amorous pursuit of the terrified Dromio (of Syracuse) by Nell, the kitchen wench.

The public life of Antipholus of Ephesus highlights the comedy still further. Clearly he is a respected man in the community, as his twin brother's comments concerning his amazing experiences in Ephesus reflect.

> There's not a man I meet but doth salute me
> As if I were their well-acquainted friend;
> And every one doth call me by my name.
> Some tender money to me; some invite me;
> Some other give me thanks for kindnesses;
> Some offer me commodities to buy.
> Even now a tailor call'd me in his shop

And show'd me silks that he had bought for me
And therewithal took measure of my body.
(IV, iii, 1-9)[4]

As the citizen of unquestioned reputation beats upon his own door
and is denied entrance, fellow citizens Angelo and Balthazar observe
their friend's growing embarrassment. Indeed, Antipholus has revealed his concern for appearances at the first of the scene with the
comment to Signior Angelo that he "must excuse us all":

My wife is shrewish when I keep not hours.
Say that I linger'd with you at your shop
To see the making of her carcanet,
And that to-morrow you will bring it home.
(III, i, 2-5)

Whether the excuse is indeed genuine or the idea of the gift is a
momentary ploy to explain his tardiness, Antipholus' comment betrays to his business associates his apprehension concerning Adriana's attitude. Moreover, to make the subsequent denial to his home
more embarrassing, he has mere moments earlier invited Balthazar
to be his dinner guest for "a table full of welcome." As Antipholus
becomes increasingly more furious and more vociferous before his
door, his friend counsels him to realize the public scene he is creating:

Herein you war against your reputation
And draw within the compass of suspect
The unviolated honour of your wife . . .
A vulgar comment will be made of it . . .
For slander lives upon succession,
For ever hous'd where 't gets possession.
(III, i, 86-88, 100, 105-106)

At this point, however, he is more than willing to endanger reputation for revenge. And to that end he leads his friends off to a "wench

of excellent discourse, / Pretty and witty, wild, and yet, too, gentle" (109-110). The chain previously ordered for his wife he now intends to bestow upon his more receptive hostess. And, as if to ensure the comic perspective for the entire affair, his final words as he stalks off to his mistress concern affairs of the pocket rather than the heart: "This jest shall cost me some expense" (123).

The chain, of course, is given by Angelo to the wrong Antipholus, and the scene is set for further humor at the expense of public reputation. Angelo, pressed for payment on another matter, in turn requests payment from Antipholus. Indignant at being called to account for what he never has received, Antipholus refuses to pay, is arrested at Angelo's suit, and sends Dromio to Adriana for bail money. In a wild melange of comic confusion, the gold is carried to the wrong Antipholus, the courtesan demands her chain from the wrong Antipholus, and Adriana sets Dr. Pinch, a conjuror, on the wrong Antipholus. The net result is the arrest of Antipholus and Dromio of Ephesus on charges of insanity with orders that they "be bound and laid in some dark room." The frantic husband, as he is being dragged away, hurls public insults at the equally frantic wife:

> Dissembling harlot, thou art false in all
> And art confederate with a damned pack
> To make a loathsome abject scorn of me;
> But with these nails I'll pluck out these false eyes
> That would behold in me this shameful sport.
> (IV, iv, 104-108)

The play has comically wrought total destruction on both the private and public life of Antipholus of Ephesus.[5] Privately, his wife has locked him out—apparently while harboring another lover. Then, too, Adriana has verified her suspicions concerning her husband's relationship with a local courtesan. Any honey of domestic love has evidently been transformed into bitter gall. Publicly, his reputation has been slandered, his credit and honesty impugned, and his mental competence denied. This complex knot the simultaneous appearance on stage of the two Antipholuses and the Dromios will unravel.

The characters, certainly much relieved to discover a reasonable explanation for the stupefying welter of events and delighted to find a brother long since assumed dead, otherwise part our company as they earlier had made it. With the possible exception of Adriana, no fundamental—or for that matter even superficial—character transformations occur. The resolving explanations will doubtless restore both the public reputation and the private equanimity. And, obviously, there is no villainy in Antipholus and Dromio of Syracuse which demands poetic redress. They have been unwitting parties to a multitude of situational confusions which have produced the comic plot. Given the constraints of identical males—one a stranger and the other married and well known in the community —and of their identical servants, the plot is dramatically feasible, albeit improbable. There is obviously no comic catharsis, that is, no measure of value and profit drawn upon the character who knows himself more fully as a result of the comic experience. Here the comic experience is no more and no less than the sheer merriment of controlled confusion resulting from mistaken identity.[6]

Adequate control of the action of the plot is a prime concern of the comic dramatist; he must in some fashion provide a perspective for the spectators sufficient to assure them psychologically that right reason has been dethroned for the sake of the comic, not the tragic, muse. While this is not to abstract from the plot every potential danger, it is to imbue it with a tone or spirit as well as with the narrative elements which will plausibly permit a comic resolution of the plot's complications. The dramatist, in other words, must create the comic distance between spectator and character—the perspective from which the viewer can effectively realize the comic experience.

The comic perspective in *The Comedy of Errors* is built upon two primary devices: stylized action—that is, action so flagrantly broad as to ensure the spectator's interest in *what* is happening (not to whom and how it emotionally affects them)—and a comic pointer

—that is, a character or, in more primitive terms, a scene which exists partially (or primarily) as an explanation and a guide for the major complications of the plot.

The basic situation with its complex improbabilities is, of course, the dominant feature of exaggeration or stylization which prevents the spectator's interest in character from passing beyond the physical events themselves. Twins separated from infancy, yet one still interested in reunion; an identical situation involving the twins' servants; parents, one facing death for lack of friends and funds, the other a leader of a religious order, also alive, active, and prime for reunion. Even without the series of farcically disastrous events occasioned by mistaken identity, the plot invites interest in the action, not the character.

Certain features further emphasize the broad quality of the action. For one thing, the action is literally replete with the farcical action of physical slapstick. At least five scenes involve a Dromio beaten by his actual or his pretended master, the servant inevitably bearing the blame for the confusions of mistaken identity. Antipholus of Syracuse also contributes to the fantastic tone of the stage-world through the references to witchery and sorcery with which numerous scenes conclude.

> They say this town is full of cozenage,
> As, nimble jugglers that deceive the eye,
> Dark-working sorcerers that change the mind,
> Soul-killing witches that deform the body,
> Disguised cheaters, prating mountebanks,
> And many such-like liberties of sin.
> (I, ii, 97-102)
>
> Am I in earth, in heaven, or in hell?
> Sleeping or waking? Mad or well-advis'd?
> (II, ii, 214-215)
>
> There's none but witches do inhabit here.
> (III, ii, 161)
>
> Sure, these are but imaginary wiles,
> And Lapland sorcerers inhabit here . . .

Thou art, as you are all, a sorceress.
I conjure thee to leave me and be gone . . .
Avaunt, thou witch!
(IV, iii, 10-11, 67-68, 79)

Utterly stupefied by the people who know him, the wife who claims him, and the merchant who gives a gold chain to him, he has no explanation other than the assumption that either he or the entire city is victim of a magical spell.[7]

Two romantic features of the plot contribute especially to the stylization. Consider first the extreme comic shifts in Adriana, wife of Antipholus of Ephesus: One moment she is the stock shrew overwhelming anyone in earshot with an enumeration of her husband's flaws and allowing him liberty only to obey her mandates (II, i); the next moment she is the moralist attacking her husband as "an adulterate blot" (II, ii, 141-146); on another occasion she is the clinging vine totally dependent upon her mate.

Thou art an elm, my husband, I a vine,
Whose weakness married to thy [stronger] state
Makes me with thy strength to communicate.
(II, ii, 176-178)

It can be argued, of course, that Adriana profits to some degree from the comic experience.[8] Goaded by the insinuations of the abbess, she proclaims that she has indeed properly chastened her husband for his extramarital feminine interest:

It was the copy of our conference.
In bed he slept not for my urging it;
At board he fed not for my urging it;
Alone, it was the subject of my theme;
In company I often glanced it;
Still did I tell him it was vile and bad.
(V, i, 62-67)

When this verbal exhibition prompts Aemilia to brand Adriana's "venom clamours of a jealous woman" as the cause "that the man was mad," the subdued shrew can reply only: "She did betray me to my own reproof" (90).

Possibly, then, Adriana is in a small way a precursor of characters like Benedick and Beatrice, who will indeed come to know themselves more fully through the action of the play. Indeed, with certain lines and scenes, the actress determined to do so can put more flesh in her role than can be comfortably accommodated throughout the play. Adriana's insistence to Aemilia, for example, that she be allowed to take her husband home and care for him, that he "have no attorney but myself" (100), and her subsequent lengthy plea that the duke release him to her care can be interpreted as the sympathetic concern of a wife for the husband she loves. But, on the other hand, this scene can also be acted as a reversion to shrewishness in her determination to have control of him. Obviously, as with certain of Katherina's lines in *The Taming of the Shrew*, or of Biron's in *Love's Labour's Lost*, the interpretation rests with the determination of the tone of the play by the director and the player.

The significant point, in any case, is that in these early comedies Shakespeare does not dwell on or build his humor from character revelation. Even if Adriana has publicly confessed her shrewishness, the humor at the end of the scene arises from the shock that she has entertained the wrong man in the privacy of her home. Confused and chagrined as her husband and his twin and the older generation look on, she no doubt should stare anxiously from one group to another. And, certainly, her broad facial expressions can do much to enhance the comic situation of this moment:

ADR. Which of you two did dine with me to-day?
ANT. S. I, gentle mistress.
ADR. And are not you my husband?
ANT. E. No; I say nay to that.

(369-371)

Such humor obviously focuses attention on the action itself and prevents emotional involvement.

20 *Evolution of Shakespeare's Comedy*

The second romantic feature of exaggeration involves the amatory interest of the Syracusan Antipholus and Dromio. That Antipholus of Ephesus should be married is not incredible, but that his twin, whom Adriana dines and woos as her own husband, should under such circumstances become enamored of the sister Luciana and pursue her hotly between moments with Adriana is convenient but fantastic.[9] And what a price Dromio of Syracuse must pay for his twin's romantic taste: the "very beastly creature," "wondrous fat," a "kitchen wench and all grease" who "if she lives till doomsday" will "burn a week longer than the whole world" (III, ii, 89, 94, 96-97, 100-102).

In short, such an exaggerated pattern of action forces characterization to the puppet level of farce: a broad doubletake or clever mugging can create humor from an otherwise somber situation; a ranting Herod or a shrewish uxor can turn a potentially serious moment to comedy; a father's pompous tirade can reduce to laughter his daughter's forbidden elopement; a Petrarchan lover through his ridiculous lamentation can translate his romantic agony into humor. Such broad action forces attention upon the physical events themselves and neither permits nor invites the spectator to consider the motivations of the characters or to become emotionally involved with them.

Regardless of the level of comic characterization, the reader must, of course, possess sufficient information to appreciate the comic confusion. If it is situation comedy, he must understand the situation to enjoy its incongruities; if it is comedy of identity, he must perceive the gap between appearance and reality to which, at least for a time, the character is impervious; if it is comedy of transformation, he must understand the nature of the evil or the adversity which purges the character and be assured that its power is only temporary. The characteristic method employed by Shakespeare to provide this information is a character or several characters who, consciously or unconsciously, develop a sufficiently objective rapport with the spectators to act as a guide or pointer. One aspect of Shakespeare's development as a comic playwright is the gradual integration of the pointer into the plot so that he performs the double function of comic guide and a character important to the plot in his own right.

Obviously, for the spectator to achieve the necessary comic perspective for *The Comedy of Errors*, he must understand the full situation; he must know that two sets of identical twins exist as master and servant, that one Antipholus is visiting a city in which the other is a well-known and reputable citizen, that these twins have been separated for a sufficiently lengthy period so as not to be able to provide a ready explanation when the complications of identity begin, that eventually the complications can be resolved with the added joy of brotherly reunion. In this respect, the comic structure of *The Comedy of Errors*—probably the clumsiest in all Shakespeare—belies its apprentice-creator. For to provide this information, Shakespeare has framed his plot (I, i; V, i) with the story of Aegeon and Aemilia, separated parents of the separated sons who likewise will be reunited. This material, appended to the Plautine sources, is not an integral part of the play; moreover, despite the duke's skillful mugging (even perhaps his falling asleep from ennui), Aegeon's lengthy opening speech is dramatically tedious and relatively ineffective. Indeed, of the one hundred fifty-nine lines in the scene, he speaks one hundred and four. Even so, by establishing the problem of familial separation and emphasizing the desire for reunion, the scene does, albeit awkwardly, create a greater depth of dramatic interest than the farce of mistaken identity could provide.[10] And, furthermore, the information it provides the spectator is essential. Aegeon has been captured while passing through Ephesus and is condemned to die unless he can pay one thousand marks. He relates at length the events of the shipwreck which twenty-three years ago separated him, one infant son, and his infant male servant from his wife, another infant son, and his infant male servant. The separation was especially painful since both the sons and the servants were sets of identical twins.

And in our sight they three were taken up
By fishermen of Corinth, as we thought.
At length, another ship had seiz'd on us.
                    (I, i, 111-113)

So strong is the hope that they are yet alive that the remaining son
and servant set out five years ago in search of their counterparts.

The plot itself, underway in scene ii, immediately provides the
connection for the spectators. Antipholus of Syracuse announces
that he is:

        like a drop of water
That in the ocean seeks another drop . . .
So I, to find a mother and a brother,
In quest of them, unhappy, lose myself.
                    (I, ii, 35-36, 39-40)

He has just sent his Dromio to deposit money at the inn (18); when
his servant's identical rushes on stage to call him home for dinner
with "his" wife (43), dramatic irony is achieved for the spectator
who, now in a position of superior knowledge, can enjoy the ridiculous complications of mistaken identity with the assurance that all
pieces are present with which to fit out a satisfactory conclusion.

The final scene provides such an ending. Aegeon, off stage since
the initial moments, returns to be rescued from his execution and
reunited with his wife as both sons and both servants appear on
stage simultaneously for the first time. Aemilia, as an abbess, appears
for the first time in the play.[11] Before casting aside her religious
garb, she acidly berates Adriana for the shrewish jealousy which
has driven her husband to take religious sanctuary.

The venom clamours of a jealous woman
Poisons more deadly than a mad dog's tooth.
                    (V, i, 69-70)

The "two Antipholuses, these two so like, / And these two Dromios, one in semblance" satisfy the comic anticipations of the spectators and resolve all problems in a fashion apposite to the moment:

> We came into the world like brother and brother;
> And now let's go hand in hand, not one before another.
>
> (424-425)

The connection between pointer and situation is admittedly clumsy in *The Comedy of Errors*. A situation comedy has been enveloped in an explanatory layer in a fashion at best peripheral. Yet, Shakespeare's method is clear. At a time when much of the contemporary comedy was still unfocused and disjointed, he approached his material with a concept of structural control not entirely dissimilar from that to be utilized a decade later by Ben Jonson for comic control of his satiric stage-worlds. And, as his comic vision grew, his method was refined. As later chapters will describe, there is a structural "explanation" for Shakespeare's "comic masterpieces."

The Comedy of Errors may or may not have been Shakespeare's first dramatic effort at comedy, but in either case, with its plot built on the intrigues of mistaken identity, it stands as a virtual anomaly in the Shakespeare canon. By the time he was again to utilize the Roman-intrigue structure significantly in *Twelfth Night*, he had adapted and molded to his own purposes the elements of romantic comedy drawn from the native narrative tradition. Indeed, with the exceptions of *The Comedy of Errors* and *The Merry Wives of Windsor*, the evolution of Shakespearean comedy through the first decade of his work—*The Two Gentlemen of Verona, Love's Labour's Lost, The Taming of the Shrew, A Midsummer-Night's Dream, The Merchant of Venice, Much Ado about Nothing, As You Like It*, and *Twelfth Night*—can be traced through his employment of "romantic" motifs. In these plays, two fundamental phases of his comedy are represented. The first four are, like *The Comedy of Errors*, comedies of "action"; characters are significant only in terms of what they do, not in terms of what they are or how they are transformed by what happens to them; they are puppets or stock characters run through the complications that temporarily prevent the success of youthful romance. In the four remaining dramas, Shakespeare moves to comedies of "identity" in which the conventional elements of romantic comedy are still employed, but in which, as aforementioned, the humor arises not from the action itself but from the character exposure arising from the action, the comic gap between appearance and reality.

The Two Gentlemen of Verona is certainly among Shakespeare's earliest attempts to adapt the material of romance to the stage and to devise a comic perspective to control it.[12] Admittedly his effort in this play is only partially successful. Intemperate young lovers, crossed by fate and fortune and caught in an emotional morass which blinds reason and leads the victim to betray friend, parent, and self in the mad pursuit of the adored; capricious yet faithful mistresses, who are nurtured by inordinate flattery and stolid fidelity but whose own faithfulness proves stronger than any adversity this side of death; an irate father, determined to wed his daughter to his own choice based on financial and social status and staunchly opposed to the heart's choice which disregards such matters; a daughter imprisoned in a high tower and a banished lover—direct results of the father's convictions in action; the father's candidate, the foolish rival wooer, whose claim to distinction is a loquacity which at least partially conceals his cowardice and fatuousness; a deceitful friend; a proxy wooing; an escape into a forest haunted by outlaw brigands, frightful lions, or whimsical fairies—such are the stock characters and motifs of the narrative comedy which in England took shape in the hands of the University Wits, especially Lyly and Greene, and which in tone is so strikingly different from the Plautine quality of *The Comedy of Errors*.

Built on the commonplace Renaissance theme of friendship versus love, *The Two Gentlemen of Verona* is a veritable repository of stock romantic motifs and characters.[13] Admittedly these characters are one-dimensional: Shakespeare is interested neither in character development nor in credible motivation. Instead he is interested in the comic potential of a situation popular with his audience. Hence, the characters in effect do not determine the events but merely perform the roles which the action has predetermined.[14] As for this action, the crossed and twisted ties of youthful affection are no less involved than those in *A Midsummer-Night's Dream*. At the outset, Valentine and Proteus are fast friends; Proteus is "deeply" enamored of Julia; Valentine flouts such passion and considers himself impervious to love. By the middle of the play the force of love has seized Valentine; in his adoration of Silvia he suffers all the more poignantly because of his previous assumption of invulnerability; Proteus, forced by his father to leave Verona and later forced by Valentine to consider the consummate virtues of the fair Silvia, promptly forgets his former love and falls hopelessly in love with her; concurrently, he determines to destroy his erstwhile friend by informing Silvia's father of the intended elopement and by dispraising Valentine before Silvia. Thus at this phase, a complete reversal has occurred for the principals of the play. And the whirlwind of events which conclude the play—completely absurd in a stage-world in which the spectators are involved emotionally with the characters but plausible in comedy which does not look beyond the humor of the situation—finds the characters manipulated through yet another reversal. Julia, in disguise as a page, pursues her errant lover; Valentine, banished from Milan, is captured by outlaws and becomes their captain; Silvia, amorously pursued by Proteus, flees with the aid of Eglamour toward Verona and Valentine only to be captured by the outlaws. When Proteus "rescues" Silvia and threatens to force her to yield to his desires, Valentine reveals himself, Silvia is rescued, and Proteus is abashed. Proteus apologizes for his beastly infidelity, whereupon Valentine offers to confer Silvia upon him as a token of their reconciliation. At this point Julia reveals her identity, and Proteus, abashed again, realizes that there is nothing in Silvia's face which is not duplicated "more fresh in Julia's with a constant eye." Silvia remains silent through this fantastic shifting of affection, though obviously her gestures and facial expressions can do much to enrich the broad comedy of the scene. At any rate, eventually Jack has his Jill and nought goes ill: Silvia rebounds to her altruistic Valentine, Julia to her retrieved Proteus. And in the spirit of romantic farce, the spectators assume that the emotions which have fluctuated so wildly through the past two hours are now stable, that for purpose of fiction true love has triumphed for now and for all time.

The dominant force which motivates the events of the plot is, of course, the lunacy of youthful, impetuous love. As Bottom remarks in *A Midsummer-Night's Dream* that "reason and love keep little company together now-a-days," so Speed speaks of "the chameleon Love" as "blind" (II, i, 76, 178) and Julia of love as "a blinded god" (IV, iv, 201); Proteus observes that love "hath dazzled my reason's light . . . There is no reason but I shall be blind" (II, iv, 210, 212). The potential humor of the play arises from the sudden and illogical character reversals prompted by this romantic compulsion.[15] Such reversals are obviously not intended to reveal either a genuinely evil nature or an incongruity of character. As Shakespeare will later depict through the juice of the flower and the Athenian lovers in *A Midsummer-Night's Dream*, the force of romantic passion is whimsical and uncontrollable, its victims hapless pawns; and in this comic vision the victims are not villains but madcaps whose antics temporarily contradict their saner judgments and sever their previous ties of affection.

Shakespeare directs emphasis upon plot through stylized characterization, hyperbolic rhetoric, and the use of comic pointers who, though admittedly peripheral to the main action, do direct the spectator's attention to that which is ludicrous and ridiculous in the actions of the principals of the play. More specifically, the stylized characterization results from caricatures manipulated to create situation comedy. Valentine appears in only six scenes; but each depicts him as a character of comic exaggeration.[16] In the opening scene, he berates Proteus for "living dully sluggardiz'd at home" and wearing out his "youth with shapeless idleness" when travel is imperative for a complete education. He mocks Proteus as "a votary to fond desire," "yoked by a fool" in his subservience to his master, Love. It is sheer fatuity:

> To be in love, where scorn is bought with groans;
> Coy looks with heart-sore sighs; one fading moment's mirth
> With twenty watchful, weary, tedious nights.
>
> (I, i, 28-31)

He prides himself on emotional self-control and on clear-sighted goals and ambitions. Love and its effects as he observes them in his friend he holds in special disdain. Valentine, in effect, is the extreme antilover, impervious to Cupid's shaft.

His remaining appearances are a veritable self-parody, for "the chameleon Love" transforms him into the thing he previously mocked so unmercifully. In II, i, he writes anonymous love letters on command only to be neglected by Silvia, the "thing divine." Mocked by his servant Speed, he has veered from one extreme to another, from the antilover to the Petrarchan fawner. Three scenes later, obviously wanting to impress Silvia's father through courteous flattery of his friend, he flatly contradicts his earlier assertions to Proteus. Instead of "homely wits" Proteus is now described as young in years but "his experience old; / His head unmellow'd, but his judgement ripe." Instead of "living dully sluggardiz'd at home," he has "Made use and fair advantage of his days":

> He is complete in feature and in mind
> With all good grace to grace a gentleman.
>
> (II, iv, 73-74)

When Proteus enters a few lines later, Valentine is forced to admit the metamorphosis which love has performed:

> I have done penance for contemning Love,
> Whose high imperious thoughts have punish'd me
> With bitter fasts, with penitential groans,
> With nightly tears, and daily heart-sore sighs . . .

Now no discourse, except it be of love;
Now can I break my fast, dine, sup, and sleep,
Upon the very naked name of love.
                        (II, iv, 129-132, 140-142)

And it is not enough that Proteus affirm Silvia's beauty; before
Valentine is satisfied, his friend must "Call her divine" and swear
her fairer than Julia.

A mocker in excess, a lover in excess, and in Act III a mourner
in excess: death itself is preferable to banishment from Silvia!

What light is light, if Silvia be not seen?
What joy is joy, if Silvia be not by?
Unless it be to think that she is by,
And feed upon the shadow of perfection.
Except I be by Silvia in the night,
There is no music in the nightingale;
Unless I look on Silvia in the day,
There is no day for me to look upon.
She is my essence, and I leave to be,
If I be not by her fair influence
Foster'd, illumin'd, cherish'd, kept alive.
                        (III, i, 174-184)

So also, when later captured by the outlaw brigands outside Man-
tua, he laments that he is a man "crossed with adversity." And, as
before, nothing occurs in moderation for Valentine. So impressed
are the outlaws with his melancholia that they offer him the choice
of captaincy of their outlaw force—or death! The hero, albeit aware
of the charges against these men, abduction, murder, and "such
like petty crimes as these," readily exercises his option to lead them.

The series of Valentine's actions in the final act provides an
emphatic capstone to the caricature. From the opening soliloquy
(iv) in which as a victim of melancholia he welcomes "This shadowy desert, unfrequented woods," he emerges at the prime moment
to rescue Silvia from being ravished by Proteus. His first thoughts

Comedies of Action 29

fly not to Silvia—his "day," "essence," "fair influence"—but to his renegade friend for whose treachery he will "count the world a stranger . . . The private wound is deepest." At the slightest sign of Proteus' sorrow, he leaps at the opportunity to forgive and, in an action by no means a crux but merely a final excessive gesture, willingly offers Silvia as token of his forgiveness.[17]

Closely considered, emotional involvement with the character of Valentine is an absurd impossibility. Shakespeare consciously builds the excessive qualities of a caricature in order to insure the absolute detachment of situation comedy. A similar pattern is evident in Proteus,[18] Julia, and Silvia, the other major figures of the plot. Indeed, Proteus' actions are even more exaggerated than those of Valentine. In his initial appearance he describes his victimization by love and takes sorrowful leave of his friend, swearing to be his "beadsman" in his "holy prayers." In his passionate devotion to Julia, he admits that he neglects "friends, and all, for love," that he has "set the world at nought; / Made wit with musing weak, heart sick with thought." Yet later, when confronted by his father and informed that he must leave Verona to further his training and pursue his ambitions, he remains silent concerning his love for fear his father will "take exceptions to [his] love." Evidently potential parental disapproval is more disagreeable than certain separation from his "honour'd love"! In II, ii, amidst Julia's tide of tears and his own volley of words, he leaves Julia with the incredibly inapposite comment, "Alas! this parting strikes poor lovers dumb."

Within the space of two brief scenes his undying affection for Julia is dead:

> Even as one heat another heat expels . . .
> So the remembrance of my former love
> Is by a newer object quite forgotten.
> (II, iv, 192, 194-195)

Reason and love are again strange bedfellows. Frenetic passion

hath dazzled my reason's light;
But when I look on her [Silvia's] perfections,
There is no reason but I shall be blind.
(II, iv, 210-212)

In a line with the infinite comic possibilities of broadly played litotes, "Me thinks my zeal to Valentine is cold," he rationalizes that "Love bade me swear and Love bids me forswear . . . I will forget that Julia is alive . . . And Valentine I'll hold an enemy" (II, vi, 6, 27, 29). Later, having betrayed Valentine to Silvia's father and feigned support for Thurio as Silvia's favored lover, he tutors his rival with what he realizes is an excess loathsome to the recipient, but which ironically neither he nor Valentine is able to see in himself:

You must lay lime to tangle her desires
By wailful sonnets, whose composed rhymes
Should be full-fraught with serviceable vows . . .
Say that upon the altar of her beauty
You sacrifice your tears, your sighs, your heart;
Write till your ink be dry, and with your tears
Moist it again . . .
After your dire-lamenting elegies,
Visit by night your lady's chamber-window
With some sweet consort.
(III, ii, 68-70, 73-76, 82-84)

Just such activities which he counsels Thurio to practice—knowing the foolish dotage will appear stupid and ridiculous to the recipient—he himself pursues in wooing Silvia (IV, ii). He serenades her, averring that both Julia and Valentine are dead (even as Julia in disguise ruefully observes his infidelity); and later he sends gifts—both of which misfire—through Launce and his page (Julia).

The multiple reversals of the final scene complete this caricature. Courage (in rescuing Silvia from rape and bragging about it), lust, shame and sorrow when Valentine stays his attempt to rape her himself—Proteus' emotions run the gamut which concludes with his perfidious rationalizations that the fluctuation of man's mind is the flaw heaven intended to prevent man's perfection: "That one error / Fills him with faults; makes him run through all the sins" (V, iv, 111-112). Then, in perhaps the most ridiculous moment of all, he listens unemotionally as Valentine establishes the double wedding date for himself to Silvia and Proteus to Julia.

Both Silvia and Julia[19] illustrate further the general pattern of exaggeration. Julia, for instance, refuses to admit any attraction to Proteus, yet coyly argues with her maid to secure a letter from her ardent wooer. Moreover, without any provocation or suspicion of Proteus' infidelity, she assumes a page's disguise, bequeaths all her possessions to her maid Lucetta, and with bold audacity pursues her amour; later she manages to faint at the critical moment which announces her true identity to Proteus in a most histrionically effective fashion. Silvia, like Julia, first parries her lover's advances with coy indifference, but later she maintains complete fidelity to Valentine against both the fatuous Thurio and the apostate Proteus. Her chief comic importance is found in her silence which contributes to the richness of the final scene. Certainly the spectator who views a skillful comic actress as Silvia perceives more than the armchair reader, for her actions and reactions as she is being passed from Proteus to Thurio to Valentine to Proteus and finally to Valentine again can create, without dialogue, the most humorous moment of the entire comedy.

Several incidental details further illustrate Shakespeare's deliberate disregard of credible character motivation. For Julia to command her servant Lucetta to enumerate her mistress' suitors and to select the best is as improbable as for Proteus' father, Antonio, to query his servant, Panthino, concerning where and how his son should be sent for further education. The Mantuan outlaws' absurd capturing and crowning of Valentine in one day has been noted previously. And two events in the final scene are noteworthy: Thurio's eager sacrifice of Silvia to avoid a fight and the duke's peremptory acceptance of Valentine as Silvia's suitor and his universal pardon to each member of the outlaw band. Certainly it is surprising when Thurio, having so arduously pursued his interest in Silvia, disclaims any interest in her when confronted by Valentine:

> I hold him but a fool that will endanger
> His body for a girl that loves him not.
> I claim her not, and therefore she is thine.
> (V, iv, 133-135)

More startling is the duke's sudden amicability toward Valentine, for whom previously his hatred was sufficiently strong to provoke banishment:

> I do applaud thy spirit, Valentine,
> And think thee worthy of an empress' love.
> Know then, I here forget all former griefs,
> Cancel all grudge, repeal thee home again . . .
> Take thou thy Silvia, for thou hast deserv'd her.
> (V, iv, 140-143, 147)

This reconciliation with Valentine, though largely unnoticed by those critics who are preoccupied with the condemnation of Valentine's forgiveness of Proteus, is no less absurd by any test of credibility. Appropriately, then, the duke's general amnesty and his concurrence in the preparation for double wedding festivities aptly conclude the plot, comic not because of plausible character development or emotional involvement but because of sheer ludicrousness of action.

In addition to the stylized characterization a second device which Shakespeare utilizes to prevent the spectator's reacting emotionally to what the characters are saying and thus to maintain the level of situation comedy is the hyperbolic rhetoric. At a potentially serious moment the characters break into conceits or elaborate puns which, even in an age addicted to word play, could only strengthen the comic distance. In the opening scene, Proteus' infatuation with

Julia is lightly set forth through puns on "boots." His is a "deep story of a deeper love"; he is "more than over shoes in love"—"over boots in love"; to Proteus' retort, "give me not the boots" (don't mess with me), Valentine replies that he will not bother him because "it boots thee not" to be involved in an unreciprocated love. When Speed attempts to locate his master Valentine, Proteus involves him in a lengthy debate as to who is the sheep and who the shepherd. Speed quips that, since he seeks the master and the shepherd seeks the sheep, he is the shepherd. Proteus' retort is that, since Speed follows Valentine for fodder and the sheep follows the shepherd for fodder, Valentine is the shepherd. The word play turns immediately to a pun on Julia's reaction to a love note which Speed has conveyed for Proteus. Speed claims to be a lost mutton (an extension of the previous image) who has given a letter to a laced mutton (a courtesan). Proteus claims the pasture too small for such mutton, that Speed is astray. His response is confused between a "nod," quickly followed by "aye," and "noddy."

Although these are random examples, they illustrate the intense verbal dexterity of the opening scene which establishes the artificial tone for the entire drama. Further examples throughout the play include the elaborate musical terminology used by Lucetta and Julia in their discussion of Proteus' love note ("sing," "tune," "note," "set," "burden," "melodious," "high," "sharp," "flat," "concord," "descant," "mean," "bass" [II, i]). Valentine's love for Silvia is compared both to a religion ("penance," "imperious," "fasts," "groans," "tears," "sighs," "humbled," "confess," "correction," "service" [II, iv]) and to a rare gem ("jewel," "pearl," "gold" [II, iv]). Silvia's father, having discovered Valentine's plans to elope with his daughter, brands him "Phaethon" ("Merop's son" aspiring to "guide the heavenly car" and with "daring folly burn the world" [III, i]). Elaborate puns are constructed upon "understand" and "stand under" (II, v), upon "mastership" and "master's ship" (III, i), upon "tide" (of tears), "tide" (of the ocean), "tied," and upon "tale" and "tail" (II, ii, iii).

Combined with the exaggerated action and the hyperbolic rhetoric is the use of servant characters as comic pointers.[20] Speed, Launce, and Lucetta appear in nine of the twenty scenes of the play with comments related specifically to the actions of the main characters which provide information necessary for the spectator to achieve his perspective of superior comic detachment. Of the three, Speed, through his conversations with both Valentine and Proteus, is the most significant as a pointer. Unassuming and basically unintelligent, he nonetheless can see things clearly which his superiors, blinded by infatuation, are unable to, or refuse to, realize. It is he who observes that impetuous love transforms a normal character into an "excellent motion!" an "exceeding puppet!" (II, i, 100-101). In his first two appearances he signals the ridiculous in both Proteus and Valentine by mocking their foolish Petrarchan poses. Proteus is told that for all his pains and protestations "you'll hardly win" Julia (I, i). "Give her no token but stones, for she's as hard as steel." Valentine, equally obsessed with Silvia, is informed that he possesses all the special marks of the foolish gallant: "first, you have learn'd, like Sir Proteus, to wreathe your arms like a malecontent; to relish a love-song, like a robin-redbreast; to walk alone, like one that had the pestilence; to sigh, like a school-boy that had lost his A B C; to weep, like a young wench that had buried her grandam; to fast, like one that takes diet; to watch, like one that fears robbing; to speak puling, like a beggar at Hallowmas. You were wont, when you laugh'd, to crow like a cock; when you walk'd, to walk like one of the lions; when you fasted, it was presently after dinner; when you look'd sadly, it was for want of money: and now you are metamorphos'd with a mistress, that, when I look on you, I can hardly think you my master" (II, i, 18-33). Speed has, in effect, provided a comic definition of the "romantic" lover. He tells Valentine flatly that "these follies are within you and shine through you like the water in an urinal . . . Because Love is blind. O, that you had mine eyes, or your own eyes had the lights they were wont to have when you chid at Sir Proteus for going ungarter'd!" (II, i, 39-41, 76-79). When Silvia enters, Speed, through asides, emphasizes the fatuity of the doting lover, realizing full well that Silvia has commanded his master to write love lines to himself ("Some lines to one she loves"). He who knows the "chameleon Love" for what it is lives by sterner stuff; he is nourished by "victuals and would fain have meat" (178, 180). It is necessary for Speed to point out to his naive master that the vainglorious Sir Thurio is his rival in love (II, iv). And later, in proving to Launce that he can read, he itemizes the virtues of Launce's love—a milkmaid who can milk, brew, sew, knit, wash, scour, spin, and above all who is "slow in words" (III, i). The entire scene, with its practical view of love involving a woman with pragmatic abilities, parodies the "impractical" passionate love for which Valentine has been banished and for which Proteus sacrifices his fidelity both in romance and in friendship.

Launce, Proteus' servant, plays a significant role in three additional instances. He is first used for parody to prevent the romantic parting of Proteus and Julia from assuming a somber emotional quality. Proteus and Julia have exchanged rings and in a "tide of tears" "true love" has pledged its "true constancy" (II, ii). Inserted between this scene and that which depicts Proteus' reunion with Valentine and his introduction to Silvia at Milan is Launce's lugubrious parting from Crab, "the sourest-natured dog that lives" because it fails to weep for him though his master, were he to "lose the tide," could "fill it with [his] tears." "My mother weeping, my father wailing, my sister crying, our maid howling, our cat wringing her hands, and all our house in a great perplexity, yet did not this cruel-hearted cur shed one tear . . . why, my grandam, having no eyes, look you, wept herself blind at my parting" (II, iii, 6-10, 13-14). He then proceeds to the use of visual aids with his shoes (his mother being the one "with a hole in it"), his staff, his dog, and himself carefully arranged to reenact the final lachrymose moments: "Now come I to my father: 'Father, your blessing.' Now should not the shoe speak a word for weeping. Now should I kiss my father; well, he weeps on. Now come I to my mother. Oh, that she could speak now like a wood woman! Well, I kiss her; why, there 'tis; here's my mother's breath up and down. Now come I to my sister;

mark the moan she makes. Now the dog all this while sheds not a tear nor speaks a word; but see how I lay the dust with my tears" (25-35). The similar situation, even the similar image of "tide of tears," though Launce may be totally unaware of it, quite obviously has functioned to preserve the comic level at a potentially dangerous moment. So again in III, i, his aforementioned conversation with Speed concerning the milkmaid serves such a function in its juxtaposition with the scene in which Proteus betrays Valentine, who is apprehended and banished from Silvia and Milan. Prior to Speed's entry, Launce points specifically to Proteus' treachery in a brief soliloquy: "I am but a fool, look you, and yet I have the wit to think my master is a kind of a knave" (III, i, 261-262). One further illustration is Launce's conversation with Speed in II, v. Here Launce anticipates Proteus' crass transformation by suggesting through bawdy jest that, now that his master is traveling, he will not make a match with Julia.

Although in a minor role, Lucetta is certainly a conscious pointer in her two brief appearances. After reciting the list of Julia's suitors upon command (I, ii), she proves her mistress' disdain for Proteus is mere hypocrisy by receiving a letter in Julia's name and manipulating her into a furious rage. Initially the maid is commanded peremptorily to take back the epistle unopened, then testily to return with it. When she carefully drops the letter in Julia's sight and counsels that it should not be read in such a belligerent mood, Julia tears it in pieces, only to be forced to attempt to reassemble them a few moments later. Obviously Lucetta knows where Julia's real affection lies: "I see things too, although you judge I wink" (139). Her perception is keener still a few scenes later when Julia determines to pursue Proteus to Milan. Lucetta tells her frankly that she had "Better forbear till Proteus make return" (II, vii, 14). Proteus "will scarce be pleas'd" with such a journey, and, to Julia's remark that Proteus' heart is free of fraud, she quips ominously, "Pray heaven he prove so, when you come to him!" (79).

All considered, there is much about the comic structure of *The Two Gentlemen of Verona* that suggests an early work in which

Shakespeare was experimenting for effective comic form. The comic pointers who help to maintain the proper rapport between spectator and stage-world by providing information necessary to a proper comic perspective, for example, appear predominantly in the first two acts. Launce and Speed appear once in III, Launce once in IV, neither in V. Obviously, the comic distance in the last half of the play depends essentially upon the exaggerated pattern of action and the rhetoric. In later comedies, the more extensive utilization of the comic pointers will frequently eliminate the need for such broad action and will make possible a more subtle depiction of the comic situation. Moreover, the pointers of this play are still peripheral to the main action; there is no full integration into the plot as will be the case with Oberon and Titania in *A Midsummer-Night's Dream* and Viola and Sebastian in *Twelfth Night*. Consequently, since the comic perspective lacks the clarity of his mature work, readers and critics have on occasion been misled concerning the playwright's intention; they have reacted sentimentally to what Shakespeare would have us laugh at—a situation which exposes the incongruities between what something really is and what it is taken to be. Nevertheless, there is a significant advancement over the comic pointers of *The Comedy of Errors,* in which Shakespeare provides the information for the situation comedy by framing the farce of mistaken identity with scenes which explain it to the spectators. In sum, although involved with the situation comedy of puppet characters, Shakespeare has begun his work with romantic comedy, a form which he will utilize for the next decade; and in his use of comic pointers who are, albeit imperfectly, an integral aspect of the plot he has begun the experimentation with a comic device, the evolution of which can be traced through his comedies of "action," "identity," and "transformation."

In *The Taming of the Shrew* as in *The Comedy of Errors,* Shakespeare utilizes an external framing device to establish the spectator's comic distance. Even though in its present form the action of the Induction is never concluded, quite probably Sly and his attendants are intended to remain on the balcony stage throughout the play to observe the action below. Thus the scene serves constantly to draw the filter of fiction before us lest we be tempted to forget that Kate is a purely artificial figure of farce and, like many an armchair critic, to become indignant that Shakespeare could consider such cruel mistreatment of womankind as comic. The lord, returning from his hunting expedition and spying the drunken Sly sprawled in front of an alehouse, determines to "practice on this drunken man" by surrounding him with lavish ornaments and convincing him he is a rich man who has for years suffered from loss of memory and obsession with poverty. The playwright, as if to provide double comic insurance, depicts now the arrival of players who, after consulting with the lord, agree to perform a shrew story, "pleasing stuff," for Sly's entertainment. Finally, the lord proclaims that he will act to control the reasonable limits of the humor:

> haply my presence
> May well abate the over-merry spleen
> Which otherwise would grow into extremes.
> (Induction, i, 136-138)

Shortly after the major action is underway, the characters of the Induction again appear to remind us of a play watched by Sly, who in turn is presumably watched by a lord, and who in turn is observed by us. Groggy and nodding, Sly awakens barely long enough to mumble to his page-wife: " 'Tis a very excellent piece of work, madam lady; would 'twere done!" (I, i, 258-259).

The major device for creating comic distance, then, like the protatic action involving Aegeon and Aemilia in *The Comedy of Errors*, is a layer of material entirely outside the main action. The machinery may indeed be crude when compared with the techniques which Shakespeare is to develop in his subsequent work, but the result is firmly to establish the perspective for situation comedy.

For that matter, were the frame omitted altogether, it is hardly conceivable that a critic *in the playhouse* could become emotionally involved with these characters in Padua. Clearly they are creatures who arouse humor directly from action, not from hypocrisy or transformation. The battle of the sexes—envisaged in the main plot through the extremes of the masculine ogre and the professed virago and mirrored in the subplot by the fatuous rival wooers—is played out to the spectator's delight as the one-dimensional characters are manipulated like pawns for maximum contentiousness. Petruchio is the same pompous and egocentric ass at the end of the play as he gloats over his wife's obedience and his resultant net gain of two hundred pounds that he was at the beginning when he stalked into Padua beating his servant for misunderstanding him and swearing his intentions to marry wealth.

> Come, Kate, we'll to bed.
> We three are married, but you two are sped.
> 'Twas I won the wager, though you hit the white.
> (V, ii, 184-186)

Nor has Kate changed one tittle! To be sure, she no longer flouts her shrewishness before Petruchio. But, far from conquering it, she has merely redirected it for greater effect. The Kate who takes up the cudgels with the widow at the drop of a word in the last act (and with Petruchio's encouragement—"To her, Kate") is the same Kate who strikes verbally at all comers in the opening scene; in the same fashion, Kate delights in the victory over Bianca which she gains through "obedience" to Petruchio just as she had previously delighted in threatening the younger sister and having her cower in fear. It is as if she has but teamed up with her husband in order to display her temperament more efficiently. Indeed, the "taming" of the title is no less ironic than the "gentlemen" of *The Two Gentlemen of Verona*.

The subplot reveals additional stock characters: the passive young maiden, the apprehensive fop, the lecherous old man who attempts to woo with money that which his body can no longer attract, the lovelorn young swain who loses every semblance of reason on his first glance at the damsel. Baptista, if taken seriously, emerges as a vicious and monstrous father figure whose perverted actions have precipitated his daughter's neurosis. Taken as a stylized figure, however, he is the stock comic father who endures his domineering daughter and is convinced that nobody in his right mind will marry the shrew. Add to these characters of farce the multiple disguises which enrich the mid section of the play (Tranio as Lucentio, Lucentio as Cambio, Hortensio as Licio, the old pedant as Vincentio), the minor comic pointer, Gremio, who as Petruchio's servant inserts numerous quips to enhance the comic potential of his master's action, and the broad humor arising from the frequent physical cuffing, and the result is a companion play to *The Comedy of Errors*. The narrative of this play may be more complex, but both the level of characterization and the structural devices which establish and control the audience's comic perspective are similar.

In like fashion, *Love's Labour's Lost* is a companion play to *The Two Gentlemen of Verona*. Both depend largely on caricature, minor characters as comic pointers, and zany figures whose action sporadically parallels that of the main plot. As *The Two Gentlemen of Verona* opens with the mocker invulnerable to love and the lover invulnerable to infidelity, each of whom is comically to pay the price of his pompous certitude, so *Love's Labour's Lost* opens with a masculine posture destined for ridiculous exposure—the vow binding the king of Navarre and his three attendant lords to Academe: three years of limited sleep, fasting, and total abstinence from women. Clearly the king, as Boyet observes after the first meeting with the French princess, is "[p]roud with his form, in his eye pride express[ing]" (II, i, 237). He has proclaimed that "Navarre shall be the wonder of the world" (I, i, 12) and that his "little Academe" will bring the fame for which all men seek. Despite Biron's doubts concerning the wisdom of the restrictions on food and feminine companionship, he, along with Longaville and Dumain, swears to the "barren tasks" with the king.

Forced to entertain the princess and her attendants, the young men predictably fall in love. The resultant scene, in which each pens a lyric to his lady fair and recites his passion in what he assumes to be solitude, only to realize that he has been overheard by his companions and thus his violation of the agreement discovered, is reminiscent of the later scene in which Benedick and Beatrice will alter their attitude toward love as a result of what they over-hear. In *Much Ado about Nothing*, of course, only the audience hears the admission of Benedick and later Beatrice that they are victims of the love they have so unmercifully mocked; the practicers who have informed each that he is passionately, if silently, adored by the other have departed. And only the audience enjoys the delicious moment when the two mockers first converse again in private and attempt to convey their newly discovered interest in each other. The situation in *Love's Labour's Lost* is more artificially contrived: Biron observes Longaville, these two individually ob-serve Dumain, and these three individually observe the king. In seriatim fashion each exposure is peeled off until only Biron is left smugly deriding those who have played false to the vow of Academe, and he in turn is exposed through his love note to Rosaline which Costard has mistakenly delivered to Jaquenetta.

The elaborate contrivance is, however, a key to the comic tone of this play. Whereas the humor of *Much Ado about Nothing* serves to purge Benedick and Beatrice of their unnatural attitudes and to prepare them for absorption into a normal society at the conclusion of the play (that is, whereas the humor arises from character and the incongruity of word and deed), the humor of *Love's Labour's Lost* serves only to deride an extreme posture which it is impossible to maintain (that is, the humor arises from the situation). Hence, the more elaborate and artificially contrived the comic trap, the greater the potential for the broadly played role appropriate to farce. To this end, Shakespeare does not, in any extensive way, motivate the passion of the king, Longaville, and Dumain or prepare us for their downfall. As with Proteus and Valentine, the spectator sees only the extreme shifts of romantic attitude, not the process of transformation, and the result is to emphasize the artificiality and the ludicrousness of it all. When we see the king and his companions in I, i, they are swearing their dedication to three years of study and in II, i, they are "of mere necessity" entertaining the princess and her attendants; our next encounter, IV, iii, finds them pouring out their devotion to love in what they suppose to be the privacy of Navarre's park. Even though the spectator might well detect the lord's more-than-passing interest in the ladies in their badinage of II, i, not even the most perceptive observer is prepared for the utter infatuation reflected in their verses. The result of depicting, with little or no credible motivation, love's mockers transformed into love's victims is obviously one of comic shock; the spectator, his emotional involvement with the young lovers blocked by the stylized pattern, reacts to the humor of the situation. It is true, of course, that Biron appears in III, i, to confess his love, and certainly, considering his earlier reservations about Academe, the spectator is not totally surprised to discover that this lord is no longer "love's whip." Even here, however, the "plague / That Cupid will impose for [his] neglect" (203-204) has struck with amusing suddenness. Certainly the new oath in favor of love which emerges from their mutual exposure ("let us embrace! / As true we are as flesh and blood can be" [IV, iii, 214-215]), the ensuing argument between the king and Biron as to which mistress is the fairer, the king's determination to fight for "Saint Cupid," the princess' exclamations that they are "wit turn'd fool" (V, ii, 70) and that their dotage reflects "gravity's revolt to [wantoness]" (74): all suggest that their defense of love is as artificial and extreme as their previous defiance.

In effect, then, the mockers are transformed into doters and, as such, are prepared for further amusement by the ladies who at this point quite candidly inform the spectator that they are playing the game for sport. Four male pawns who mock love are set against four female pawns who are receptive to love; the master strategist moves, and the chess board is rearranged: four male pawns who dote on their mistresses are set against four female pawns who are determined to "mock them still" in a "civil war of wits." If the description is oversimplified, it nevertheless captures the comic flavor.

As with Adriana in *The Comedy of Errors*, the king and his companions apparently profit to some degree from their comic experiences. Biron at one point suggests to Navarre that by "losing" their oaths they can "find" themselves (IV, iii, 361) and sometime later he admits the transforming quality of Rosaline's wit (V, ii, 373 ff.). And it is he who, in his own way, admits to Rosaline the pretentiousness of their previous posture:

> O, never will I trust to speeches penn'd . . .
> Nor never come in vizard to my friend,
>   Nor woo in rhyme, like a blind harper's song!
> Taffeta phrases, silken terms precise,
>   Three-piled hyperboles, spruce [affectation],
> Figures pedantical; these summer-flies
>   Have blown me full of maggot ostentation.
> I do forswear them, and I here protest . . .
> Henceforth my wooing mind shall be express'd
>   In russet yeas and honest kersey noes.
>   (V, ii, 402, 404-410, 412-413)

The king, too, requests of the princess that she "Teach us . . . for our rude transgression / Some fair excuse" (431-432).

Again, however, Shakespeare does not permit the humor to develop from any kind of character revelation. The ladies' mockery of the confession, arising from each lord's having pledged his devotion to the "wrong" lady, a scheme devised and executed by the princess (V, ii, 127 ff.), and the subsequent parade of the "nine worthies" across the stage tend to focus the humor on situation rather than character. So also, when Navarre and Biron reiterate their devotion a few moments later, the princess retorts that "our maiden council" never regarded the courtship as more than "pleasant jest and courtesy, / As bombast and as lining to the time" (789-791).

Indeed the master touch is the one-year penance imposed on each of the lords, with Biron instructed to "Visit the speechless sick, and still converse / With groaning wretches" (861-862) and the king pledged to "go with speed / To some forlorn and naked hermitage, / Remote from all the pleasures of the world" (804-806). Navarre is, in short, to prove his sincerity through a period of fasting, contemplation, and abstinence from the opposite sex. That ridiculous vow for which the antilovers were mocked at the beginning of the play becomes now the vow by which he is to succeed! Ironic indeed, but how more effectively could the playwright maintain the comic focus upon the hilarious situation and prevent the spectator's emotional involvement with the young lovers? There is, of course, the subtle implication that the four young men by abiding the year's test will achieve the necessary growth or development in character which will make them capable of real love. But this is a growth which, if at all, will occur beyond the limits of the stage-world.

Boyet among the ladies of France and Biron among the lords of Navarre function as comic pointers. Boyet, while never a central part of the action, does provide comments which direct our attention to the absurdity of Navarre's schemes. Moreover, it is he who is largely responsible for inciting the romantic warfare. He, for instance, first informs the princess of the lords' susceptibility to Cupid, and he later prepares her for the visit of the Muscovites and assists her in mocking the disguised men. He observes also, as the men abandon their defenses in the final act, that the "tongues of mocking wenches are as keen / As is the razor's edge invisible" (V, ii, 256-257). Biron, on the other hand, is in function a foretaste of such Shakespearean characters as Viola, Helena, Vincentio, Paulina, and Prospero. These characters, aside from their significance to the main plot, provide comments which establish and control the spectator's comic perspective; a primary device for comic distancing is thus functionally integrated, not peripheral to the main story as in *The Comedy of Errors* and *The Taming of the Shrew*. Biron, to be sure, is only partially successful as a pointer, his comments sporadic; yet in his early predictions that Academe involves "barren tasks, too hard to keep, / Not to see ladies, study, fast, not sleep!" (I, i, 47-48) and his comment that "all delights are vain" which are purchased with pain (72) and that "Necessity will make us all forsworn" (150), he reflects a greater degree of self-knowledge than his colleagues possess and directs the spectator's laughter upon himself and the cult of the intellect. Likewise it is Biron who in the final act first forswears the Petrarchan pose and avers that henceforth his wooing shall be "In russet yeas and honest kersey noes" (413). And it is Biron who voices the appropriate concluding comment that "Our wooing doth not end like an old play; / Jack hath not Jill" (V, ii, 884-885) because the ladies who "Might well have made our sport a comedy," (886) have refused to give their hands in marriage.

Shakespeare also utilizes subplot characters who through their parallel antics enhance the comic potential of the major action. As Navarre and his companions pursue their ladies fair, Costard and Don Adriano de Armado contest for Jacquenetta, the country wench. Indeed Costard's arrest by Dull, the bumbling constable, on the charge of cavorting with a woman in defiance of the law of Academe, preplots the similar fall of the male principals. Even our *miles gloriosus* falls victim to the petticoat despite his vaunted invulnerability! Additional subplot characters such as Holofernes and Nathaniel are somewhat heavy-handedly and peripherally introduced into the plot. Nevertheless, the inept performance of the Nine Worthies—including those who are mocked as a result of their inability to remember their lines and those who, even in their august garbs, continue their rivalry over the country wench—reinforces the farcical tone at the moment at which the death of the King of France must conclude the merry war of the sexes and the ladies impose their final mandate.

Throughout the early comedies, then, Shakespeare, to create a comic perspective, is experimenting with caricature, loosely related parallel action in the low characters, servants who, wiser than they seem, speak revealingly of their masters, framing devices which provide the spectator superior knowledge and emphasize the fictional nature of the action, broad physical action and bawdy dialogue, and occasional stock comic characters whose relation to the narrative itself is quite incidental. At times the comic machinery is too plainly visible, the effect a bit strained. And, at all times the flavor of farce is largely dependent upon stylization of character and action, which is for many people a quality more easily realized on the stage than in the imagination. In this respect these early comedies share a common disadvantage, for they are staged relatively infrequently; and thus armchair critics or readers more easily fall prey to the tendency to seek in the character a credibility and consistency which belie his dramatic purposes and destroy the comic tone.

Shakespeare's final situation comedy, A *Midsummer-Night's Dream*, does not, however, suffer these difficulties. In this play, one of the most frequently produced, the dramatist achieves a successful integration of technique and plot, a comic perspective which is functional as well to the developing narrative. The characters who form the narrative center are again one-dimensional.[21] Like the Dromios and Antipholuses, Proteus and Valentine, Kate and Petruchio, the Athenian quartet are basically static characters manipulated into humorous contradiction and incongruity. Indeed, they are virtual caricatures of lovesick youth, comic proof that "reason and love keep little company together now-a-days" (III, i, 147-148). Stylized for situation comedy, they have no identity aside from their love-interest, and their victimization by whimsical passion is no less at the conclusion of the play than at the beginning; that is, they have gained no new insights into the nature of love and no greater self-control as a result of their experience. Their romantic confusion, generated to be sure by natural impulses, is both intensified and resolved by supernatural forces visible only to the audience.

The comic tone is immediately established in the first scene through farcical repartee and action. Egeus charges that Lysander has bewitched his daughter with moonlight verses "at her window sung" and with locks of his hair and other such "knacks." Theseus concurs, and to his observation that Demetrius is indeed "a worthy gentleman," Hermia retorts: "So is Lysander . . . I would my father look'd but with my eyes" (I, i, 53, 56), and in a similar vein Lysander quips to his rival a few lines later: "You have her father's love, Demetrius, / Let me have Hermia's; do you marry him" (93-94). Later, alone with Lysander and faced with the unlikely options of the tomb or the nunnery for disobedience, Hermia laments the obstacles confronting "true love." In a stichomythic conversation replete with comic potential if played broadly, the couple catalogue love's barriers at length and agree that, since it "stands as an edict in destiny," they must accept this "customary cross" with "patience" (151-153). Yet, within three lines the impetuous lovers are laying elaborate secret plans for defying "destiny" by eloping to a house "from Athens . . . seven leagues" remote. So excited are they about these plans that, the importance of secrecy notwithstanding, they blurt the news to the first passerby, who happens to be Helena, with her own vested interests in their arrangement. All told, the first appearance of the Athenian lovers, long before fairy whimsicality can be blamed, is a veritable travesty of reason.

The fay machinery, of course, compounds the confusion and the humor in the middle of the play by creating situations for arrant contradictions of the sacred vow. Helena, for instance, doting on Demetrius, chases into the woods her lover, who in turn is chasing Hermia. Helena is mercilessly insulted by Demetrius, and at the exact moment she convinces herself that she is "as ugly as a bear" (II, ii, 94) and that her pursuit is futile, she is dumbfounded by his sudden reversal of romantic interest, his desire to "change a raven for a dove," and the hunter becomes the hunted. A similar reversal by Lysander in Act III is the final step in the farcical *reductio ad absurdum*; each youth now is miserable: Hermia loves Lysander, Lysander loves Helena, Demetrius Helena, Helena hates both men for mocking her (or so she assumes), and both men hate Hermia. Much of the humor at this point arises from the physical differences between Helena, the tall blonde, and Hermia, the short brunette. When Helena chides her companion for allowing love to destroy their friendship, Hermia brands her a "juggler" and "canker-blossom" (III, ii, 282); to win Lysander, the blonde:

        hath urg'd her height;
And with her personage, her tall personage,
Her height, forsooth, she hath prevail'd with him . . .
Because I am so dwarfish and so low?
    . . . thou painted maypole? Speak,
        . . . I am not yet so low
But that my nails can reach unto thine eyes.
                        (291-293, 295-298)

With Helena imploring the men for protection ("Let her not hurt me"), she is chased offstage, yelling:

Your hands than mine are quicker for a fray;
My legs are longer though, to run away.
                        (342-343)

The men, only a few steps behind, also exchange threats, and the act concludes with the four, unable to locate each other, wandering aimlessly through the forest, yelling insults until they fall asleep from exhaustion. When they awaken the next morning to the sound of Theseus' hunting horn, all romantic confusions are forgotten "as a dream." The lovers are properly paired; Theseus denies Egeus' complaints; "Jack shall have Jill; / Nought shall go ill" (III, ii, 461-462).

   Whatever the occasional critic may say about the characterization in A Midsummer-Night's Dream,[22] these are not characters so much as they are pawns. Certainly the height and hair color, even the temperament, distinguishes the heroines, but these traits are no more substantial than the fiery Adriana and the passive Luciana, or than the Antipholus twins from different lands, one single and one married, or than the polarized temperaments of Baptista's daughters in Padua. As in Shakespeare's previous comedies, the characters are funny for what they do, not for what they pretend to be and certainly not for some transformation in personality. Determined by the preconceived situation, not as in later plays giving rise to the action as a result of their personality, these characters are maneuvered from above rather than motivated from within. As such, the comic detachment is preserved; the spectator is never tempted into emotional involvement with the quartet and their frantic romantic escapades.

Yet the success of this play, in which Shakespeare is universally credited with his first comic masterpiece,[23] is obviously the result of more than stylization of character. The advancement is primarily in structure—the arrangement of the plot strands to achieve the most effective comic perspective. The comic pointer or controller and the subplot as a comic comment upon the main action are more fully integrated than in the playwright's previous work.[24] And the result for the spectator is a firm and clear perspective through which to realize the full comic potential of the drama.

Scholars have delighted in explaining this structure in terms of "layers" of action, which is claimed to be the consequence of Shakespeare's artistic fusion of diverse borrowings from his own age and earlier. Certainly, literary source hunting is productive in providing information concerning the author's personal reading habits and also in shedding possible light on the purposes of the work under consideration. Yet, the results are hardly worth the effort when, by surrounding Shakespeare with a hoard of works, one turns him into what Quiller-Couch has described as "a shadowy Prospero" darting here for a motif, there for a characterization.[25] Everything we know about Shakespeare suggests a more pragmatic and direct creative process.

The case is, of course, overstated in the previous paragraph, for Shakespeare did borrow frequently and extensively from others; in virtually no instance did he create his plot whole cloth. Nevertheless, it is somewhat disconcerting to read that, for *A Midsummer-Night's Dream*, the dramatist consciously drew the hint for Theseus and Hippolyta from Chaucer's "The Knight's Tale" and North's translation of Plutarch, verbal bits from Marlowe's *Dido*, the name Titania from Ovid's *Metamorphoses*, Oberon from the *Huon of Bordeaux* or Greene's *James IV*, Puck's characteristics from Scot's *The Discovery of Witchcraft*, the fairies from Drayton's "Nymphidia" (borrowing—as Edmund Malone first pointed out—in the other direction if at all, since Drayton's mock heroic fairy tale was not composed until 1627), the magic juice from Montemayor's *Diana*, and the happy idea of Pyramus and Thisbe from Pettie's *The Petite Palace of Pettie His Pleasure*, the miscellany *A Gorgeous Gallery of Gallant Inventions*, and Thomas Mouffet's didactic poem *The Silke-Wormes and Their Flies*.[26] To be sure, this is only a partial listing, but perhaps the predicament is sufficiently illustrated in a single remark by Professor Kenneth Muir concerning the Pyramus and Thisbe episode, two hundred and fifty lines of Act V: "It is enough for my purpose if the reader is willing to concede that Shakespeare consulted six or seven versions of the Pyramus story before writing his tedious brief scene."[27] It is always possible, of course, that Shakespeare was working from a lost play by a sixteenth-century T. S. Eliot who had indeed fused a narrative from such multiple and diverse sources,[28] but with no evidence to support it, such an assertion is manifestly unconvincing.

Shakespeare's structural artistry in *A Midsummer-Night's Dream* has a less complex and much more logical explanation. Instead of fusing three or four disparate strands of action, he was apparently adapting "The Knight's Tale," the prototype of these narrative lines, to the purposes of romantic comedy. Admittedly, the concept that Shakespeare drew from Chaucer is not new; numerous critics (see footnote 26) have observed a general similarity of plot, and Shakespeare's debt has been both rigorously asserted and denied. Israel Gollancz, for instance, argues for a direct Chaucerian influence, while H. Staunton maintains there is no resemblance between the play and the metrical romance except that both tales are set in the court of Theseus at Athens.[29] But the fact remains that the basic structure and sequence of events in the two stories run parallel from end to end. (1) The narrative begins with a state wedding, either consummated or projected. (2) Problems posed by individuals seeking Theseus' aid and advice attract the attention of the royal lovers, and (3) the duke intervenes to proffer a solution. (4) From this settlement involving physical authority arises an even more intense romantic factionalism in which (5) supernatural powers intervene and (6) ultimately impose a solution more whimsical than justifiable. (7) The story then concludes with an explanation of the turn of events, an additional marriage ceremony, and the establishment of a romantic aura in which peace and joy reign supreme.

If one were asked to summarize either "The Knight's Tale" or *A Midsummer-Night's Dream,* it would be naive to describe the plot in this manner. Even so, such a sketch does illustrate the remarkably similar narrative structure of the two. In Chaucer's tale (1) Theseus, Duke of Athens, has wed Hippolyta, Queen of the Amazons, and returns to Athens with his bride. (2) His homecoming is stayed at the outskirts of the town by a group of ladies, widowed queens and duchesses in black, who beseech him to attack Creon in order to gain revenge for the desecration of their husbands' bodies. (3) The noble duke rides off posthaste to do battle with Creon, defeats him, and conquers Thebes. (4) From this apparent solution arises the rivalry in love of Palamon and Arcite, who, brought to Athens as perpetual prisoners, fall desperately in love with Emily from the vantage point of the window in their prison cell. (5) Following Arcite's escape and Palamon's release from prison, as the rival wooers prepare to settle the issue by tournament combat, each invokes divine aid: Arcite, Mars; Palamon, Venus; Emily, Diana. In turn, a rivalry develops between Mars and Venus, (6) with the wily Saturn providing a stratagem by which both can be victorious. Mars appropriately aids Arcite in defeating Palamon in war, yet Venus prevails in love, as Palamon eventually gains the lady following Arcite's fatal accident arranged by Saturn. (7) Theseus, as later in Shakespeare's comedy, is unaware of the activities of the gods, whose solution has been whimsically imposed upon the mortal world. And, as later he must draw an observation on the comic activities of the lovers, so here he must attempt to read purpose and meaning into the seeming welter of tragic events. The Duke, in a speech of Boethian consolation, determines that it is "wysdom . . . / to maken vertu of necessitee, / And take it weel that we may not eschue," trusting that "the Firste Moevere of the cause above"[30] controls and orders all events in a providential scheme incomprehensible to the finite faculties. Thus the metrical romance concludes on a solemn note of philosophic didacticism.

Clearly there are three significant layers of the action: the Theseus and Hippolyta relationship, which frames the central action; the romantic struggles of Palamon and Arcite, which is the heart of the action; and the intervention of the gods, which is the motivating force both to complicate and to resolve the question of the romantic struggles. In Shakespeare's play both the arrangement of the plot strands and the sequence of events are similar: The Theseus-Hippolyta relationship frames the action, the romantic struggles of Lysander, Demetrius, Hermia, and Helena form the heart of the action, and the intervention of the fairy-gods motivates, complicates, and resolves their struggles. A fourth strand of action —the rustics with their bumbling rehearsals and even more inept dramatic performance—is apparently original with Shakespeare and, as described later, is a primary device by which the dramatist sharpens the comic perspective.

More specifically, (1) Theseus returns to Athens with his intended bride Hippolyta, Queen of the Amazons. (2) His address of love is abruptly terminated by Egeus, Hermia's enraged father, who demands the judgment of the state upon his disobedient daughter. (3) Theseus concurs with Egeus in principle if not in spirit, informing Hermia that within three days she must either accept the suitor favored by her father, vow herself to eternal chastity, or die for disobedience to her father's will. (4) This apparent solution intensifies the rivalry in love between Demetrius and Lysander, a situation made further complex by the attempted elopement of Lysander and Hermia, the doting Helena who informs Demetrius of such plans, and the subsequent gathering of all four love-sick Athenian youths in the woods, "a league without the town." (5) At this point comes the intervention of the supernatural agents, Oberon and Titania, the King and Queen of the fairies, their own estrangement reminiscent of the struggles between Mars and Venus.[31] (6) With the mischievous aid of Puck[32] and the juice of the magic flower, Oberon transforms the rival wooers from suitors of Hermia to suitors of Helena and ultimately rights the situation so that "Jack shall have Jill; / Nought shall go ill" (III, ii, 461-462). (7) As Theseus in "The Knight's Tale," unaware of the whimsical actions of the gods, interprets the subsequent turn of events philosophically, and thus establishes the dominant tone of that narrative, so Theseus in *A Midsummer-Night's Dream*, by refusing to believe the lovers' tales are more than fabrications of the passionate mind, passes tolerant and romantic judgment upon the Athenian quartet and their fancied dreams: "The lunatic, the lover, and the poet / Are of imagination all compact" (V, i, 7-8). Indeed, in the harried world of romantic comedy, "reason and love keep little company together now-a-days" (III, i, 146-147).

In effect, Shakespeare has utilized Chaucer's tale in a much more extensive fashion than previous critics have articulated. Certainly there are modifications—but such that Shakespeare, whether faced with providing marital entertainment or not,[33] would devise by way of adapting the plot to the purposes of romantic comedy and creating a proper perspective for the spectator. For instance, by adding Helena to the group of young lovers, Shakespeare intensifies the rival wooing theme and enriches the comic potential of the lovers' confusion (Demetrius and Lysander → Hermia; Demetrius and Lysander → Helena; Lysander → Hermia, Demetrius → Helena). Also, of course, the addition of the girl obviates the necessity of ultimately removing one of the young men when the author is resolving the romantic complications. The fairy court of Titania and Oberon provides song and dance, for instance the songs of Titania's attendants in II, ii; the addition of Egeus[34] provides the irate father who attempts to block the progress of young love: both are conventional elements of romantic comedy.

Such alterations, however, are relatively minor. Two further structural modifications provide the basic transformation of Chaucer's tale of chivalric romance into the fun and farce of romantic comedy and create the perspective through which we are to view it—the addition of the rustics as parodic machinery and the substitution of fay rulers for Olympian deities. Through Bottom and his associates Shakespeare is obviously burlesquing his own profession:[35] the play they produce (*The Most Lamentable Comedy and Most Cruel Death of Pyramus and Thisbe*), utterly inappropriate in tone and title if not in theme; the ridiculous casting, with Bottom demanding every role and Flute embarrassed at having a female part; the pompous manner of delivery, combined with actors who confuse actual lines with cues, the endless death scene in which the protagonist loses more breath than blood, and the doggerel rhythm certain to turn the most serious of themes to laughter.

More important to the comic perspective, the subplot parallels and burlesques the major action and thus reinforces the comic detachment for the spectator. Specifically, the handicraftsmen appear five times in the play, their action in each instance directly related to the misadventures of the Athenian youth. The first appearance (I, ii) occurs immediately after our lovers have established their roles —the rejected maiden, the pursued damsel, the rival wooers; the two who have planned an elopement foolishly tell the third, who in turn plans to tell the fourth. If for even a brief moment Helena's determination to mar the elopement blunts the comic edge, the handicraftsmen sharpen it through their bumbling casting scenes; they too will assume the roles of young lovers victimized by love, and their decidedly fictional quality—largely the result of Bottom's enormous ego and his desire to play all parts, or at least to describe interminably his fatuous costume plans for the lead—gives comic emphasis to the equally stylized creations in the main plot.

Their next two appearances burlesque the harried romantic confusions of the Athenian lovers. With the chase underway in the moonlit woods as Helena pursues Demetrius, Quince and his company begin their rehearsal. Just as Helena, having convinced herself that she is "as ugly as a bear," becomes the object of Demetrius' affection, so does Bottom, literally as ugly as an ass—at least in part —become the object of Titania's affection. His first words following his transformation ("If I were fair, Thisby, I were only thine" [III, i, 106]) echo Helena's self-disparagement. And, as Lysander, awakening, vows that he will "run through fire . . . for thy sweet sake. / Transparent Helena!" (II, ii, 103-104), so Titania, awakening, sighs, "What angel wakes me from my flowery bed? . . . I pray thee, gentle mortal, sing again" (III, i, 132, 140). Bottom's "delicate" song leads the fairy queen to declare:

> So is mine eye enthralled to thy shape;
> And thy fair virtue's force perforce doth move me
> On the first view to say, to swear, I love thee.
>
> (142-144)

Titania's love-at-first-sight, of course, parallels the frantic and frequent interchange of such passion among Demetrius, Lysander, Helena, and Hermia. In similar fashion, Bottom's appearance in IV, i farcically anticipates the lovers' reconciliation, which is to occur later in the same scene. Ministered to by Titania's court, the befuddled weaver revels in such lavish attention; if inexplicably he desires his head scratched or "good dry oats" or a trip to the barber, he nonetheless can appreciate the romantic interest of a female who is able to supply comforts at will.[36] Meanwhile, Oberon, having secured the changeling boy from his queen and now pitying her condition, applies to her eyes the ointment of Dian's bud, the antidote for love-in-idleness. Starting as if from a dream, she exclaims, "Methought I was enamour'd of an ass" (80). So also Theseus and his hunting party come upon the sleeping lovers, who "Half sleep, half waking . . . cannot truly say how [they] came here" (151-152). Likewise released from their spells, each claims an appropriate partner, and Theseus proclaims that his nuptial plans shall be expanded to include theirs.

The final action of the handicraftsmen in Act V provides the entertainment for this wedding festival. A brief appearance at the conclusion of Act IV sets the proper comic tone for the "merry and tragical" play; Bottom, rushing in at the last moment to rejoin his troupe and flatly refusing to describe what he thinks he remembers of his "dream-like" experiences, charges his companions to prepare themselves for performance: "let Thisby have clean linen; and let not him that plays the lion pare his nails, for they shall hang out for the lion's claws. And, most dear actors, eat no onions nor garlic, for we are to utter sweet breath; and I do not doubt but to hear them say, it is a sweet comedy" (IV, ii, 39-46). As for the performance itself, the inept acting—numerous malapropisms, confusion of cues with lines, misreading of punctuation, interpolated conversation with the audience, histrionic gesturing and ad-libbing—coupled with the high seriousness of the Pyramus and Thisbe legend creates a travesty of the tribulations of youthful passion and provides a hilarious capstone comment on the major theme of the play.[37] We read frequently that this seriocomic rendition is perhaps a parody of *Romeo and Juliet*. How much more certainly it sharpens the comic vagaries of romantic love as the spectator observes this mockery of the plight of the Athenian lovers. Hermia and Lysander, like Pyramus and Thisbe, face parental opposition to their love and thus are forced to meet in secret and to place themselves at the mercy of fate (happily in the form of fairy rather than lion). Like that of Pyramus and Thisbe, their love encounters numerous miscalculations and misjudgments, and like their ancient counterparts they are impelled to rebellion and risks by a reason clouded by impetuous passion.

The subplot, then, is far more than occasional farce inserted for diversion. While it certainly reflects Shakespeare's use of material which he knew intimately from first-hand observation,[38] it also illustrates his increasing ability to achieve a firm comic perspective through elements functional within what the spectator perceives to be the total dramatic fabric.

The substitution of whimsical fairy for Chaucer's Olympian gods, however, most clearly establishes the proper fictional tone for the spectator.[39] For this is not a world governed by stern gods who, engaged in their own quarrels, are willing to destroy mortals in order that their wills might prevail; it is not a world in which death is an actuality. Instead it is a world controlled by fairies, themselves taunting and estranged lovers, who at worst suck up contagious fogs from the seas, rot the crops, or produce late frosts—fairies who are content to rectify all mortal problems once their own lover's quarrel is settled.[40] And, of course, the rulers have come to Athens to grace the wedding of their favored mortal (Titania → Theseus, Oberon → Hippolyta). Whereas the wedding in Chaucer involves a bitter struggle between Mars and Venus through Arcite and Palamon, the wedding in Shakespeare is a matter of mutually pleasant consent to the fairy rulers.

Much of the second act is devoted to the exposition of Oberon and Titania as benevolent rulers of this fictional stage-world. The powers of Puck, as Oberon's jester, are described at length (II, i, 33-41, 43-58), after which the estranged king and queen enter from opposite sides of the stage, each chiding the other for interest in the opposite sex. The central speech is that of Titania (81-117), who attributes the various mortal ills to their "jealousy" and "brawls."

> The human mortals want their winter [cheer];
> No night is now with hymn or carol blest.
> Therefore the moon, the governess of floods,
> Pale in her anger, washes all the air,
> That rheumatic diseases do abound . . .
> And this same progeny of evils comes
> From our debate, from our dissension;
> We are their parents and original.
>   (101-105, 115-117)

With Oberon's additional comments to Puck (155-174, 176-187) concerning the miraculous powers of love-in-idleness and Dian's bud and his intentions to use them to win his point with Titania, our *deus ex machina* is securely established. The only connection still necessary is the fairy king's interest in the Athenian lovers, and this concern a few lines later results from his observation of the forlorn Helena and the disdainful Demetrius. To be sure, Puck's misapplications of the love potion, both intentional and unintentional, will create the full circle of romantic confusion, but it is now inconceivable that the spectator be apprehensive over the outcome. The intervention of the deities to manipulate the mortal affairs of the heart is, of course, corollary to the solution of their own quarrel. In his own strange way, the ass-headed Bottom becomes a parodic rival wooer for Oberon's queen, thereby making the estrangement of the royal fairies the more ridiculous. The argument, however, is only the generating circumstance; the emphasis of the play for them, and for the Athenian youth, is reconciliation. Appropriately, following his command to Puck to correct the mortals' romantic confusion, Oberon delivers the final words of the play, a blessing on the wedding and a prophecy that the lovers shall ever be true and that their issue "Ever shall be fortunate" (V, i, 413). In effect, there is no real evil in this play; there are no fully developed characters; but this world of Athens is Oberon's as firmly as the island world of *The Tempest* is Prospero's. Both men stand in full view of the audience, if not the surrounding characters, as they direct their subjects to a predetermined happy conclusion, of which the audience shares a vision.

Once it is established that Shakespeare is refashioning "The Knight's Tale" to his own purposes, there is obviously nothing to prevent us from perceiving any number of further "sources" which he might incidentally have drawn upon in the adaptation. But, such modification of a single tale is far indeed from assuming—as most critics do—that Shakespeare was weaving disparate plot strands into the fabric of *A Midsummer-Night's Dream*: that he was achieving "a satisfactory blending" of "four plots" derived "from such diversified sources as classical myth and legend, native English fairy lore, and his own intimate knowledge of amateur theatricals," "exercising great ingenuity to unify a hotch-potch of material."[41] Moreover, it goes without saying that Shakespeare's use of the prototype of a complete narrative in no way minimizes his artistry. The prime significance is that Shakespeare, with a talent which makes of adaptation no less a talent than originality, has achieved his most fully integrated and effective comic perspective to date and, as a consequence, his greatest success in situation comedy.

"By my foes, sir, I profit in the knowledge of myself"

3 *The* Comedies of Identity

With his final plays of the sixteenth century, Shakespeare rejects comedy based upon action alone and moves toward the development of a comic vision through which to relate credible development of character. Only in *The Merry Wives of Windsor,* which might well have been produced hastily upon royal command, does he again rely on the farce of situational intrigue in which one-dimensional characters are manipulated into cleverly arranged comic complications. Ford, for example, is the stock jealous husband all too ready to believe himself a cuckold and Falstaff a villain. Disguised as Brooke, he gullibly devours Falstaff's pompous claims of masculinity and sets one trap after another in his futile efforts to apprehend his wife in her guilt. His conversion to patience and trust at the end of the play—announced peremptorily rather than dramatically experienced—is much like that of Adriana, or of Ferdinand and Biron, or of Kate. Again, the humor arises not from any credible alteration in character but from the jealous man fed the fuel of his dissension, comic because the reader shares with Mistress Ford and Mistress Page their determination to practice upon Falstaff for his foolish presumption and on Ford for his unfounded jealousy. The other characters are likewise one-dimensional: Dr. Caius and Hugh Evans, raging furiously about a duel which never comes off; the fatuous Slender, willing to woo but not really aware of what it is all about; Mistress Quickly, willing to speak a good word to Ann Page for anyone who will pay well for it; Fenton, the aristocrat who woos for love rather than for material gain; Bardolph and Nym, the seedy retainers of a decadent knight. And above all, of course, there is Sir John himself. Yet, if *The Merry Wives of Windsor* has the presence of the "huge bombard of sack" to commend it, the pawn here is far indeed from the witty and pragmatic buffoon who so perfectly embodies the sardonic political realities of sixteenth-century England; the counterpart in Windsor is a fat fool who, envisioning himself as a *fine amour,* is led in rapid succession into three predicaments involving a tumbling while in a dirty laundry basket, a buffeting while in disguise as Mother Prat, and a roughing up by "fairies" while decked out as Herne the Hunter. The humor of Falstaff, in short, as of the characters in the early comedies, results from what he as a stock character does, not from how what happens alters or affects his personality.

The Falstaff of the chronicle plays, on the other hand, is of significance in the evolution of Shakespeare's artistry. Like the earlier principals of *The Merchant of Venice,* he, as a character who apparently develops in the course of the action of the play, is among the playwright's first flesh and blood comic creations. It may well be that the development is more apparent than real—that Shakespeare is actually creating a series of scenes which through the course of *1, 2 Henry IV* control and manipulate the spectator's attitude toward the character by progressively revealing the dissipation concealed for a time by his high degree of wit. If so, the development of character is not in any alteration or transformation in Falstaff himself, but in the depth of the spectator's vision of him and the realization of his artistry in using the verbal retort to make the worse appear the better. But the technique of controlling the perspective of the audience in such a fashion is only one step removed from a controlled perspective in which actual character development does occur. In effect, whether by design or by accident, the Falstaff of *Henry IV* is apparently the result of Shakespeare's experimentation in comic technique and as such broadly reflects the general transition from the one-dimensional characters of the comedies of action to the two-dimensional characters of the comedies of identity, in which the humor arises from the development of character in that the action of the play focuses on the character's being forced to recognize or to acknowledge his true nature and his being supposedly permanently affected as a result of his comic experience.

In *The Merchant of Venice,* much as in *A Midsummer-Night's Dream,* Shakespeare is interweaving various strands of action which in their cumulative effect provide a more powerful statement than that of any single strand. The theme quite overtly concerns the quality of ideal love and its effects upon the human personality.

The experiences of Bassanio-Portia (Gratiano-Nerissa) and Lorenzo-Jessica depict love's powers to overcome barriers created on the one hand by the "will of a dead father" and on the other hand by a hatred bred of centuries of racial enmity, in each case the relationship at some point reflecting the sacrificial selflessness of ideal love. Here and in the subsequent romantic comedies, the playwright develops his comedy primarily not from the situation of the wooing but from the manner in which the characters come to learn their true identity in the process of the courtship. Admittedly Jessica and Lorenzo are stylized in that they never waver in their devotion; ready to sacrifice friend, family, wealth, and country for each other, they leave little room for "growth" in their conception of love and their awareness of its powers. Portia and Bassanio, on the other hand, do experience a self-revelation as evidenced by their actions during the course of the play.

Bassanio at the outset is by his own admission a gallant who has "disabled [his] estate / By something showing a more swelling port / Than [his] faint means would grant continuance" (I, i, 123-125). The wooing of Portia, for which he borrows three thousand ducats from Antonio by way of Shylock, he broaches primarily as a plan to render himself debt free, "to get clear of all the debts I owe" (134). Portia's love, however, kindles the best sparks in his character. Certainly by the time he is forced to choose between three caskets, his scale of values has undergone a significant change. The "gaudy gold, / Hard food for Midas" (III, ii, 101-102), the earlier Bassanio would never have been able to bypass; and his reflection that "outward shows" are but deceptive ornament to true worth hardly suggests the gallant of "swelling port." So too, following the marriage and the return to Venice, his magnanimity toward Antonio reaches its greatest heights with the offer of his life for that of his friend:

> The Jew shall have my flesh, blood, bones, and all,
> Ere thou shalt lose for me one drop of blood.
> (IV, i, 112-113)

His "life itself . . . wife, and all the world" he would "lose . . . aye, sacrifice them all" to save his friend (284 ff.).

Portia, too, realizes her finest moments as a result of love's influence. Throughout the early scenes, as suitors virtually parade before the three caskets, she is melancholy and irritable, "aweary of this great world" because she "may neither choose who [she] would nor refuse who [she] dislike[s]" (I, ii, 2, 24-25). Delighting only in mocking her suitors as Nerissa names them over, she exclaims that "there is not one among them" whose absence she does not "dote on" (119-120). It is a new Portia indeed who wishes herself "A thousand times more fair, ten thousand times / More rich" (III, ii, 155-156) so that she might stand higher in Bassanio's account, and who excitedly presents herself to him as "an unlessoned girl, unschooled, unpracticed":

> Happiest of all is that her gentle spirit
> Commits itself to yours to be directed,
> As from her lord, her governor, her king.
> Myself and what is mine to you and yours
> Is now converted.
>
> (165-169)

Significantly, as Bassanio's growth in love finds fullest expression in his attempts to save the life of his friend, so Portia, for the love she bears her lord, assumes the role of Balthasar and, in effect, does save the merchant.

Antonio, then, is the recipient of the selfless actions to which the power of love has raised both Bassanio and Portia. Each through the catalyst of love has recognized true identity more completely. And, interestingly enough, Antonio also is forced to recognize the limitations in his view of love and consequently to profit from the experience of the play. In the first act, the merchant opens his "purse, [his] person, [his] extremest means" (I, i, 138) to his friend in need of money for the wooing of Portia; to his friends he is the paragon of integrity and generosity. Yet, this "ideal" friend harbors a detestation of the Jew equally as vehement as any Shylock feels for the Christian: in the Rialto he "rails" on Shylock's dealings (I, iii, 48 ff.), calls him a "misbeliever, cut-throat dog, / And spit[s] upon [his] Jewish gaberdine . . . void[s] rheum upon [his] beard / And foot[s] [him] as . . . a stranger cur" (112-113, 119, 126, 131 ff.; III, i, 56-60). Later, while for a time in the Jew's clutches, Antonio witnesses the awesome ugliness of sheer hate as Shylock demands his pound of flesh. And apparently he recognizes the like passion within himself as he sees it reflected in another. For certainly the Antonio who, following Portia's legal maneuvering disguised as Balthasar, forgives Shylock and remits to him his possessions (IV, i, 381-390) is a man whose vision of love has grown and expanded. The insistence that Shylock become a Christian need not disturb us, because to most Elizabethans this would be an act of mercy.

Perhaps, then, in Antonio one perceives in a small way the kind of moral rehabilitation which Shakespeare will later emphasize in his comedies of transformation. In any event, Bassanio and Portia might indeed agree: "How many things by season seasoned are / To their right praise and true perfection" (V, i, 107-108). With Shylock portrayed consistently as a comic villain, with the incidental appearances of the zany Launcelot Gobbo, with the pointed remarks of Gratiano, and with the stylization of Lorenzo and Jessica, Shakespeare is relatively successful in providing an effective comic perspective for such character development.

In Rosalind and Orlando of *As You Like It*, the dramatist again depicts a growth in the comprehension of love which subsequently leads them to a fuller realization of their true personality. At the outset Orlando, filled with anger and frustration, rebels against his brother's tyranny. Forced to flee for his life into the Forest of Arden, he carries with him the memory of the fair maiden who smiled upon him in the momentary encounter earlier at the wrestling match at court. He carves her initial and posts rather lame verses on trees throughout the forest. Oblivious to Rosalind's presence in Arden, the swain pours forth his sentiment in high Petrarchan fashion. In time, his passion is tempered through the "schooling" he receives from Ganymede (Rosalind in disguise) concerning the female temperament and the fatuity of his moping and pining for unrequited love (IV, i; V, ii); and his affection apparently achieves a degree of maturation when he ceases to regard it as a bittersweet game, informing Ganymede that he no longer can be satisfied with the pretense of wooing by proxy (V, ii, 55). With this maturation comes the corollary ability to forgive the elder brother and literally to save the brother's life at the expense of his own personal safety. Obviously, then, through the catalyst of love, Orlando's personality is purged and his highest qualities realized. In a similar fashion, Rosalind's personality develops throughout the action of the play. Hesitant at first to admit her vulnerability to love (I, iii), she for a time will do so only through her disguise as Ganymede. Consciously or unconsciously, she, like Orlando, is "schooled" in affection as she twice observes in Phebe's disdainful repudiation of Silvius (III, v; IV, iii) the cruelty of feminine pride in mocking sincere overtures of love. Hence she, too, is prepared for the final moments of the action in which she will offer herself in love to Orlando. Both Frederick, the usurping duke, and Oliver, the tyrannical eldest son of Sir Roland de Boys, are also influenced by the power of love—Frederick through a holy friar, Oliver through the sacrificial love of Orlando. While the drama does not focus realistically on these latter alterations in character, their presence does serve to intensify the pattern of development in Rosalind and Orlando.

As a vehicle for maintaining an effective comic perspective for the development of the two young lovers, Shakespeare provides a variety of comic pointers. The idyllic pastoral life touted by Duke Senior (mocked by Jaques, II, i), the virtues of court life to which others of his party would return (mocked by Jaques, II, vii; and by Corin, III, ii), the Petrarchan love conventions implicitly accepted by Rosalind and Orlando (mocked by Touchstone, II, iv, and parodied through his devious attempts to win physical pleasure with Audrey, III, iii), specifically the roles of Orlando as a lovesick swain (mocked in William, whose failure to act aggressively in his affair of the heart costs him his sweetheart) and of Rosalind as a lofty she-sun (caricatured in Phebe's haughty disdain, III, v; IV, iii)—all such devices block the spectator's emotional involvement and thus create the distance necessary to the comic vision.

It is in *Much Ado about Nothing* and *Twelfth Night* that the evolution of Shakespeare's comic vision is most effectively exemplified. In *Much Ado about Nothing*, Benedick, Beatrice, and Don John are depicted on the level of identity. The personality of Don John, like that of Malvolio, does not alter in the course of the play, but the action results in exposing him to the surrounding characters for the hypocrite and would-be villain that he is. On the other hand, Benedick and Beatrice do develop; at the outset both consider themselves impervious to love—indeed their greatest pleasure is in mocking the opposite sex—and each regards marriage as the most purgatorial experience conceivable. The action of the play humorously mocks them from this unnatural position, and, although there is no basic transformation of spiritual values such as will occur in the final comedies, the result is nonetheless a development or growth in self-knowledge. Each, convinced he is the object of the other's adoration, chides himself for prideful disdain and, though not without some difficulty, accepts the affection and amazingly finds himself reciprocating.

To be sure, Shakespeare has previously capitalized upon the humor of love's mocker becoming love's victim.[1] But, as we have previously observed, the characters of the earlier comedies, like Valentine and Biron, for example, are maneuvered from a position of antilover to that of Petrarchan fawner or from a posture of fawning fidelity to one of crass infidelity in such broad and rapid fashion as to discourage any credibility of characterization. With no credible motivation, the emphasis is upon the humor of the situation; the characters are merely pawns whose changes in attitude are peremptorily announced, not lived through. Moreover, in the cases of Ferdinand, Biron, Longaville, and Dumain, the drastic alteration in their attitude toward romance is not immediately accepted by the opposite sex, though by implication it will be reciprocated one year later; the unnatural pledge of social abstinence for one year sworn by the king for the sake of love at the end of the play is, after all, only two years less ridiculous than a similar unnatural pledge for three years against love at the beginning. In any event, if there is indeed a growth in social wisdom which is ultimately to make the lords and ladies compatible in love, it is, as implied by the ladies, a character development which will occur *outside* the play during the year's penance, after which each lady will accept her lover if he has remained true to his vow. The effectiveness of the play again arises from the stylized inconsistencies of one-dimensional characters who are funny because of the situation in which they are placed.

Benedick and Beatrice, however, are presented as realistic human characters, who with credible motivation develop in their attitude toward love during the course of the play. Instead of creating broad comedy at the expense of plausible characterization, the playwright dramatizes the stages of their social maturation, and the humor arises from character rather than from action.

In the opening scene, the "merry war" between these two mockers is clearly established as the dominant theme.[2] Certainly before tacitly accepting Hero and Claudio as the main characters of the play, we should reconsider the centrality of Benedick and Beatrice to the plot. For one thing, Shakespeare specifically introduces the theme of the sparring mockers before the theme of melodramatic romance. Nowhere else does he give such primary emphasis to a "subplot"; obviously, when all principals first come on stage together, our major interest is not in the love-at-first-sight which develops between two relatively pallid characters, but in the development of the "merry war" between the witty sparks. For another thing, it is Benedick and Beatrice who sustain our dramatic interest through the mid-portion of the play; once their comic traps are set, we as spectators merely bide our time for the next private encounter of Benedick and Beatrice as we observe the fortunes and misfortunes of Hero and Claudio. And, quite frankly, it is their fate which much more viably concerns us than that of the gullible "hero" and the passively victimized "heroine."

Beatrice's first words mock her male adversary and squarely establish the comic foundations for their subsequent verbal parrying.[3] As a messenger informs Leonato, Governor of Messina, of the imminent arrival of the Prince of Arragon and his forces, she mockingly inquires: "I pray you, is Signior Mountanto return'd from the wars or no? . . . I pray you, how many hath he kill'd and eaten in these wars? . . . for indeed I promised to eat all of his killing" (I, i, 30-31, 42-45). Obviously her tilt with this "very valiant trencherman," this "stuff'd man" (51, 58-59), antedates the play.[4] In their last encounter, she reports, "four of his five wits went halting off . . . if he have wit enough to keep himself warm, let him bear it for a difference between himself and his horse; for it is all the wealth that he hath left to be known a reasonable creature" (66, 67-71). ". . . not till a hot January" will she ever abide him or any other man! When Benedick comes on stage, her railing tongue is quick to continue the attack. He has no more than opened his mouth when she blurts: "I wonder that you will still be talking, Signior Benedick. Nobody marks you" (117-118). Such is his personality that "Courtesy itself must convert to disdain, if [he] come in her presence" (123-124). With ominous bluntness she proclaims herself an antilover: "I had rather hear my dog bark at a crow than a man swear he loves me" (132-133).

Benedick is no less adept with the insulting barb. Expressing surprise that "my dear Lady Disdain" is still living, he mocks her for hiding her romantic interest in him and pompously avers that, for the sake of the ladies, "I would I could find in my heart that I had not a hard heart" (127-128); though "loved of all ladies . . . truly, I love none." A few moments later, asked by Claudio to comment on Hero's beauty, Benedick seizes the opportunity to broaden his attack upon the fatuity of love: "Is't come to this? In faith, hath not the world one man but he will wear his cap with suspicion? Shall I never see a bachelor of three-score again? . . .Because I will not do them the wrong to mistrust any, I will do myself the right to trust none; and the fine is, for the which I may go the finer, I will live a bachelor" (199-202, 244-248). Should he ever fall victim to love, he proclaims that the bull's horns are to be set on his head and that he is to be placed on exhibit with the appropriate placards: "Here is good horse to hire . . . Here you may see Benedick the married man" (268-270).

While the actual skirmish between the antilovers is brief, Benedick and Beatrice have clearly revealed that they have far more than a casual interest in one another but that their pride will never allow them to admit it. Act II provides repetition and intensification of this theme just prior to the central exposure scenes. Each antilover appears to restate his convictions to a friend who is contemplating marriage, and again a momentary encounter adds spice to their charges. Beatrice, chiding Hero as love's fool, asserts that she thanks God morning and evening that he has sent her no husband. She can "not endure a husband with a beard on his face" (II, i, 30-31), yet a youth without a beard is too young for her. By remaining a maid she will avoid hell and gain heaven. Not until men are made of something more valiant than dust and not until she is convinced that a man, descended like her from Adam, is not her kindred will she be "fitted with a husband." As a realistic and pragmatic person, she prides herself on being able to "see a church by daylight" (85-86): "wooing, wedding, and repenting, is as a Scotch jig, a measure, and a cinque pace; the first suit is hot and hasty, like a Scotch jig, and full as fantastical; the wedding, mannerly-modest, as a measure, full of state and ancientry; and then comes repentance and, with his bad legs, falls into the cinque pace faster and faster, till he sink into his grave" (76-83). As for Benedick, smarting from Beatrice's remarks during a masked ball that he is "the Prince's jester, a very dull fool" (142), he would not marry this "infernal Ate in good apparel" (263), "though she were endowed with all that Adam had left him before he transgress'd" (258-260). He would undertake any mission "rather than hold three words' conference with this harpy . . . I cannot endure my Lady Tongue" (279-280, 283-284).

The playwright, in effect, has provided both antilovers sufficient rope to become totally ensnared in their unnatural postures. Yet he applies the slip knot in such a way as to make their victimization by Cupid thoroughly plausible.[5] Each thinks the other dotes on him and suffers as a consequence of the unrequited passion; hence, each, gratifying his own ego, is able to justify through reason the attitude to which passion is leading him. At least for the moment, neither is forced to swallow his pride whole cloth. Benedick overhears that Beatrice "loves him with an enraged affection" (II, iii, 104-105); she is up "twenty times a night" falling, weeping, sobbing, beating her heart, tearing her hair, praying, cursing: "O sweet Benedick! God give me patience!" (154-155). Beatrice, in turn, overhears that Benedick loves her "entirely"; he is "Consume[d] away in sighs, waste[d] inwardly" (III, i, 37, 78). She hears herself branded "self-endeared," hardhearted, disdainful, and scornful (49-56). With her "carping" she

> turns . . . every man the wrong side out,
> And never gives to truth and virtue that
> Which simpleness and merit purchaseth.
>> (68-70)

Both profit from the net prepared for them. Forced to admit their stubborn pride to themselves, they for the first time can recognize affection for what it is. As Benedick exclaims in soliloquy: "Love me! why, it must be requited . . . I did never think to marry. I must not seem proud. Happy are they that hear their detractions and can put them to mending . . . I will be horribly in love with her . . . When I said I would die a bachelor, I did not think I should live till I were married" (II, iii, 232, 236-238, 243-244, 250-252). So likewise Beatrice in soliloquy proclaims:

> Stand I condemn'd for pride and scorn so much?
> Contempt, farewell! and maiden pride, adieu! . . .
> And, Benedick, love on; I will requite thee,
> Taming my wild heart to thy loving hand.
>> (III, i, 108-109, 111-112)

If the spectator is to be convinced of the validity of this change in attitude, the verbal warriors must successfully overcome two obstacles: the next confrontation with their friends, who can be expected to mock them mercilessly, and their next private meeting, in which for a critical moment each will probe for signs of affection in the other while his own wit will be poised for self-defense. Benedick's first test comes almost immediately, and, in the face of his companions' laughter, his forthright intentions to reveal all ("Gallants, I am not as I have been" [III, ii, 15]) wither to a transparent subterfuge ("I have the toothache" [21]). But he swallows his pride and by submission admits the truth as his friends mock his new clothes, his combed hair, his shaved and scented face, and his subdued wit, "which is now crept into a lute-string and now govern'd by stops" (60-61). Beatrice, too, bites her tongue and her pride a few scenes later. Claiming that she is "out of all other tune," "exceeding ill," "stuff'd" (III, iv, 43, 53, 64), she must abide the mocking prescription that she obtain "distill'd Carduus Benedictus, and lay it to your heart. It is the only thing for a qualm" (73-75).

Shortly thereafter, their brash cynicism gone, they are able, albeit clumsily and hesitatingly, to declare their mutual love: "I will swear by it that you love me; and I will make him eat it that says I love not you" (IV, i, 278-279); "You have stayed me in a happy hour. I was about to protest I loved you" (285-286). Beatrice's sudden command that Benedick prove his love by killing Claudio signals more than the spectator realizes at first glance: having escaped his egotistical shell in which wit was literally a defensive weapon, each is able for the first time to act compassionately on behalf of another—Beatrice, in giving the command, on behalf of the wronged Hero; Benedick, in finally accepting it, on behalf of Beatrice, who has become painfully convinced of Claudio's villainy.[6] Heretofore, the spectator has viewed only the sharply disdainful sides of both mocking warriors. Now Beatrice reveals a sensitivity and concern for her cousin which points significantly toward those finer qualities of spirit with which love is allied. So, too, Benedick's acceptance in all seriousness of the charge to kill Claudio, erstwhile his best friend, graphically indicates the surrender of his previous values to a new control.

To be sure, the merry warriors are trained for combat, not romance, and their wooing is at times woefully inept. Benedick, for instance, attempting to pen his affection for his mistress, can produce only doggerel. In utter frustration he exclaims: "Marry, I cannot show it in rhyme. I have tried. I can find out no rhyme to 'lady' but 'baby,' an innocent rhyme; for 'scorn,' 'horn,' a hard rhyme; for 'school,' 'fool,' a babbling rhyme; very ominous endings. No, I was not born under a rhyming planet, nor I cannot woo in festival terms" (V, ii, 35-41). And both would willingly disown the epistles produced by their companions in the final moments of the play—the "halting sonnet of [Benedick's] own pure brain, / Fashion'd to Beatrice" (V, iv, 87-88) and "another / Writ in [Beatrice's] hand, stol'n from her pocket, / Containing her affection unto Benedick" (88-90). To the last the lovers continue their verbal sparring. But the words no longer have a sting; instead the quip—that is, the form of dialogue which is second nature to them—serves as a device for the final personal and public declaration of their love:

> BENE. Come, I will have thee; but, by this light, I take thee for pity.
> BEAT. I would not deny you; but, by this good day, I yield upon great persuasion; and partly to save your life, for I was told you were in a consumption.
> BENE. Peace! I will stop your mouth.
> [*Kissing her.*]
> (V, iv, 92-99)

Benedick has the apposite concluding remarks. If he is not the man he was at the beginning of the play, "Man is a giddy thing, and this is my conclusion" (108-109). If the fidelity of woman is an uncertain factor, at least "There is no staff more reverend than one tipp'd with horn," so "get thee a wife, get thee a wife" (124-126).

In short, Benedick's and Beatrice's recognition of their true nature as normal, healthy lovers is credibly experienced in the course of the play. The humor arises from the character development which reveals their true identity to themselves. As in *The Merchant of Venice* and *As You Like It*, Shakespeare's concern is to create a dramatic structure which will enhance the comic potential of the romantic self-revelation and at the same time will prevent moments of sentimentality from blurring the spectator's comic perspective—in effect, a comic vision which will successfully accommodate character development on the level of identity. To this end, he surrounds the "merry war" with a melodramatic plot so stylized that it is virtually impossible for the spectator to become emotionally involved with any part of the action.[7] In effect, the Hero-Claudio affair functions as a veil of fiction which maintains the clarity of the viewer's comic perspective on Benedick and Beatrice. Then, too, several minor figures, such as Leonato and Don Pedro, function sporadically as comic pointers to direct our laughter upon these mockers of love. Finally, in Dogberry and Verges, the playwright creates the bumbling constables who, like the keystone cops later, delight us even while they unwittingly disrupt the law they represent.

The stylized melodramatic action is established immediately following the first skirmish in the "merry war." In the face of Benedick's mockery of love, Claudio[8] peremptorily announces to his friend his romantic interest in Hero ("a jewel" [I, i, 183], "the sweetest lady that ever I look'd on" [189-190]), whom he desires to be "my wife" (198). This passion he relates to Don Pedro who for no ostensible reason proclaims that he will woo her for him by "assum[ing] thy part in some disguise / And tell[ing] fair Hero I am Claudio" (323-324). Into this fantastic scene now stalks Don John announcing that he was "born under Saturn . . . I cannot hide what I am . . . I am a plain-dealing villain . . . seek not to alter me" (I, iii, 12, 14, 33, 39).[9] Welcoming "any model to build mischief on" (48-49) which "may prove food to [his] displeasure" (67-68), he leaps at the least opportunity for evil. The lovesick swain, the pliant and submissive heroine, the proxy wooing, the arrant villain for whom "Any bar, any cross, any impediment will be med'cinable" (II, ii, 4-5), each performing a role for which there is no credible motivation—Shakespeare has indeed taken the kingdom of melodrama by storm.[10]

Furthermore, this material is structured so as to provide maximum comic distancing at significant moments in the Benedick-Beatrice action. Specifically, the two major points of melodramatic complication, occurring as needed to offset any tendency on the part of the spectator to react sentimentally to the young sparrers, fantastically mock the misprisions, the observations, the *notings*,[11] which direct them first to the height of their disdain, then to the height of their passion. As previously described, both Benedick and Beatrice make two appearances early in the play in which they verbally flail each other with increasing intensity. The second of these appearances involves a masked ball with each, behind the disguise of a vizard, leveling his most telling insults (II, i, 134-136, 142-148); not realizing that his assailant is actually within earshot, each assumes he cannot defend himself with the verbal retort, smoulders over the charges, and swears he will get revenge one way or another. As by deception and misprision their merry war reaches its fever pitch, so by misprision Don John makes his first melodramatic attempt to destroy Claudio's happiness. Learning of Don Pedro's intention to woo Hero for Claudio by proxy, he determines to practice upon Claudio by reporting that Don Pedro actually woos for himself, indeed that the intention is to "marry her to-night" (II, i, 176-177). The playwright makes the confusion all the more fantastic for the spectator through the "honest" misrepresentation of Antonio, who by eavesdropping learns of the wooing, but assumes the prince is to woo for himself (I, ii) and so reports his news to Leonato. Even though Don John knows nothing of this misreporting, he is able, despite his saturnine temperament—which is clearly apparent to all—to lead the gullible Claudio to condem his friend with incredible rapidity:

'Tis certain so; the Prince wooes for himself.

> Friendship is constant in all other things
> Save in the office and affairs of love.
>
> (181-183)

Both Claudio's suspicion and Don John's intended villainy melo-dramatically come to nought, as, a few lines later, Don Pedro blithely proclaims: "Here, Claudio, I have wooed in thy name, and fair Hero is won . . . Name the day of marriage, and God give thee joy!" (309-312). Shakespeare, by obviously ignoring plausible motivation, has stylized the action and thereby provided a kind of comic insulation against the spectator's emotional reaction to the intensity of the wit combat being waged by Benedick and Beatrice.

As by "noting," Benedick and Beatrice in the mid-section of the play become convinced of the other's passionate affection, and through the remainder of the action come haltingly to recognize a reciprocal emotion within themselves, the playwright again uses the subplot for comic distancing. Indeed, Don John's second attack upon Claudio is more obviously stylized than the first. Both the lovesick swain and Don Pedro lend a willing ear to the rogue's slanderous charges against Hero and unquestioningly accept as ultimate proof of her guilt a nocturnal scene which they "note," obviously from such a distance that they cannot determine her facial features. By confronting her with her "shame" at the altar and, with Don John's aid, verbally attacking her with pharisaical gusto, they deny her any reasonable opportunity for self defense. That Claudio would choose to shame her by publicly impugning her character at the altar,[12] that the fair Hero would swoon away into such a deep trance that for a time she was presumed dead, that her own father would likewise condemn her peremptorily and pray that she "not ope thine eyes" for fear that he himself would "strike at thy life," that Beatrice would not expose the inconsistency between the charge that Hero is guilty of "vile encounters . . . a thousand times in secret" and the fact that "until last night, / [she has] this twelvemonth been her bedfellow," that Margaret should not clear up the whole confusion:[13] all such features combine to make the action sheer absurdity by any measure of plausibility. But just such exaggeration of action and neglect of motivation is, of course, the key to successful melodrama. The bewildering bevy of events which follows provides a fitting capstone to this action: Hero's feigned death, the seriatim challenges to a duel which confront Claudio, his maudlin contrition which leads him to serenade her at the tomb, Leonato's incredible request that since Claudio cannot marry his daughter he marry his niece, the almost bizarre production of "another Hero" at the second altar.

Surrounded by this action, the spectator, however much he becomes interested in Benedick and Beatrice as they quite credibly experience the youthful joys and agonies resulting from ego's conflict with romance, is never permitted to lose his comic perspective or detachment. As we have seen, the transition from love's mocker to love's victim clearly is sincere and gradual and not without those occasional moments of personal frustration arising from a character's being forced to eat his words, to recognize and admit his faults of pride and spite, in short, to expose his vulnerability at the very point of his erstwhile strength. It can hardly be a mere coincidence of revision that Shakespeare in this section of the play has so carefully bolstered the comic perspective through the stylized postures of Hero and Claudio.

Apparently for the same reason, Dogberry and Verges are introduced in the last half of the play. If Shakespeare can be criticized for rather clumsily and peripherally thrusting these characters into the action at such a late stage, as is the case later with Autolycus, the results are not debatable. He gets away with it because the bumbling constables, living virtually in a world of their own, comically endear themselves to the spectator through their general stupidity and through Dogberry's specific linguistic ineptness.[14] This material bears upon our present approach to Shakespeare's artistry in two primary ways. First, the buffoons are introduced precisely at the crucial moment at which Benedick and Beatrice begin to experience their self-revelation; their four appearances in the play span the period during which the jesting warriors must make their initial comments of self-recognition and must individually bear up under the taunting gibes of their companions who are responsible for the earlier eavesdropping scenes. By the time the constables make their final exit (V, i), Benedick and Beatrice are well on their way to becoming lovers as they attempt to pen their affection in lyric form only to find themselves virtually as inept as Dogberry in the use of the King's English. In effect, then, Shakespeare has further reinforced the dramatic perspective during this significant portion of the play. Both the high melodrama of Hero-Claudio and the clumsy antics of Dogberry-Verges create the detached comic veil through which we observe the humanization of character without a consequential loss of comic rapport. Second, Dogberry and Verges, through the verbal misprision that prevents their conveying information concerning Don John's dastardly deeds, create another layer of the mis-noting which prompts much of the action of this play, and which, for example, has earlier served as a romantic catalyst for Benedick and Beatrice. As the end result of one misprision is ultimately to transform Benedick's mockery of love into an admission of love, so the other is to maneuver Borachio from freedom to prison, as he, from sheer frustration at having been arrested and tried in such inarticulate fashion, voluntarily admits his guilt rather than endure any longer the sheer fatuity of his captors. By the time the bumbling constable departs, however— with his malapropian gems, his smug assurance that, in calling him "tedious," Leonato has paid him the highest of compliments, and his furious incredulity that anyone would have the gall to call him an "ass"— he has endeared himself to all in the playhouse save his prisoner.

In addition to these narrative layers, Shakespeare utilizes minor comic pointers who help to focus and to guide the spectator's laughter upon Benedick and Beatrice.[15] No single character serves this function, and the result is an only partially successful scattering of comments from minor characters who at one moment are obviously to be accepted as comic pointers and at another moment as stylized caricatures. Specifically, though, Leonato, Don Pedro,

Claudio, Hero, Margaret, and Ursula sporadically provide significant comments as they share with the spectator a practice upon the merry warriors.

In the first portion of the play leading to the eavesdropping scenes, Leonato and Don Pedro are the comic pointers. Leonato, for instance, caught up at the outset in Beatrice's gibes about Benedick, explains: "There is a kind of merry war betwixt Signior Benedick and her. They never meet but there's a skirmish of wit between them" (I, i, 62–64). He is quick to remind her that, when Benedick returns, she will have met her match (46-47) and later he avers that, despite her shrewd tongue, "I hope to see you one day fitted with a husband" (II, i, 60-61). In similar fashion, Don Pedro taunts Benedick as "an obstinate heretic in the despite of beauty" (I, i, 236-237) and tartly prophesies that "I shall see thee, ere I die, look pale with love . . . [I]f ever thou dost fall from this faith, thou wilt prove a notable argument" (249-250, 257-258). Leonato and Don Pedro, then, clearly set the personalities for the spectator. And, appropriately, it is they who implement the scheme by which the mockers will be transformed. Beatrice, who "mocks all her wooers out of suit" (II, i, 364-365), "were an excellent wife for Benedick" (366-367): "O Lord, my lord, if they were but a week married, they would talk themselves mad" (368-369). Thus Don Pedro is led to devise the plan as difficult as "one of Hercules' labours": "to bring Signior Benedick and the Lady Beatrice into a mountain of affection the one with the other . . . I will teach you how to humour your cousin, that she shall fall in love with Benedick; and I, with your two helps, will so practise on Benedick that, in despite of his quick wit and his queasy stomach, he shall fall in love with Beatrice" (380-383, 395-400).

The additional pointers begin to function at the time of the actual deceptions. Though Leonato and Don Pedro provide most of the conversation which feeds Benedick's passion, Claudio inserts occasional asides to sharpen the comic flavor: "stalk on, stalk on; the fowl sits . . . Bait the hook well; this fish will bite . . . If he do not dote on her upon this, I will never trust my expectation" (II, iii, 94-

95, 113-114, 219-220). Similarly, as Don Pedro has instructed, Hero and Ursula pour Benedick's adoration into Beatrice's willing ears. Hero observes wryly, "Cupid's crafty arrow . . . wounds by hearsay . . . Some Cupid kills with arrows, some with traps" (III, i, 22-23, 106). And Ursula, like Claudio, provides sporadic progress reports: "The pleasant'st angling is to see the fish . . . greedily devour the treacherous bait . . . She's lim'd, I warrant you. We've caught her, madam" (26, 28, 104). Each group pointedly mocks its victim on the next appearance for the alterations in personality which belie the passion of love, Margaret joining with Hero and Ursula for this purpose (III, ii; III, iv).

The major function of the pointers in the play, then, is to maintain the proper comic perspective while establishing the young mockers as antilovers and then arranging and executing the scheme by which their mockery will be tamed and eventually transformed. Once the practice is applied and each victim humorously derided, the pointers as such are removed from the stage, returning in this guise only briefly in the late moments of the action, mockingly to produce love poems as irrefutable evidence that Benedick and Beatrice love each other just prior to their final acceptance of and acknowledgment of love:

> LEON. Come, cousin, I am sure you love the gentleman.
> CLAUD. And I'll be sworn upon't that he loves her; For here's a paper written in his hand,
> A halting sonnet of his own pure brain,
> Fashion'd to Beatrice.
> HERO. And here's another
> Writ in my cousin's hand, stol'n from her pocket,
> Containing her affection unto Benedick.
> (V, iv, 84-90)

In sum, while the pointers and the low-comedy characters of *Much Ado about Nothing* lack the total thematic integration which Shakespeare is to achieve in *Twelfth Night*, these devices, along with a stylized, melodramatic subplot, do serve to block the spectator's emotional involvement and thereby to provide him a detached

perspective through which to enjoy the humanization of two delightful—if brash and egotistical—young people who pay the price
for defying love's powers.

In *Twelfth Night* Shakespeare achieves his most successful
comedy of identity;[16] as in *The Merchant of Venice, As You Like It,*
and *Much Ado about Nothing,* the basis for comedy is the revelation
of character incongruity, the devices for exposure here forming an
integral part of the narrative. Through association with Viola, Sebastian, Feste, and Maria, each of the other characters reveals his abnormal or hypocritical posture, and each, except Malvolio, comes to
understand his true nature and is absorbed into a normal society.
The twins Viola and Sebastian, separated in a storm antecedent to
the action of the play and reunited in the fifth act, are the primary
comic pointers in that they establish the proper comic perspective
for the spectator by providing the information necessary to create
the dramatic irony.[17] Their apparent shifts in personality—Viola's
disguise and the subsequent mistaken identity—produce actual exposures in the surrounding characters. Feste and Maria, a second
pair of comic pointers outside the primary action, serve a similar
function for the low characters. These four characters, in no way
self deceived, create a rapport with the spectator; and their comments function to provide information about others necessary to
guide the laughter.

Concerning the level of characterization in *Twelfth Night,* the
basis for comedy, more specifically, is the incongruity between action and identity.[18] Major characters at the outset attempt to hide
their real nature behind a facade of physical action which is eventually revealed as a mere pose—Olivia as a victim of fashionable
melancholia, Orsino as the disconsolate and unrequited lover,
Malvolio as the puritanical jack-in-office.

The duke, like Romeo in love with the idea of love, strikes an immediate tone of hyperbolic sentimentalizing as he revels in the
music which feeds his passion. In love with Olivia at first sight, he
delights in the fancy of puns to describe his languishment:

That instant was I turn'd into a hart;
And my desires, like fell and cruel hounds,
E'er since pursue me.

                    (I, i, 21-23)

Informed in no uncertain terms that Olivia is unreceptive to his suit, he is nonetheless determined to pursue his love when we see him three scenes later unclasping to Viola (Cesario) "the book even of [his] secret soul." Now, however, he is to woo by deputy because he assumes Olivia "will attend it better in thy [the page's] youth" (I, iv, 27); as for himself he, "best / When least in company" (37-38), prefers—again like Romeo—to languish in solitude. Thus the spectator is confronted with a melodramatic count who avows an overwhelming love even as he commands another to press his suit.

In the duke's next appearance, two remarks in the midst of his continued pose signal his true identity as a prideful man infatuated with the social pose of the romantic lover. For one thing, his description to Cesario of feminine beauty simply does not correspond with his Petrarchan posture. Even while he mouths praise to Olivia's immortal and unfading beauty, he advises Cesario to take a young lover, since women are "as roses, whose fair flower / Being once display'd, doth fall that very hour" (II, iv, 39-40). For another, in the course of his conversation he flatly contradicts himself in comparing the quality of a man's love to that of a woman's. At one point he says:

Our [men's] fancies are more giddy and unfirm,
More longing, wavering, sooner lost and worn,
Than women's are.

                    (II, iv, 34-36)

Yet, a few lines later he avers:

There is no woman's sides
Can bide the beating of so strong a passion
As love doth give my heart; no woman's heart

So big, to hold so much. They lack retention . . .
        Make no compare
Between that love a woman can bear me
And that I owe Olivia.

(II, iv, 96-99, 104-106)

Even though the duke again calls for music to feed his passion and listens to Feste's song describing the melancholy death of a distraught lover, his contradiction in advising one concept of love for Cesario and claiming another for his personal commitment reflects intellectual toying with the idea of love rather than a direct emotional involvement in it.

When Orsino appears again in the final act, his actions render his character revelation complete. Both the rapidity with which he can turn angrily on Olivia and the poised alacrity with which he can accept Cesario (now Viola) as his heart's substitute reveal how deeply indeed has been his commitment to the stakes of love! When the countess first enters in Act V, Orsino speaks metaphorically of heaven walking on earth. But, his suit again rejected as "fat and fulsome," he suddenly alters his metaphor to "perverseness," "uncivil lady," and, instead of heaven and its shrines, speaks of her "ingrate and unauspicious altars" (V, i, 115-116). The "marble-breasted tyrant" has made his thoughts "ripe in mischief" as he threatens to tear her minion (Cesario) out of her cruel eye as a sacrifice to her disdain. In effect, within the space of a few short lines his unbounded love has been exploded by an equally unbounded temper. The second shift is even more revelatory of the true quality of his love. When Olivia's husband is produced, Orsino, at the point of being outfaced altogether, determines to "share in this most happy wreck" by receiving the love which Viola has for some time been anxious to offer: "Give me thy hand, / And let me see thee in thy woman's weeds . . . You shall from this time be your master's mistress" (279-280, 333-334). In short, Orsino's Petrarchan pose for Olivia stands revealed as merely the cover for a man enjoying the fascination of his romantic adventure and too proud to accept rejection.[19]

The incongruities in Olivia's character are developed even more extensively throughout the drama. Her true identity is that of a normal young lady capable both of loving and being loved and possessing a sense of humor which enables her to understand and appreciate the good fun in a practical joke. This personality she attempts to conceal, however, through her actions. And, as a result of this melancholy pose, her reputation for morbid solemnity has grown throughout the land.

Although the countess does not appear on stage until the final scene of the first act, her haughty posture is established through prior conversation. For instance, in Scene ii the spectator is told that, because of the recent deaths of her father and brother, Olivia "hath abjur'd the [company / And sight] of men" and "will admit no kind of suit" (40-41, 45). More specifically, we learn in Scene i that she intends to wear the veil of mourning for full seven years and to "water once a day her chamber round / With eye-offending brine" (29-30). When the jocularity of her household in Scene iii appears inappropriate to her pose, she remains in character through a mild reprimand to Sir Toby Belch delivered by Maria: "Your cousin, my lady, takes great exceptions to your ill hours . . . That quaffing and drinking will undo you. I heard my lady talk of it yesterday, and of a foolish knight that you brought in one night here to be her wooer" (I, iii, 5-6, 14-17). Olivia's posture, then, is clear before she appears on stage. Determined to mourn her brother beyond normal bounds, she will reject all suitors and will soberly hold herself aloof from the slightest merriment. Her household, excepting the "grave steward" of course, is utterly unaffected by her melancholy; nor is Sir Toby deterred from assuring the gullible Aguecheek of her availability.

This facade of character dissolves, at least for the spectator, upon her initial appearance on stage. For in the lengthy final scene of Act I, Feste flatly proclaims the absurdity of her attitude, and, later, with Cesario she is unable to maintain the posture she has so carefully cultivated. At first glimpse, she is irritable and impatient, testily chastizing the clown for his continued foolishness. Feste, however, as Cesario is to do later, confronts her with polite but firm rebuttal, mockingly proving her a fool for her protracted melancholy.

> CLO. Good madonna, why mournest thou?
> OLI. Good fool, for my brother's death.
> CLO. I think his soul is in hell, madonna.
> OLI. I know his soul is in heaven, fool.
> CLO. The more fool, madonna, to mourn for your brother's soul being in heaven. Take away the fool, gentlemen.
>
> (I, v, 72-78)

Her genuine nature is further revealed as she, not altogether displeased with Feste's wit, defends his catechism against Malvolio's charges. Even so, she is in no way ready to drop her demeanor. When a messenger arrives to plead Orsino's case, she orders Malvolio to report that she is sick or not at home. And, when Cesario's persistence prevails, she calls for her veil—the physical symbol of her artificial pose. Not awed by Olivia's cold and haughty disdain, Cesario frankly accuses her of being "the cruell'st she alive" and "too proud." The countess, though supposedly abjuring the sight of men for the sake of her brother's memory, listens with obvious delight, but her interest is in the messenger, not the message. The result is a flagrant reversal of her earlier determination as she not only displays a normal and healthy interest in what she assumes to be the opposite sex, but also is willing to act the aggressor's role in her affair of the heart. To that end she encourages Cesario to come again for further consultation and sends him a ring on the pretense that she is returning what he had earlier forced upon her. In the final moment of the act, she voices her dilemma in soliloquy:

> Even so quickly may one catch the plague?
> Methinks I feel this youth's perfections
> With an invisible and subtle stealth
> To creep in at mine eyes.
>
> (I, v, 314-317)

Her two appearances in Act III develop further the contrast between her true nature and her assumed posture. Her pursuit of Cesario more pronounced, she is not without moments of remorse as she realizes the indignity of her actions. For instance, in Scene i she tells Cesario not to be afraid, that she will pursue no further (141, 143), and in Scene iv she laments that there is "something in me that reproves my fault" (223). She is unable to contain her love, however, and at another point openly declares her affection so strong that "Nor wit nor reason can my passion hide" (III, i, 164). Moreover, a short time later she becomes ridiculously flustered at Cesario's very approach:

> I have sent after him; he says he'll come.
> How shall I feast him? What bestow of him?
> For youth is bought more oft than begg'd or borrow'd.
> I speak too loud.—
>
> (III, iv, 1-4)

In truth, her love for Cesario—at least to the audience—is far more outrageous than Malvolio's for her, once the steward has become convinced that he is the secret object of her attention.

By the end of the third act, Olivia's true identity has been fully revealed to the spectators. Her remaining actions leading to marriage will complete the revelation to the other characters as well. For, in the following scenes, Sebastian, who has replaced Viola and who admittedly is bewildered by the advances of the beautiful countess, is nevertheless willing to receive them and to tell her that he, "having sworn truth, ever will be true."

Malvolio is perhaps the most obvious illustration of comic character incongruity. As Olivia's steward, he pulls moral rank on everyone in her household and delights in contrasting his grave prudence with their apparent hedonism. Even Olivia, herself engrossed in somber lamentation for her deceased brother, perceives the excess prudishness in his manner: "O, you are sick of self-love, Malvolio, and taste with a distemper'd appetite. To be generous, guiltless, and of free disposition, is to take those things for bird-bolts that you deem cannon-bullets" (I, v, 97-101). Similarly, Maria, in a later scene, expresses concern that Toby's late carousals have awakened Malvolio, who, as anticipated, rushes in and exclaims against the "caterwauling" and the "gabbl[ing] like tinkers at this time of night." He in effect orders them out of the house unless greater self-discipline is exercised, singling out Maria for especial chastisement. The steward's gravity is obviously suited to Olivia's disposition: "He [Malvolio] is sad and civil, / And suits well for a servant with my fortunes" (III, iv, 5-6). Hence, as he for those very qualities is later summoned to entertain Cesario, he is prepared for his moment of comic deflation.

For, when Malvolio appears before the countess, his true nature is showing as a result of his avarice. His puritanical facade, labeled time-serving by Maria, has been profitable only so long as he has been convinced such posture was desired by his employer. Since he is motivated by ambition rather than by principle, he now hesitates not a moment to accept an opposite pattern of action. His erstwhile grave face is lined with the wrinkles of a plastered smile; his conservative attire is replaced with cross-gartered yellow stockings. As commanded in the note which he assumes to be Olivia's, he is "opposite with kinsmen, surly with servants," and his "tongue tang[s] arguments of state." Olivia, amazed at Malvolio's antics and shocked at the effrontery of his remark that he will come to her bed, declares "this is very midsummer madness." Later, Feste (Sir Topas) exorcises the evil spirit from the steward, who refuses to pray in his new role as a festive gallant. And, as from the dark room Malvolio accurately parrots the orthodox answers to the theological questions posed by Sir Topas, the spectator observes how distant indeed is this religion of action from his religion of words. The action, then, has flayed the pious cover and revealed the obsession of ego and ambition from which his personality suffers.

Revelation of the disparity between action and identity in *Twelfth Night* involves Sir Andrew and Sir Toby as well. Aguecheek, for instance, masks his cowardice behind a volley of words and fatuously challenges the reluctant Cesario to a duel, but his courage persists only as long as his aggressor's timidity does.[20] So also, Belch stakes his pursuit of the jolly life on his ability to control any situation which he creates, and here he fails physically in his inability to manipulate Sebastian (whom Aguecheek has unwittingly provoked) and emotionally in his inability to control his fascination for Maria (to whom he loses the freedom of his bachelorhood).

Incongruity between a character's surface action and his true identity is, of course, only the basis for comedy. The realization, as previously described, depends upon the success with which the dramatist uses comic devices to achieve a perspective from which the spectator will enjoy the situations which dislodge the characters from their abnormal posture. In *Twelfth Night,* the comedy of the first three acts results from the spectator's awareness, through the comic pointer, of the role that each character is playing and of the fact that the role is a pose; the humor of Act IV arises from the pointer's forcing each character into action contradictory to his pose which reveals his true nature to the other characters. And, in Act V with both twins on stage and with each character forced to eat the humble pie of exposure, the comic catharsis is achieved and each character restored to normality.

Shakespeare carefully sets up his pointers early in the play. In Scene ii, Viola describes the shipwreck which she has survived, a twin brother of whose life she is uncertain, and the disguise of eunuch which she will assume for reasons of safety as she travels to Orsino's court. Her ability to moderate her grief for Sebastian provides a foil for the excessive nature of Olivia's mourning. The following scene introduces Olivia and her household, with Maria tolerantly chiding Toby for his late hours and openly flouting the fatuousness of Sir Andrew. In Scene iv, Viola assumes her disguise as Cesario and quickly gains favor with her new master. At this point the dramatic irony becomes significant for the function of the comic pointer, as Orsino unwittingly sends female to woo female. The final scene of the act introduces Feste as a clown who travels in the households of both Orsino and Olivia. He immediately establishes himself as one who dispassionately observes this circle from the outside, with remarks such as: "Those wits, that think they have thee, do very oft prove fools; and I, that am sure I lack thee, may pass for a wise man" and "Better a witty fool than a foolish wit" (I, v, 36-40). And his first action is mockingly to reveal to the countess and to the audience the foolishness of her inordinate mourning. In the ensuing scene, Shakespeare inserts a brief revelation that Sebastian is indeed alive. Since he too is moving toward Orsino's court and since Viola's disguise is masculine, the comic trap of mistaken identity is constructed, and the middle acts will bait virtually every aspect of the trap in order that the catastrophe or resolution of the final act will be more effective.

The comic pointers introduced, the major portion of the plot now utilizes the rapport created between Viola (later Sebastian) and the spectator to effect the comic exposure of Olivia, Orsino, Aguecheek, and Belch. Feste and Maria will successfully exploit Malvolio's presumptuous nature. The steward—whether patterned after William Ffarrington,[21] Sir Ambrose Willoughby,[22] Sir William Knollys,[23] or none of these—functions in the context to heighten the absurdity of Olivia's romantic liaison with Cesario in Act III by himself becoming her lover.[24] To carry out Malvolio's duping and derision, Shakespeare prepares these servant figures who move in his circle and have the best opportunity to know his true nature.

Viola, although not self-deceived as are the other principals, also stands to profit from her experience in Illyria. For one thing, she observes first-hand the destructive effects of inordinate mourning. Facing (or so she assumes) the loss of a brother, she perceives in Olivia the unnatural posture of attempting to live so intensely in the memory of the past that the vitality and meaning of the present are destroyed. Then too, once she has consciously assumed her disguise, she comes to realize the difficulties—and the dangers—of living a lie. Unable to meet even the cowardly Sir Andrew on his own physical terms, and enamored of Orsino but able only to suffer in silence or to utter an occasional pointed remark which the spectator comprehends far more clearly than the duke, she becomes increasingly victimized by her masculine attire. Certainly when Sebastian's sudden appearance provides the opportunity for freedom, she, like those who have been mocked from their abnormal pose, is in a position to appreciate more richly the dignity of being herself and of sharing the love which the duke now reciprocates.

One of Viola's most important functions in the play, however, is to reveal Olivia's inconsistencies to the spectator so that he can fully perceive the process of comic deflation which will restore the countess to normality. To this end, once the touchstone relationship is established, Viola in soliloquy carefully identifies Olivia's infatuation for the spectator:

> Fortune forbid my outside have not charm'd her! . . .
> She loves me, sure. The cunning of her passion
> Invites me in this churlish messenger . . .
> Poor lady, she were better love a dream . . .
> How will this fadge? My master loves her dearly;
> And I, poor monster, fond as much on him;
> And she, mistaken, seems to dote on me.
>   (II, ii, 19, 23-24, 27, 34-36)

In two later scenes (II, i; III, iv) as Olivia becomes increasingly the aggressor, Cesario warns her that "I am not what I am" and that, in light of her haughty pose of immunity to romance, she is pitifully deceiving herself; "you do think you are not what you are" (III, i, 151).

Once Shakespeare has set in motion Olivia's passion, which is to result in her ultimate exposure and which will be all the funnier for the delay, he diverts the focus by manipulating the comic pointer into a series of intrigues by which to expose the surrounding characters. Throughout the third act the trap is set which is to be sprung in Act IV *as Sebastian replaces Viola* upon the scene. In Scene ii, for instance, Aguecheek is goaded into challenging Cesario to a duel. Toby and Fabian persuade the fop that Olivia really loves him and that she is feigning interest in Cesario to test the mettle of his manliness The ridiculous challenge is subsequently forced upon the distraught Viola, who declares she "will return again into the house and desire some conduct of the lady. I am no fighter . . . I am one that had rather go with sir priest than sir knight" (III, iv, 264-265, 297-299). Viola, of course, realizes the danger of her disguise, which Shakespeare has no intention of destroying before the full range of exposure is effected. Aguecheek, on the other hand, senses in her reaction an even greater coward than himself, and in Act IV flagrantly pursues the challenge.

Thus, at the end of Act III, each character has exploited his character facade to its height. And, even though the twins are meaningfully integrated into the plot in their own right, their sudden reversal in Act IV presents the comic shock which will transform each of the characters and will reveal his true identity. Aguecheek, for instance, rushes upon "Cesario" to "cuff him soundly," but the tables are turned as Sir Andrew moans, "We took him for a coward, but he's the very devil incardinate" (V, i, 184). Similarly, Sir Toby, intent upon fostering the mock combat but equally intent upon preventing either party from actually drawing a sword, now finds "Cesario's" wrath quite unmalleable and consequently gets his head bloodied for his mischievous connivances. So also, Olivia suddenly finds "Cesario" amazingly susceptible to her charms and rushes the docile youth off to a priest. Meanwhile, lest any spectator be confused and the ironic humor lessened, Sebastian, clearly functioning as Shakespeare's comic pointer, explains in soliloquy his confusion at Olivia's behavior and his inability to locate his friend Antonio at the Elephant:

> Yet doth this accident and flood of fortune
> So far exceed all instance, all discourse,
> That I am ready to distrust mine eyes
> And wrangle with my reason.
> (IV, iii, 11-14)

And, in turn, Olivia's inconsistency in coveting the affection of Cesario despite her original pose, provokes the sudden transformation of Orsino, in which he denounces her haughty disdain and snatches Viola to his heart, a heart which only a few moments earlier was abjectly prostrated before his self-constructed altar of undying love for the countess.

Shakespeare's comic device, apparent to the spectator since the second scene in the play, is fully revealed to the characters of the plot in the final scene as a capstone to the character revelations.

> One face, one voice, one habit, and two persons,
> A natural perspective, that is and is not! . . .
> An apple, cleft in two, is not more twin
> Than these two creatures.
>
> (V, i, 223-224, 230-231)

The close integration of the subplot reveals further the careful construction of the plot of *Twelfth Night*. Malvolio's puritanical posture as the zealous moralist and the flagrant exposure of his hypocrisy by Feste and Maria reinforce both the theme of character revelation and the tone of tolerant mockery. The group of Maria, Feste,[25] Toby, and Fabian, planting deceptive information and observing from the side as Malvolio is duped into rejecting his original pose, suggests a group of spectators who, cognizant of the deceptive twins which the author has planted in the main plot, look on as the major characters are run through similar paces. Thematically, Malvolio is a third suitor for Olivia in Acts II and III, his presumptuous wooing occurring as a corollary to Olivia's ridiculous pursuit of Viola-Cesario. Structurally, Shakespeare utilizes the gulling and exposure of Malvolio (II, iv; III, iv) as a prelude to the major character revelations in Act IV.

Malvolio sets himself in enmity with Feste in his first appearance on stage. As he gripes about the clown's foolishness, Feste quips: "God send you, sir, a speedy infirmity, for the better increasing your folly! Sir Toby will be sworn that I am no fox, but he will not pass his word for twopence that you are no fool" (I, v, 83-86). More specifically, Maria brands Malvolio "a kind of Puritan": "[A] time-pleaser; an affection'd ass, that cons state without book and utters it by great swarths; the best persuaded of himself, so cramm'd, as he thinks, with excellencies, that it is his grounds of faith that all that look on him love him; and on that vice in him will my revenge find notable cause to work" (II, iii, 160-166). She then, both to inform her cohorts and to establish the comic irony for the spectators, carefully describes the device by which she will drop a forged love-note in his way. And, two scenes later, she directs Toby, Andrew, and Fabian to get "into the box-tree; Malvolio's coming down this walk" (II, v, 18-19). Throughout the scene the pompous and gullible Malvolio is taken in completely, while his prepared audiences in the galleries and on the stage delight in watching his vaunted sobriety and conservative manner sacrificed for the opportunity of social and financial gain. Similarly, as he parades himself before Olivia in ridiculous attire, and later as he is accused by Feste-Sir Topas of being a puritan possessed of the devil, Feste and Maria deliver a steady volley of comments designed to focus the spectator's attention on the humor arising from Malvolio's hypocrisy, an inversion of values so drastic that as Fabian remarks, "If this were played upon a stage now, I could condemn it as an improbable fiction" (III, iv, 140-141).

Malvolio's role, then, forms the subplot of the play; it has no direct narrative connection with the primary comic device of Viola-Sebastian.[26] Once Maria and Feste have goaded him into exposure through his wooing Olivia, he is conveniently removed to the dark room as the action of the major plot resumes. And he returns to the stage only after the full range of character revelations has occurred. His presence in Act V is not insignificant, however, because it enables Shakespeare to maintain a comic tone. It may be true that Malvolio's refusal to take his ignominy in the spirit of a joke and his determination to "be revenged on the whole pack" forfeits any opportunity for our ultimate sympathy, but his action also maintains the comic perspective of the play. Through restoring a character to his true nature, the comic catharsis achieves a harmonious social relationship: Orsino weds Viola, Olivia weds Sebastian, Toby weds Maria, Sebastian's friendship with Antonio is restored, Sir Andrew accepts his cowardice. Malvolio's singular unwillingness to learn through laughter provides the spectator a final chuckle at one who remains a comic butt. And, for that matter, his action is not exceptional to the theme of the play: He has, like the others, been forced to face the revelation of his true personality, and in his case, as with Aguecheek, the revelation is not an idyllic one.

Character revelation, of course, does not involve actual transformation. While the characterization is indeed more complex than the mere manipulation of the Antipholuses and the Dromios of *The Comedy of Errors,* there is no innate alteration of personality such as is to be depicted in Leontes of *The Winter's Tale* and in Alonso of *The Tempest.*[27] In Illyria no crimes have been committed; nothing needs to be forgiven. The characters, motivated at best by a cultivated social dilettantism and at worst by an obsession for social status and wealth, make asses of themselves as a result of their failure to use common—not moral—sense. But the characters socially know themselves more fully at the end of their experiences. They have faced the therapy of exposure, have been laughed from their abnormal postures, and, presumably, have every reason to expect a richer and more productive life as a consequence of their self-knowledge. With Feste, they might all say: "by my foes, sir, I profit in the knowledge of myself" (V, i, 21-22).

Shakespeare in his subsequent plays will move toward a deeper comic vision involving a society in which evil is a reality and in which characters are spiritually transformed through the quality of love's forgiveness. His continued efforts in these comedies to establish an effective perspective—with varying degrees of success—will reveal his persistent concern for comic control over a narrative replete with potential tragedy. But *Twelfth Night* has no potential tragedy; it is among Shakespeare's most successful realizations of "romantic" comedy based on character revelation. And clearly this success results in a large measure from the effective comic perspective—the creation of characters who, while playing a significant narrative role, also serve as comic pointers by providing vital information for the spectator and by functioning as the primary device for character exposure.

"My project may deceive me, but my intents are fix'd"

4 The Problem Comedies

Whatever the motivation—personal emotional problems, a practical eye for the kind of drama popular with the audiences of the early years of the seventeenth century, or artistic determination to deal with profound moral issues—Shakespeare, after the completion of *Twelfth Night*, moves persistently, if somewhat unsteadily, toward a vision of comedy involving characters on the level of transformation who will experience the complete range of human emotion. And, as suggested earlier, when his concept of character expands, so also does his problem of maintaining a comic perspective for his stage-world. Not until *The Winter's Tale* and *The Tempest* is he to achieve a degree of success commensurate with that of *Twelfth Night*. But much is taking place artistically in the interim, and in *All's Well That Ends Well, Measure for Measure, Pericles*,[1] and *Cymbeline*, he is consciously and creatively experimenting with structural and narrative devices through which comically to control this larger vision of evil.

The result is a series of partial successes as comedy. In some cases the flaw is narrational, the spectator's interest in character blocked by a superficial development or subsumed in a literal flurry of events which boggles the imagination; the perspective is, in effect, uncontrolled, involving no meaningful anticipation of the basic direction of the narrative. *Pericles*, for instance, depicts events scattered over six kingdoms and the better part of two decades. Both Pericles and Marina are totally flat; they do not develop as characters, but, more sinned against than sinning (Pericles by nature and Marina by man), they simply endure the events of their adverse fortune. Moreover, neither Cleon and Dionyza in Tarsus nor Boult and the pander and the bawd in Mytiline are developed in sufficient detail to emerge as provocative antagonists. As a consequence, the play lacks the conflict built on character which by this point has come to be the hallmark of Shakespearean comedy. The spectator remains outside, as it were, observing the amazing events which entertain for their own sake, not because they arouse interest in what happens to a certain character or how he is affected.

The problem of *Cymbeline* is one of focus and, consequently, of lack of intensity. Shakespeare again centers the interest on character, and through the comments and actions of Imogen, Pisanio, and the second lord, he achieves a relatively effective comic perspective for action—admittedly sensational—involving a beheaded scoundrel prince and a queen's suicide by poison. But, instead of an extensively developed transformation in character, the play superficially sketches several characters achieving a new degree of self-knowledge through the humility of spiritual exposure and repentance. Cymbeline immediately suggests himself as the major focus of the play, yet his experience lacks intensity because to only a slightly greater degree than Pericles is he responsible for his ill fortunes. It is possibly true that in action antecedent to the play he has unwisely and unjustly banished Belarius, that he never should have been so naive as to be blind to the duplicity of his queen and stepson, and that his misjudgment of Posthumus in refusing Imogen's marriage reveals a pride and arrogance which breed tragedy. But these are minuscule indeed compared with the scathing jealousy which leads Leontes to imprison his wife and order his infant child abandoned to the elements or with the political greed which has led Antonio and Alonso to usurp Prospero's dukedom. Then, too, Cymbeline's experience merely frames the action of the play; we see the price his sins have cost him, his repentance, and his eventual happiness in the final act, but there is no progressive development of his moral self-revelation. So also Iachimo, having played his villainy to the hilt, experiences a change of heart, but hardly one which can claim the major interest of the audience. The best case is made for Posthumus Leonatus, who, banished unjustly, so allows his mind to feed on jealousy that he ultimately destroys his young bride, or so he presumes. The fury of passion, the misery of doubt, and the agony of contrition, humility, and repentance precede his reunion with Imogen and his pardon by an equally revivified Cymbeline. Here, in a play abounding in physical action and numerous changes of scene, Shakespeare has created a powerful comic vision of a society replete with evil, but a vision which is only partially succesful, because in its attempt at inclusiveness, it sacrifices focus and depth.

In the comedies which evidently immediately precede *Pericles* and *Cymbeline,* the flaw is more fundamentally structural—the spectator's comic omniscience or, at least, assurance destroyed or blurred by the ambiguity of the comic pointer. *All's Well That Ends Well* and *Measure for Measure* share a number of essential similarities which suggest that, in their present form at least, Shakespeare composed them at approximately the same point in his artistic development.[2] Superficially we are struck by the names Mariana, Isabella (Isbel), and Escalus which appear in both plays. More significant, these plays represent Shakespeare's first attempts at a comically controlled delineation of character on the level of transformation, a central character who falls to sin but is eventually pardoned after experiencing a comic catharsis on the moral level. In each case a young man, the victim of prideful self-esteem, encounters a woman who outmaneuvers him and exposes him for the moral hypocrite he is. Central to the design is the bed trick, through which the man's lust becomes the means for both his destruction and regeneration; for in both cases a wronged wife makes good her legal claim upon her mate, a claim which ultimately leads to pardon, reconciliation, and happiness. Finally, in both plays, Shakespeare falls short of his apparent intentions for the same reason. While he creates a provocative vision of character caught in a moral and ethical dilemma, he fails to achieve what he is ultimately to accomplish in *The Winter's Tale* and *The Tempest*—a clear perspective through which the experience for the audience, despite the presence and power of evil, will be a comic one.[3]

Bertram is presumably the result of Shakespeare's first attempt to create comic characterization on the level of transformation.[4] At any rate, he is the only character in *All's Well That Ends Well* to experience a spiritual conversion predicated on a reversal of values which permits his resorption into a society governed by the love of mercy and grace. The surrounding characters are essentially static, their values constant. Helena quite certainly is intended to be the gracious heroine possessed by a love whose forgiveness knows no bounds; Lafeu, the elderly and obedient subject of his king and his countess; the Countess of Rousillon, the matronly aristocrat whose genuine concern for her ward is reflected in her pride of family heritage and her reaction to her son's flagrant disobedience; even Parolles, the arrant braggadocio whose ignominious exposure merely forces him to a more palpable level of parisitism. By contrast, Bertram—at the outset apparently an honorable young man expected like his father to bring additional accolades to the family name—is faced with decisions which destroy his personal integrity and his public reputation. During the closing moments of the action he experiences a profound transformation; shocked into right reason, he repents his rash deeds and is appropriately forgiven by all whom he has wronged.

The plot, then, quite literally centers on Bertram.[5] At the outset he appears, completely without malice, mourning his father and comforting his mother as he leaves by royal command to attend the king at court. Obedient both to the king, to whom he is "evermore in subjection" (I, i, 5-6), and to his mother, whose "holy wishes" he "desire[s]" (68) and of whose comfort he is solicitous (86-87), he receives the charge to

> succeed thy father
> In manners, as in shape! Thy blood and virtue
> Contend for empire in thee, and thy goodness
> Share with thy birthright!
>
> (70-73)

Only the passing references to his being inexperienced ("an unseason'd courtier" [80]) and to his companionship with the "notorious liar" Parolles (111) mar our first impressions of the young count. Certainly Helena's secret admiration speaks implicitly to his advantage. And his brief appearance in the next scene does nothing to impair this image. To the king, who recounts his fast friendship with Bertram's father, the son "bear'st [his] father's face," his "[f]rank nature," and his "moral parts." The king, in brief, reads the full range of his father's excellencies into Bertram and proffers him a warm welcome: "My son's no dearer" (I, ii, 76).

In Act II, however, the young count, at court for the first time and faced with the sin of family pride, proves doubly false. First, he flagrantly disobeys the king's orders to stay home from the Florentine wars because of his youth; secondly, he is false to Helena, whom he grudgingly weds by royal command but immediately deserts with callous lies. Both violations involve his following the advice of his rogue companion, advice on the one hand to "steal away bravely" (II, i, 29) in defiance of the king, and on the other hand to use his friendship for pragmatic and timeserving alliance with those who "wear themselves in the cap of the time" (54-55).

When with the king's blessing Helena chooses Bertram as husband, he responds: "give me leave to use / The help of mine own eyes" (II, iii, 113-114); that she has the king's favor is no reason for which "I should marry her" (117). The moment is powerful, provoking both admiration and disdain for the young count. There is certainly some justification, for example, in his defiance of the king's high-handed demand that he "take her . . . My honour's at the stake" (112-113, 156). For one thing, he has the courage to speak out against what he feels to be an injustice; for another, he never directly lies to the king: at the point of acquiescence he agrees to "take her hand" but he pointedly does not, as the ruler suggests, "tell her she is [his]." On the other hand, Bertram clearly loses both dignity and integrity during this confrontation. Contemptuous of Helena's low breeding ("at my father's charge," "A poor physician's daughter"), he proclaims flatly, "I cannot love her, nor will strive to do't" (152). Yet, when the king's wrath makes it apparent that continued royal favor will not condone such an attitude, Bertram—however ingeniously—diametrically reverses his posture: "Pardon, my gracious lord; for I submit / My fancy to your eyes" (174-175).

The central dramatic issue—to the seventeenth- or the twentieth-century audience—is not whether the ruler is psychologically or morally just in exercising such a marital choice, but rather Bertram's arrant duplicity, his obedience feigned for the sake of currying royal favor. Since Parolles is at this point the dominant influence on Bertram, it is appropriate that the count first confess his intentions to him.[6] "Although before the solemn priest I have sworn, I will not bed her . . . O my Parolles, they have married me! I'll to the Tuscan wars, and never bed her . . . I'll send her straight away. To-morrow I'll to the wars, she to her single sorrow" (II, iii, 286-287, 289-290, 312-313). And, rather than face her himself, he sends his companion with word that "my lord will go away to-night . . . [on] serious business" and that she is to take her instant departure to Rousillon. Moments later, taking personal leave of Helena and refusing even a token kiss, Bertram becomes a skilled liar, avowing his "respects are better than they seem . . . 'Twill be two days ere I shall see you" (II, v, 71, 75).

This degradation which we have observed directly in Act II is confirmed in Act III by the remarks of the surrounding characters. His mother, for instance, twice denounces his dastardly actions. When she receives his note of explanation, she exclaims:

> This is not well, rash and unbridled boy,
> To fly the favours of so good a king,
> To pluck his indignation on thy head
> By the misprising of a maid too virtuous
> For the contempt of empire.
> (III, ii, 30-34)

She excoriates him again after Helena has secretly left Rousillon:

> What angel shall
> Bless this unworthy husband? He cannot thrive,
> Unless her prayers, whom Heaven delights to hear
> And loves to grant, reprieve him from the wrath
> Of greatest justice. Write, write, Rinaldo,

To this unworthy husband of his wife.
. . . set [her worth] down sharply.
(III, iii, 25-30, 33)

Similarly, Mariana in Florence speaks of Bertram as full of "prom-ises, enticements, oaths, tokens, and all these engines of lust" (III, v, 19-21), and Diana remarks: "I would he lov'd his wife. If he were honester / He were much goodlier" (82-83).

It is ironic, then, that as his moral infamy develops, so does his martial fame. The duke of Florence appoints him "The general of our horse"; as a "lover of . . . drum, hater of love" (III, iii, 11), the count is credited with "most honourable service" (III, v, 3-4). A similar and more pervasive irony in the play is the frequent equation of peace and sickness; the kingdom without war is said to fail to provide an adequate training field for the young aristocrats. So, for instance, a lord comments to the king that the Florentine-Senoy conflict "well may serve / A nursery to our gentry, who are sick / For breathing and exploit" (I, ii, 15-17). Later, the duke of Florence is told by one of his young French volunteers: "I am sure the younger of our nature, / That surfeit on their ease, will day by day / Come here for physic" (III, i, 17-19).

With the fall to sin clearly established, Bertram's wheel of fire turns through four stages prior to his repentance at the conclusion of the play. These stages involve, in turn, Parolles, Diana Capilet, his mother (the Countess of Rousillon), and the king. In each case, Bertram painfully achieves a degree of self-knowledge which is to culminate in his final humility. In the first phase, the count is forced to acknowledge the crass ignobility of his erstwhile confidant. A group of French lords carefully arrange and execute a plan by which Parolles' vaunted courage is revealed as a facade for cow-ardly fear, his integrity a pretense for treason, or whatever action might for the moment be necessary to save his skin. "Arrested" as he seeks to recover the drum, Parolles is to be interrogated by those whom he will assume to be enemy troops. Bertram is told: "Be but your lordship present at his examination; if he do not, for the promise of his life and in the highest compulsion of base fear, offer to betray you and deliver all the intelligence in his power against you . . . never trust my judgment in anything" (III, vi, 29-35). As he later hears his companion—whose advice he previously has solicited—brand him "a fool" (IV, iii, 258), "a dangerous and lascivious boy," "a whale to virginity [who] devours up all the fry it finds" (248-250), his remarks reflect the difficulty of admitting (as one lord phrases it) that "this is your devoted friend, sir, the manifold linguist and the armipotent soldier" (264-265). "Come, bring forth this counterfeit module, has deceiv'd me, like a double-meaning prophesier . . . What a past-saving slave is this! . . . Damnable both-sides rogue!" (IV, iii, 112-115, 158-159, 251).

Bertram, not realizing that he is an object of a far more complex ruse than that to expose Parolles, experiences purgatorial indignity in his lust for Diana. Given what he assumes to be ready access to her, he woos in a manner appropos to his self-designed aristocratic posture, like a courtly lover vowing eternal love—outside marriage (for Diana, like Helena, is his social inferior). Thus he terms her a "goddess," a "fair soul," a "monument," swearing "By love's own sweet constraint" forever to "Do thee all rights of service." "Love is holy"; she is "holy-cruel." But Bertram is not permitted to maintain his facade of dignity. Diana is careful to remind him that the same vows he makes to her, he owes to his wife:

> 'Tis not the many oaths that makes the truth,
> But the plain single vow that is vow'd true.
> What is not holy, that we swear not by,
> But take the High'st to witness . . .
>   therefore your oaths
> Are words and poor conditions, but unseal'd.
> > (IV, ii, 21-24, 29-30)

Finally, no longer with the pretense of dignity, Bertram implores Diana to "give thyself unto my sick desires" (35); and, when she by prearrangement with Helena insists on the ring which "is an honour 'longing to our house, / Bequeathed down from many an-

cestors" and "which were the greatest obloquy i' th' world / In me
to lose" (42-45), he in utter frustration exclaims: "Here, take my
ring! / My house, mine honour, yea, my life" (51-52). We should
also remember the procedure arranged for consummation. With
both visual and aural communication banned, the sex act is animalistic, lacking the least semblance of dignity. The arrangement is
obviously necessary to the plot; even so, it is also significant in
what it tells us about Bertram, for the method can only be de-
grading to one who possesses such a high opinion of his importance.

The following scene provides reported action in which Bertram
visibly begins not only to react to his guilt, but also to sacrifice the
public honor of his name. In a discussion between two French
lords, we are informed that the Countess of Rousillon has sent her
son a letter "that stings his nature; for on the reading it he chang'd
almost into another man" (IV, iii, 5-6). The letter, however, which
lays "much worthy blame . . . upon him for shaking off so good a
wife and so sweet a lady" (7-9) and for "incurr[ing] the everlasting
displeasure of the King" (10-11), only momentarily deters the
count, who is even now perverting the honor of "a young gentlewoman here in Florence" (17-18). So, as the lords remark, are we
in rebellion traitors to ourselves: "And as in the common course of
all treasons, we still see them reveal themselves, till they attain to
their abhorr'd ends, so he that in this action contrives against his
own nobility, in his proper stream o'erflows himself" (25-30). Could
he be anatomized, he "might take a measure of his own judgements"
(39-40) and thus perceive how hollow indeed is martial glory in
the absence of moral integrity: "The great dignity that his valour
hath here acquir'd for him shall at home be encount'red with a
shame as ample" (IV, iii, 80-82). These remarks, coupled with the
moment of remorse—albeit brief—anticipate Bertram's shame,
humility, and contrition.

In the final scene, the count, before the king, is to meet his moment of truth. With both his mother and Lafeu as advocates, he is
forgiven before he enters. The king's comments ("I have forgiven
and forgotten all; / Though my revenges were high bent upon him"

[V, iii, 9-10], "We are reconcil'd" [21], "[t]he time is fair again" [36], "All is whole" [37]) set the tone· for general amnesty. Bertram's penitential statement pertaining to his actions ("My high-repented blames, / Dear sovereign, pardon to me" [36-37]) and his assertion that he now realizes how much he loved Helena (44-55) appear to produce the proper posture for reconciliation. But he has repented only of his public sins, revealing nothing; his rejection of Helena and disobedience of the king are, after all, common knowledge. Moreover, with Helena dead, the sting of contrition concerning his dastardly relationship is less painful. Of course, he has no reason to assume that any of his acquaintances in France are concerned with his moral latitude in Florence. Thus, when his foreign escapades come to light, the sudden public confrontation with his private sins sets his defense mechanism in motion again and reveals that he is not yet ready to face the total truth. He denies that the ring he wears was ever Helena's, that he has ever sworn to marry Diana. In reality we have never seen Bertram make the oath which Diana avers, yet—however brash her methods—it is no less distasteful that his pride leads him publicly to impugn her character with such vehemence:

> My lord, this is a fond and desp'rate creature,
> Whom sometime I have laugh'd with. Let your Highness
> Lay a more noble thought upon mine honour
> Than for to think that I would sink it here.
> . . . She's impudent, my lord,
> And was a common gamester to th' camp.
> . . . Certain it is I lik'd her,
> And boarded her i' th' wanton way of youth . . .
> Her [infinite cunning], with her modern grace,
> Subdu'd me to her rate. She got the ring.
> (V, iii, 178-181, 187-188, 210-211, 216-217)

Having vented these insults, Bertram is awestruck and totally subdued by the sudden "resurrection" of Helena. His sin and immorality laid completely bare, he now repents anew—this time with nothing to hide—to the king and Helena, the two whom he has wronged through deceit and disobedience:

> Both, both. O, pardon!
> If she, my liege, can make me know this clearly,
> I'll love her dearly, ever, ever dearly.
> (309, 316-317)

With Helena's acceptance and the king's pardon, Bertram—apparently purged as a result of his experience—is resorbed into the normal society. And the king, promising Diana her choice of husband from his young noblemen at court, provides the apposite concluding comment:

> All yet seems well; and if it end so meet,
> The bitter past, more welcome is the sweet.
> (333-334)

Bertram, clearly, is a kind of comic characterization which Shakespeare has not previously attempted. Neither a pawn manipulated for the humor of situation, nor a social hypocrite in whom the comic gap between appearance and reality is exploited, the French count is, as it were, a spiritual hypocrite, exposed and transformed. Shakespeare has not previously depicted realistic characters contending with such issues, nor has he attempted in his comic vision to delineate character growth on the spiritual or moral level. The playwright, in brief, is now concerned in his comedy with the fully developed character who must make real decisions and face the real consequences; rather than comedy of escape from the total human condition, this is comedy of involvement in the total human condition. And Bertram's dramatic experience is comically plausible —certainly not vastly dissimilar to that of Leontes, or of Alonso, Antonio, Sebastian, or of Cymbeline.

Yet, the play pleases virtually no one as comedy; somewhere along the line the comic experience breaks down for most spectators and critics. It is easy enough to blame this failure on the twentieth-century attitude toward arranged marriages. While obviously the attitude toward arranged marriages has changed, the argument makes two dangerous assumptions concerning *All's Well*: first, that the play used to be popular, but no longer is so because we do not condone such marital guardianship; second, that Shakespeare's attitude on this matter is fundamentally different from ours—a view hardly borne out by his depiction of arranged marriage in, for example, *Romeo and Juliet* or *A Midsummer-Night's Dream* or *The Two Gentlemen of Verona* or *The Winter's Tale* (Polixenes' parental opposition to the love of Perdita and Florizel). The failure of the play can also be blamed on the incongruous mixture of realistic and romantic elements,[7] or on Shakespeare's use of a narrative pattern familiar to his audience involving the clever and gracious young woman, a pattern which we do not readily accept because it is unfamiliar to us,[8] or on Shakespeare's sacrifice of narrative integrity for the sake of dramatizing scriptural allegory,[9] or on Shakespeare's somewhat imperfect adaptation of another's play or a clumsy revision of his own,[10] or on Shakespeare's deliberate attempt to create an ironic or satiric play somewhat in the Jonson-Marston vein,[11] or on Shakespeare's following the fashion with a prodigal son play,[12] or, if one is willing to stretch the date sufficiently, on Shakespeare's determination to please James I by creating a fantastic situation solved by the mercy and wisdom of the king.

A greater or lesser degree of truth is possible in each of these suggestions. Yet, for whatever other motivations are involved, the more basic and fundamental explanation is that this play—along with *Measure for Measure*—is structurally faulty.[13] We have previously observed the various devices which Shakespeare utilizes to block the spectator's emotional involvement and thus to produce the comic dramatic experience—devices such as a close rapport between the spectator and a comic pointer, a character who observes and comments or who manipulates and controls the action and thereby provides superior knowledge; or stylized characters and hyperbolic action; or a subplot, frequently involving zanies or low-life characters, which mocks or burlesques the main action. In moving from comedy of identity to comedy of transformation, Shakespeare finds the problem of maintaining an effective comic perspective an acute one. Given the greater tendency toward emotional involvement with any character who is realistically presented —that is, who is caught up in a situation demanding fundamental moral and ethical decisions which ostensibly, at least, control the welfare of both body and soul—the spectator's view must be carefully conditioned. If for any reason the comic perspective breaks down, the play turns to melodrama, perhaps even tragedy, and the spectator's reaction, at least momentarily, is confused.

In *All's Well That Ends Well*, Shakespeare establishes the comic perspective through the use of Helena as the major comic pointer, Lafeu and Lavache as secondary pointers, and an extensive parallel to Bertram's actions in the sardonic exploits of Parolles. Structurally, the drama is quite similar to *Twelfth Night*, perhaps the comedy immediately preceding it. Helena, like Viola-Sebastian, plays an integral role in the narrative itself, yet provides for the spectator information essential to his viewing comically the actions of the surrounding characters—primarily Bertram. Like Malvolio, Parolles is involved in action which constitutes an extensive parallel to the action of the major character. As Maria functions in *Twelfth Night* as a secondary comic pointer to expose Malvolio, so Lafeu functions primarily throughout the play to insert touchstone remarks concerning Parolles and his relationship to Bertram and to effect the rogue's initial exposure for the audience. And finally, as Feste provides occasional choric commentary on the whole pattern of character hypocrisy, so Lavache, albeit less consciously, performs this service in *All's Well That Ends Well*.

More specifically, the clown—although appearing in only six scenes and quite briefly in each of these—tolerantly mocks, frequently with bawdiness, the major themes and the major characters of the play and in this manner helps to strengthen the comic perspective by blocking the spectator's emotional involvement.[14] In several instances, to be sure, the bantering is unconscious; however, the result of the juxtaposition of his comments and attitudes with the dominant issues of the play is comic distancing. The clown's first appearance, for example, mocks romance just at the moment when Helena is admitting her secret love for Bertram. Instead of a passion which is noble, enduring, and sacrificial, he views love as sensual and inconstant. He begs permission to marry because his body requires it and because Isbel needs to be made an honest woman. Since he assumes cuckoldry to be the natural state of the married man, he asserts that he will be able to use his wife to gain new friends. To the countess' reproval that he is a "foul-mouth'd and calumnious knave," he retorts, "A prophet I, madam; and I speak the truth the next way" (I, iii, 62-63). Similarly his next appearance satirizes the court, where both Bertram and Parolles expect to develop the clever ingenuity of witty repartee and the charm and the integrity of the true aristocrat. Lavache bluntly proclaims that the key to success at court is fashionable time-serving, not integrity: "Truly, madam, if God have lent a man any manners, he may easily put it off at court. He that cannot make a leg, put off's cap, kiss his hand and say nothing, has neither leg, hands, lip, nor cap; and indeed such a fellow, to say precisely, were not for the court" (II, ii, 8-14). In such high society it is much safer to have an answer which will serve all men and offend none, "like a barber's chair that fits all buttocks." A well-placed "O Lord, sir" will get the fashion seeker further than any honest answer! Later he describes the marvelous habits which reflect the fashionable melancholia in a courtier—the way one will "look upon his boot and sing; mend the ruff and sing; ask questions and sing; pick his teeth and sing" (III, ii, 6-8). And his newfound cavalier habits are now reflected in his whimsical feminine interests; the rustic girls are no longer to his taste: "I have no mind to Isbel since I was at court. Our old [ling] and our Isbels o' th' country are nothing like your old ling and your Isbels o' th' court. The brains of my Cupid's knock'd out, and I begin to love, as an old man loves money, with no stomach" (13-18). In our first glimpse of the countess following the presumed death of Helena, the clown attempts to distract her from her sorrow through sheer bawdiness, and Shakespeare, through the wit, avoids a potentially tedious moment. When asked whether he considers himself a fool or a knave, the clown babbles that he is a knave in a man's service but a fool in a woman's. For, fool to a woman, he can proffer his bauble "to do her service." He claims moreover that he serves a lord with an English name— "The Black Prince . . . alias, the prince of darkness; alias, the devil" (IV, v, 44-45), who surely is "the prince of the world," since the nobility flock to "the flow'ry way that leads to the broad gate and the great fire" (56-57).

At times the clown points directly to laughter at Parolles' expense. In the scene immediately following Bertram's decision to abandon Helena for the battlefield, as Parolles has advised, Lavache bluntly brands him a pompous knave who has misled the count: "[M]any a man's tongue shakes out his master's undoing. To say nothing, to do nothing, to know nothing, and to have nothing, is to be a great part of your title; which is within a very little of nothing" (II, iv, 23-27). When the braggadocio retorts that the clown is a fool, Lavache reminds him that the role of the fool is to act as a mirror in which others will see their true qualities reflected: "Did you find me in yourself, sir, or were you taught to find me? The search, sir, was profitable; and much fool may you find in you, even to the world's pleasure and the increase of laughter" (33-37). At the conclusion of the play, Parolles must solicit the favor of the clown, whom with deference he calls Lavache—an indication both of the ignominy which Mars' stalwart has suffered and also of the perceptive shame by which he now admittedly intends to thrive. Once more the clown, before referring him to Lafeu, uses to good advantage the opportunity to berate him with invective: "Fortune's displeasure is but sluttish, if it smell so strongly as thou speak'st of. I will henceforth eat no fish of Fortune's butt'ring. Prithee, allow the wind . . . [P]rithee, stand away. A paper from Fortune's close-stool to give to a nobleman!" (V, ii, 7-10, 17-18). The clown, then, though a minor figure, makes his appearances at significant moments for strengthening the comic perspective through irony, sarcasm, and bawdiness.

More extensively, Parolles' exposure as a braggadocio directly parallels the exposure of Bertram as a moral reprobate and thus reinforces the comic tone of the play.[15] Bertram receives praise from both family and ruler—in the first scene from his mother for his blood, virtue, goodness, and birthright, and in the second scene from the king for the friendship, soldiership, and wit which he presumably inherits from his father. In the intervening moments, Parolles, lacking such admirers, touts himself with equal fervor. Claiming that he was born when Mars was predominant, he avoids Helena's retorts by exclaiming "I am so full of businesses, I cannot answer thee acutely" (I, i, 220-221). Each man prepares for court with grandiose expectations of what the royal company can do for him: Bertram is expected to "succeed [his] father," but he is warned of the pitfalls for the "unseason'd courtier"; Parolles boasts that he "will return perfect courtier" and thus be able to thrust instruction and advice upon all around him. Both count and companion, then, convinced of their self-importance, are primed for pride's fall at court.

Once at court, each takes his leave for the battlefield under false pretenses. Bertram, incensed when his youth is urged as a cause of his staying home from the wars, decides on Parolles' advice to steal away in defiance of royal advice. His departure becomes doubly damning after his marriage to Helena; with the blatant lie that business requires him to be away from her for two days he departs for the battlefield assuming he will never see her again. With similar lies, the braggadocio, no less verbal than before concerning his valor, claims he is anxious to get to the field where many already bear the marks of his sword: "Noble heroes, my sword and yours are kin . . . you shall find in the regiment of the Spinii one Captain Spurio, [with his cicatrice, an] emblem of war, here on his sinister cheek,—it was this very sword entrench'd it;—say to him, I live; and observe his reports for me" (II, i, 40-46). Calling France a dog-hole and a stable inhabited by jades, he rushes "To th' wars" where his arms might "sustain the bound and high curvet / Of Mars's fiery steed" (II, iii, 299-300).

Through the remainder of the play, Parolles' actions are directly correlated with Bertram's. We hear of Bertram's designs upon Diana, and, two scenes later, Helena plots with Diana to catch him in his moral cowardice. In between, the French lords plot to expose Parolles' physical cowardice. Convinced that he is "an infinite and endless liar, an hourly promise-breaker" (III, vi, 10-11), the lords convince Bertram to allow Parolles to recapture the regimental drum. Though the count is hesitant to believe he is "so far deceived in him," he agrees to be present at the examination and hear the betrayal. ". . . for the love of laughter," the lords inform their captain, "you shall see his fall to-night" (36, 107-108).

The scene depicting Bertram's commitment to sin with Diana is inserted between the two scenes in which Parolles is apprehended, confesses, and repents. Clearly Shakespeare, through the subplot, is providing comic insulation for Bertram's morally critical moment. For Parolles' fate is comic in the fullest sense of the word. Mumbling as he comes on stage that he has now talked himself into a terrible predicament, he is seized and blindfolded. Without ascertaining who his enemies are, let alone waiting for their charges against him, he blurts that he will tell all he knows: "I'll / Discover that which shall undo the Florentine" (IV, i, 79-80); "And all the secrets of our camp I'll show" (93). In the subsequent scene, the "gallant militarist" answers question after question, broadcasting vital intelligence information while the astonished Bertram mumbles angrily in the background. As one lord remarks of the chameleon pragmatism of this *miles gloriosus*: "I will never trust a man again for keeping his sword clean, nor believe he can have everything in him by wearing his apparel neatly" (IV, iii, 165-168). One by one Parolles describes the French lords—Bertram included—as foolish and incompetent. Just prior to the full disclosure of identities, Parolles is privately swearing to be more wary of his foolhardy escapades, but second thoughts are now too late. Stripping off his blindfold, his companion-interrogators stand around him in mocking anticipation of Parolles' flailing attempts to extricate himself from a situation which would perplex even a Falstaff. Cornered and bewildered, Parolles can only moan, "Who cannot be crush'd with a plot?" (IV, iii, 360).

If Parolles were to be either emotionally crushed or morally converted, his value as a device by which Shakespeare keeps a comic edge on the parallel events of Bertram's fate would be sharply diminished. The playwright, consequently, allows the scamp the final words in the scene, and these words, delivered in soliloquy only four lines after his public admission of defeat, reveal that he and his roguery are very much alive. The effect is to retain Parolles as the object of derision and to block the spectator's sympathy for and emotional involvement with him and, by extension, the count—who is shortly to experience a similar exposure. Parolles, to be sure, has achieved a greater degree of self-knowldge; he now knows himself to be a fool, just as he has long since known himself to be a braggart. Hence, like Bertram, he profits from the comic experience, but not with the end result of any sort of moral transformation. He has no intention of altering his life; he is simply determined to play his chosen role the more expertly:

> Yet am I thankful. If my heart were great,
> 'Twould burst at this. Captain I'll be no more;
> But I will eat and drink, and sleep as soft
> As captain shall. Simply the thing I am
> Shall make me live. Who knows himself a braggart,
> Let him fear this; for it will come to pass
> That every braggart shall be found an ass.
> Rust, sword! cool, blushes! and, Parolles, live
> Safest in shame! Being fool'd, by fool'ry thrive!
>   (366-374)

And we see Parolles in action again as the play concludes. Immediately prior to the king's promise of pardon to Bertram and the subsequent mercy of Helena which will make that promise good, the rogue plays the pitiful penitent, "a man whom Fortune hath cruelly scratch'd" (V, ii, 28-29), and after weathering a barrage of insults achieves his pardon from Lafeu: "Sirrah, inquire further after me. I had talk of you last night. Though you are a fool and a knave, you shall eat; go to, follow" (55-58). Obviously Parolles is finding it profitable to "live safest in shame" and to thrive "by fool'ry."

The parallel, in sum, has been carefully constructed. Certainly, to speak of Parolles' "innocence" and "repentance" is to overstate the point; his initial pride is deflated, however, and he "profits" from the experience. As such, his dramatic experience preplots and anticipates the stages of Bertram's experience. And in the final stages, we are again reminded of Malvolio, who remains the comic victim and offsets the potential sentimentality of the reunion scene in *Twelfth Night*. Parolles' reaction to his exposure—his refusal to be transformed in nature and his determination to be revenged upon the entire lot by profiting in roguery in the future from the mistakes which have led to his present downfall—leaves him a comic butt and provides Shakespeare a means of maintaining the comic tone at the moment Bertram's exposure and repentance are making dangerously sentimental demands upon the emotions of the spectator.

Both the function of Lavache and the development of an extensive subplot clearly contribute to the comic perspective. Shakespeare's difficulty in achieving a successful comic perspective occurs in the additional devices, in the function of Lafeu and, more crucially, of Helena as comic pointers.

Lafeu's role does not emerge clearly until the middle of the play, from which point he is the primary device for exposing Parolles as the *miles gloriosus*. Prior to that moment, however, he himself has unconsciously been the object of the spectator's laughter. Hence there is at least momentarily an emotional dislocation before the spectator can realize that the elderly courtier is in a position to control and direct his attitudes toward the major comic butt of the play. Certainly this inconsistency in character, coupled with the ambiguity of Helena, contributes to the difficulty in tone during the early scenes.

In Lafeu's initial appearance, he comforts both the countess and her ward, assuring the countess that the king will be a second father to her son and comforting Helena through praising the wisdom and skill of her deceased father. Yet in his next two appearances, we are amused by his Polonius-like senility. As Lafeu brings news of Helena's medical talents, the king tolerantly mocks his obsequious bowing and his demeanor of amazed credulity. Of this badinage the king remarks, as the courtier leaves to accompany Helena before the throne, "Thus he his special nothing ever prologues" (II, i, 95). Even more obviously he is the object of ridicule when he rushes out proclaiming the king's cure. Standing to the side and speaking directly to the audience, Parolles raises chuckles with taunting interruptions of the lugubrious and garrulous report which Lafeu delivers:

> LAF. I may truly say it is a novelty to the world.
> PAR. It is, indeed; if you will have it in showing,
> you shall read it in—what do ye call there?
> LAF. A showing of a heavenly effect in an earthly actor.
> PAR. That's it; I would have said the very same.
> LAF. Why, your Dauphin is not lustier. 'Fore me, I speak in
> respect—
> PAR. Nay, 'tis strange, 'tis very strange, that is the brief
> and the tedious of it; and he's of a most facinerious spirit
> that will not acknowledge it to be the—
> LAF. Very hand of Heaven.
> PAR. Ay, so I say.
> LAF. In a most weak—
> PAR. And debile minister, great power, great transcendence;
> which should, indeed, give us a further use to be made
> than alone the recov'ry of the King, as to be—
> LAF. Generally thankful.
>
> (II, iii, 22-43)

In both instances, a director may choose to de-emphasize Lafeu's foolishness and to soften the king's and Parolles' mockery, perhaps even to turn the jest upon the rogue, but clearly the comic potential of the scenes arises in part at the lord's expense.

This same Lafeu, however, controls the comic potential in his remaining scenes and begins clearly to direct our derision toward Parolles at the moment Bertram has accepted Helena under protest and is to follow the rogue's advice to abandon her. By providing a pointer to expose Parolles as clearly laughable at the point he becomes more insidiously dangerous because Bertram falls under his influence, Shakespeare is again reinforcing the comic tone at a critical moment. When Parolles rankles at being labeled Bertram's man, Lafeu quickly calls his bluff: "I must tell thee, sirrah, I write man; to which title age cannot bring thee" (II, iii, 208-209). To Parolles' quip that Lafeu's age is his salvation, the lord retorts: "Do not plunge thyself too far in anger, lest thou hasten thy trial; which if—Lord have mercy on thee for a hen! So, my good window of lattice, fare thee well! Thy casement I need not open, for I look through thee" (222-227). The braggadocio regains his courage when Lafeu walks off stage and swears to swinge him on their next encounter: "scurvy, old, filthy, scurvy lord! . . . I'll beat him, by my life, if I can meet him with any convenience, an he were double and double a lord. I'll have no more pity of his age than I would have of—I'll beat him, an if I could but meet him again" (250, 252-256). Lafeu's entrance on these very words utterly melts his courage and provides the capstone for the exposure of his arrant cowardice as he receives another verbal laceration: "Methinks, thou art a general offence, and every man should beat thee" (267-268). Two scenes later, Lafeu flatly reproves Bertram for the faith which he places in his boon companion. To the count's claim that Parolles is a gallant soldier, Lafeu retorts, "Then my dial goes not true. I took this lark for a bunting" (II, v, 6-7). And to Bertram's claim that his companion is knowledgeable and valiant, the lord exclaims: "there can be no kernel in this light nut: the soul of this man is his clothes. Trust him not in matter of heavy consequence; I have kept of them tame, and know their natures" (47-50). Later, his vilification of the rogue has hardly moderated, as he brands him a "red-tailed humble-bee" and exclaims to the countess: "your son was misled with a snipt-taffeta fellow there, whose villanous saffron would have made all the unbak'd and doughy youth of a nation in his colour" (IV, v, 1-4).

Because Lafeu provides our major comic insight into Parolles, it is appropriate that the braggadocio must appeal to him for forgiveness: "It lies in you, my lord, to bring me in some grace, for you did bring me out" (V, ii, 49-50). And, as we have seen, Lafeu's pardon precedes the general reconciliation among the major characters in the final scene.

While there is minor inconsistency in the characterization and function of Lafeu, the play might well have succeeded as comedy but for the enigmatic quality of Helena. Clearly, she is in the major position to control our attitude. For it is she who early takes us into her confidence concerning her love for Bertram; who informs us she is travelling to court to seek his love; who, obedient to her new husband's command, returns to Rousillon alone and later takes leave of her home rather than force him into exile; who by accident, or design, turns up in Florence and arranges (with the audience fully aware of it) the bed trick involving Diana Capilet through which she will regain a husband by fulfilling his own stated conditions; and whom, finally, the spectator knows to be alive as she plans her *coup de theatre*—the amazing reappearance before Bertram and the king at the conclusion of the play. Obviously Bertram is practiced upon, and the moment there is doubt or ambiguity concerning the practicer, her character and motivation, the spectator's "comic" detachment from Bertram is destroyed. The spectator, consequently, finds himself confusedly sympathizing with Bertram in one scene against a shrew who appears to act from selfish presumptuousness, yet forced in the next scene to acknowledge the count's gross transgressions against a gentlewoman who appears to act from selfless grace and mercy.

Unless we assume that Shakespeare was purposefully creating a melodramatic situation—a view hardly tenable in light of his demonstrable concern for comic control in the drama both preceding and following this work—we must assume that Helena is intended to be totally sympathetic.[16] With this character the audience presumably would develop a basic rapport, accepting her as a comic controller to provide the essential information and the attitude necessary to creating and maintaining the comic tone. But, however she was intended, she comes across ambivalently when set against the emotional demands placed on the spectators as they observe Bertram placed into situations which require decisions affecting his basic spiritual values—demands which arise in part, to be sure, from his own egocentricity, but also in part from her practice upon him.

The point is unarguable, of course, that by creating some semblance of sympathy for Bertram in the opening scenes of the play Shakespeare is able more convincingly to make him acceptable to the spectator at the conclusion. That is, were Bertram to be delineated throughout as arrogant and corrupt, his "conversion" at the end would be far less credible. And to the extent that a temporary rapport with the count is to be developed, the spectator must have only a partial realization of Helena's motives and of the ultimate scope of her power in controlling the comic perspective. Admittedly, then, it may well have been the playwright's intention to reveal only a partial view of her personality and her intentions in the early acts. If so, his failure is one of degree; for, in fact, instead of merely withholding the spectator's judgment, he suggests such duplicity in her motives or involves her in such ambiguous means (especially since the end which might conceivably justify them is not perceived) that the spectator in later scenes finds it extremely difficult to develop with her the rapport which is so vital to the successful comic dramatization of the theme.

In the first act, even while not actively pursuing Bertram, Helena appears to be inconsistent, and hence the cornerstone for the comic perspective is unsteady. We first see her as an apparently utterly innocent maid, "bequeathed to [the countess'] overlooking" (I, i, 43-44) as a result of her father's death. As Bertram comforts his mother concerning the death of his father, Helena weeps, as the countess assumes, in "remembrance of her father" (56). And Helena assures her foster mother that the grief is indeed genuine (60-61). It is somewhat disconcerting, then, to hear Helena in soliloquy less than thirty lines later revealing that Bertram's departure is the actual cause for her grief with the rather blunt remarks "I think not on my father . . . I have forgot him" (90-93). If there is nothing flagrantly malicious in her comments, there is nonetheless a distasteful ambiguity which colors our first impressions. And, her rather ribald conversation with Parolles before she gets off stage does nothing to help. Although she knows him "a notorious liar," a "fool" and a "coward" (111, 112), she does nothing to avoid the company, engaging him in a lengthy dialogue about sex and the most effective uses to which a maiden might put her virginity. Again, if we are impressed by her talent for repartee, we are surprised by her apparent lack of taste in the subject of their conversation. Indeed, it is she who almost invites the smutty conversation by asking Parolles how woman might "barricado [virginity] against" men. Through an extensive description of man's sexual pursuit in military images (barricado, enemy, assails, defense, warlike resistance, undermine, blow up), the braggadocio proclaims that virginity is a commodity which must be used if it is to preserve its gloss: "the longer kept, the less worth. Off with't while't is vendible" (166-167). Ironically, she is in effect to accept his advice, whether she realizes it or not, in her decision a few lines later to pursue Bertram (231 ff.). Moreover, her decision to become the aggressor makes rather ironic her adamant concern for protecting virginity against the dominant male.

The spectator also, from her first three appearances on stage, is unable to determine Helena's basic personality. At times she is modestly shy; cognizant of her lack of noble blood, she is readily obedient to the wishes of her social superiors and accepts her lot with apparent docility. At other moments she is aggressively determined to chart her own path, fearless and frankly confronting countess and king alike. More specifically, in the initial moments of the play she stands reticently to the side as the countess describes her honesty, goodness, and fair disposition (I, i, 45-52). Similarly, two scenes later, when the countess has discovered her affection for Bertram, Helena stands apologetically before her guardian, thrice begging pardon and pity (I, iii, 160, 191, 192) and freely acknowledging her humble birth (161-162). Swearing specifically that her motive in traveling to Paris is to "cure the desperate languishings whereof / The King is render'd lost," she implies she would never be so presumptuous as to consider further designs upon the count:

I am from humble, he from honoured name . . .
My master, my dear lord he is; and I
His servant live, and will his vassal die.
    . . . I follow him not
By any token of presumptuous suit.
                    (162, 164-165, 203-204)

Following an unpleasantly catechismic interrogation—a quality suggested in part by the general tone and in part by the extensive religious imagery (pardon, gross, passion, confess, sin, hellish obstinacy, on my knee, before high heaven, adore, grace, sovereignty) —the countess grants the submissive Helena her leave and love to travel to Paris. And, in like character, Helena comes before the king with extreme deference: "I come to tender [the cure] and my appliance / With all bound humbleness" (II, i, 116-117). When the king refuses her offer, she weakly responds:

My duty then shall pay me for my pains.
I will no more enforce mine office on you;
Humbly entreating from your royal thoughts
A modest one, to bear me back again.
                    (128-131)

The other Helena, however, is no less in evidence. On the heels of her submissive posture in the first scene, she in soliloquy proclaims her determination to fulfill her desires:

Our remedies oft in ourselves do lie,
Which we ascribe to heaven. The fated sky
Gives us free scope . . .
Impossible be strange attempts to those

That weigh their pains in sense and do suppose
What hath been cannot be.

(I, i, 231-233, 239-241)

Similarly, in the scene before the king—to whom in an unfortunate image Lafeu introduces her with the quip "I am Cressid's uncle,/ That dare leave two together" (II, i, 100-101)—less than ten lines following her proclamation of humility, she assumes the role of god's minister, chastizing the ruler for refusing "the help of heaven" which she proffers:

He that of greatest works is finisher
Oft does them by the weakest minister:
So holy writ in babes hath judgement shown,
When judges have been babes.

(II, i, 139-142)

At this point, despite what she has told the countess, she demands her choice of husband as payment for success and offers her life in forfeit if she is unsuccessful.

The spectator's reaction to these initial scenes is understandably confused.[17] It may well be that this brief discussion has exaggerated the inconsistency, and it is presumably true that Shakespeare did not intend the character to be ambivalent, at least to this extent. Nevertheless, even the most astute performance of the role cannot conceal these inconsistencies without skillful cutting. And, with Helena as the central practicer or the major pointer in the play, the degree of ambiguity is fatal to a clear comic perspective which would prevent an emotional involvement with Bertram.

The problem of perspective with Helena is primarily centered on these first three appearances. While there are two further occasions during which her actions tend to erode the necessary rapport with the spectator, the ambiguity in her motivations stems directly from the difficulties in our first impressions. That is, the traces of the designing woman which correctly or incorrectly color the first scenes quite naturally feed the spectator's suspicions at these later moments.

One such occasion is Helena's sudden appearance at Florence, disguised as a pilgrim. There have been various explanations for Florence as a point en route to the shrine of Saint Jaques, that is Florence (Italy) as a point between Rousillon (France) and the shrine of St. James of Compostella (Spain), and the final answer probably lies hidden in the revision of the play. At any rate, it is highly unlikely that Shakespeare intended to imply that Helena has used the idea of the pilgrimage merely as a ploy to rush to Florence and Bertram; after all, Diana's mother informs her that "There's four or five, to great Saint Jaques bound, / Already at my house" (III, v, 98-99). Yet the spectator is prone to believe the worst because of his ambiguous impressions of her at the outset.[18] Furthermore, if she is indeed willing to adapt the pilgrimage to serve her purposes later, as she does in the reports that she has accomplished her undertaking and subsequently died from grief (IV, iii, 56-63), the spectator might well suspect that she has devised the entire plan from the outset.

The second occasion on which a sympathetic rapport is at least momentarily difficult is in her manipulation of Diana Capilet in the final act. It gives the uncomfortable impression that Diana's personal sensitivity is being sacrificed to the construction of the properly charged dramatic moment when Helena herself will enter. Following Bertram's embarrassing inability to explain the presence of his wife's ring on his finger, Diana, directed by Helena, enters with charges against the count which will add further confusion to the scene. Diana, instructed to flout Bertram as his wife by bed right, is subjected to public contumely by the flailing count. First protesting that he would never stain his honor by such low acquaintance (V, iii, 180-181) and then admitting his knowledge of her as "a common gamester to th' camp" (187-188), he exclaims:

> Certain it is I lik'd her,
> And boarded her i' th' wanton way of youth . . .

> Her [infinite cunning], with her modern grace,
> Subdu'd me to her rate. She got the ring;
> And I had that which any inferior might
> At market-price have bought.
>
> (V, iii, 210-211, 216-219)

Interrogated by the king but apparently forbidden to reveal the full truth, Diana so exasperates the ruler that he orders her arrested and imprisoned. It is difficult for the spectator to condone Helena's forcing Diana to claim deeds which she is not in fact guilty of but which, once a matter of public record, will injure her reputation. And, if there is some comfort in the assumption that Helena will shortly set the record straight, the end hardly seems to justify the means. In order to establish an extremely difficult situation which, almost goddess-like, she will be able to rectify (thereby clearing the fair name of Diana and bringing more drastic recriminations upon Bertram), she is apparently quite willing to manipulate another to serve her self-appointed purposes; and, in doing so, there are reminiscences of the duplicity observed in her first appearances on stage.

Essentially, though, the relationship between Helena and spectator is a compatible one from the middle of the second act, and her role as comic pointer comes more sharply into focus. This greater rapport results, in part, from the further development of Bertram's character; as the count's depravity becomes more obvious, he loses any sympathy which the spectator has initially felt for him. But, more important, the selflessness of Helena's motivation becomes more clearly apparent, and hence her control of the action more desirable.

This selfless love is signalled in her scene with the king following his recovery. Seeking her reward, her choice of husbands from the young gallants at court, she claims nothing but instead offers herself to Bertram:

> I dare not say I take you; but I give

Me and my service, ever whilst I live,
Into your guiding power.

(II, iii, 109-111)

When Bertram refuses to receive her, she modestly requests the
king not to press her demand: "That you are well restor'd, my lord,
I'm glad. / Let the rest go" (154-155). The king, however, whose
"honour's at the stake," forces the point, Bertram ostensibly con-
cedes to the royal mandate, and Helena, however unfortunate the
circumstances, gains a husband. If her duplicity in the initial scenes
were intended to reflect her true personality, we should now expect
a virago who, having achieved a legal marriage, would reap its
social and material advantages. In fact, her reaction is the opposite
extreme; she proves Griselda-like in her obedience to her husband
throughout the remainder of the play, whether it be in following
his orders to return home alone or in fulfilling his enigmatic conditions for sharing his friendship. Instead of a wedding bed, she faces
the ignominy of her husband's rebuttal by means of his boon male
companion. Yet, in the face of Parolles' peremptory remarks that
"my lord will away tonight" and that she is to take her discreet leave
of the king she replies only: "In everything I wait upon his will"
(II, iv, 55). In the following scene, as Bertram takes leave of her,
every comment reiterates her desire to please him through obedience—despite his disdainful denial of a parting kiss:

I have, sir, as I was commanded from you,
Spoke with the King and have procur'd his leave
For present parting . . .
        Sir, I can nothing say,
But that I am your most obedient servant . . .
        And ever shall
With true observance seek to eke out that
Wherein toward me my homely stars have fail'd
To equal my great fortune . . .
I shall not break your bidding, good my lord.

(II, v, 59-61, 76-77, 78-81, 93)

Rapport with Helena reaches perhaps its strongest point for the spectator in the mid-portion of the play. As the abandoned young wife comes home to Rousillon, she finds a mother-in-law who welcomes her with open arms and praises her as "too virtuous / For the contempt of empire" (III, ii, 33-34), while berating her "rash and unbridled boy" (30). More significant, Helena describes to the audience in a key soliloquy her unbounded love for Bertram, accusing herself for forcing him into exile and into the dangers of the battlefield:

> Poor lord! is't I
> That chase thee from thy country and expose
> Those tender limbs of thine to the event
> Of the none-sparing war? And is it I
> That drive thee from the sportive court, where thou
> Wast shot at with fair eyes, to be the mark
> Of smoky muskets? . . .
> though I kill him not, I am the cause
> His death was so effected.
> (III, ii, 105-111, 118-119)

Rather than destroy his happiness, she determines to sacrifice her own, stealing away from family and friend:

> come thou home, Rousillon,
> Whence honour but of danger wins a scar,
> As oft it loses all. I will be gone.
> My being here it is that holds thee hence.
> (123-126)

This selfless love is clear also in the letter she leaves for the countess. Branding herself her husband's "despiteful Juno" who "sent him forth / From courtly friends, with camping foes to live" (III, iv, 13-14), she claims he "is too good and fair for Death and me, / Whom I myself embrace, to set him free" (16-17). And, assuming we can honestly take what she says at face value, she becomes "Saint Jaques' pilgrim":

Ambitious love hath in me so offended
That barefoot plod I the cold ground upon,
With sainted vow my faults to have amended.

(5-7)

The countess through her tears blesses the departed "angel" and predicts that Bertram's salvation, if at all, must come through her. Later, in a conversation with Diana before her true identity is revealed, she defends the count and in similar fashion berates herself as the true cause of their marital unhappiness:

O, I believe with him.
In argument of praise, or to the worth
Of the great Count himself, she is too mean
To have her name repeated.

(III, v, 60-64)

From this point of strong rapport, Helena proceeds somewhat unevenly, as we have noted, to reclaim Bertram's company and presumably to capture his affection. And, in effect, as the spectator's relationship with Helena goes, so goes the play. Basically the plot revolves on two major devices, each of which Helena perpetrates and each of which the spectator enjoys from her vantage point. Her plan secretly to pursue Bertram as her heart's choice she explains first in soliloquy and then ambiguously to the countess. Thus her conditional offer to the king—though she has every desire to cure his malady—is observed as a part of her total efforts to win her love, and the profound shock which Bertram experiences can be anticipated. After she is repulsed by her "legally procured" husband, her second scheme evidently grows out of her self-imposed exile. The spectator next meets her in disguise in Florence, for a time sharing this level of perception only with her. When she explains her identity to Diana and her mother and requests their aid, Bertram—like Parolles—inevitably moves toward a trap of exposure from which there is no honorable escape. And in the concluding events of the play the audience looks on the flurry of events fully cognizant of the final revelations which will so profoundly shock the count, the king, and the inhabitants of Rousillon.

Shakespeare in this work has moved to a new dramatic plane in his creation of comedy which depicts moral aberration and in which the comic shock resulting from exposure produces a comic catharsis of a spiritually transformational nature. In a play which permits actual evil to exist, control is critical if a truly comic perspective is to be maintained for the spectator, and the playwright, clearly sensitive to this fact, has utilized essentially the same devices as in his preceding success—the double comic pointer, the clown, and the parodic subplot. Of these devices, obviously Helena as the primary comic pointer, although victimized momentarily, controls the bulk of the action and exercises the major control on our attitude toward it. But, in sum, the character of Helena is more firmly conceived than executed. While the pattern of the play requires a noble and selfless creature whose true love will save the antagonist from himself and from his depraved companions in spite of himself and whose control of the action will provide the appropriate comic perspective for the spectator, and while Helena in some moments quite satisfies these demands, there are other moments of ambiguity in her actions and motivations which erode the comic faith and blur the comic perspective. Shakespeare's "problem" comedy, in short, is admittedly a powerful exploration of human values, but as comedy the structural flaws preclude its total success.

As previously suggested, the "problem" of *Measure for Measure* is similar. Angelo is presumably Shakespeare's second comic vision of character developed on the level of transformation. From a position of Angelo's initial innocence—albeit a "sequestered virtue"— to the disastrous revelation of the inadequacy of his moral determination when put to the practical test, to the spiritual quagmire in which publicly his tyrannical misuse of power and privately his ignominious lust for Isabella involves him, to the shock which humbles his pride and leads to his contrite repentance, to the dispensation of mercy through which his evil deeds are abrogated and his life spared, the playwright attempts comically to trace the destruction and regeneration of a character and his moral values.[19] Indeed the pattern of degradation is more vivid in Angelo than in Bertram because his innocence and his fundamental integrity are more sharply emphasized in the opening scenes of the play. In the first place, that Vincentio would delegate virtually absolute power to his young deputy attests to the high confidence which Angelo inspires; if Vincentio lacks the confidence that Angelo will succeed, certainly there is no indication to the audience in the first two scenes.[20] Thus the audience, with Escalus, concurs:

> If any in Vienna be of worth
> To undergo such ample grace and honour,
> It is Lord Angelo.
>
> (I, i, 23-25)

Undergirding this reputation of high esteem are obedience, humility, and courtesy, qualities which in the first scene convince the spectators of his nobility and integrity. His first words, for example, reflect his deference to the duke: "Always obedient to your Grace's will, / I come to know your pleasure" (26-27); his second, after he is informed of his new appointment, suggest a basic modesty:

> Now, good my lord,
> Let there be some more test made of my metal
> Before so noble and so great a figure
> Be stamp'd upon it.
>
> (48-51)

When the duke insists that his decision is final, Angelo at least begs permission to escort him a portion of the way and, denied this request, bids him Godspeed: "The heavens give safety to your purposes!" (74).

Angelo's every word and deed in the first scene, then, contribute to the image of youthful preeminence. Hence the peremptory manner in which he arrests and sentences Claudio through a law which has not been enforced for fourteen or nineteen years—depending upon whose calculation one accepts—is at best a discomfiting shock. Of course, it is true that the first complaints come from Mistress Overdone, who stands to lose a lucrative trade by Angelo's restrictive measures, and that the major invective comes from Claudio, the victim who stands to lose his life. No doubt to some degree we consider the source as Claudio brands the deputy "the demigod Authority" more interested in reputation than in equity:

> Whether it be the fault and glimpse of newness,
> Or whether that the body public be
> A horse whereon the governor doth ride,
>   . . . this new governor
> Awakes me all the enrolled penalties
>   . . . and, for a name,
> Now puts the drowsy and neglected act
> Freshly on me. 'Tis surely for a name.
> (I, ii, 162-164, 169-170, 173-175)

Moreover, despite the regrettable absence of gracious as well as pragmatic vision in Angelo's authoritarian posture, he has not as yet broken faith with his idealistic vision of man. Our basic rapport with him begins nevertheless to erode as we hear Claudio proclaim that Juliet "is fast my wife, / Save that we do the denunciation lack / Of outward order" (151-153). And our suspicions are compounded when we suddenly learn that Vincentio, far from being in Poland, has remained in Vienna to observe this "precise" Angelo, who:

> Stands at a guard with envy, scarce confesses
> That his blood flows, or that his appetite
> Is more to bread than stone; hence shall we see,
> If power change purpose, what our seemers be.
> (I, iii, 51-54)

Lucio similarly views Angelo as an incredible prude. Having determined to make a public example of Claudio, the deputy is

a man whose blood
Is very snow-broth, one who never feels
The wanton stings and motions of the sense.

(I, iv, 57-59)

Angelo, then, is not at the end of the first act overtly hypocritical and cruel; to the contrary he is a man of conviction and ideals. But, by the same token, he is a man literally untainted by the duplicity of man's nature, apparently untouched by sexual temptation. It is understandable that many a critic has taken the name Angelo almost literally—as if reminiscent of prelapsarian man.[21] For indeed, he is a man primed for a fall, or more precisely, a spiritual collapse. He legalistically proclaims "We must not make a scarecrow of the law" (II, i, 1), pompously but with honest sincerity observing that " 'Tis one thing to be tempted . . . Another thing to fall" and ominously inviting the same rigidity of the law should he ever bear such guilt. Spurning the advice of both Escalus, who suggests that a milder application of the law could have the same therapeutic effect, and of the provost, who warns that many a ruler has later regretted such harsh judgment, Angelo demands that Claudio "[b]e executed by nine to-morrow morning" (34). So also, to Isabella's pleas, he retorts: "Your brother is a forfeit of the law, / And you but waste your words . . . It is the law, not I condemn your brother . . . Be satisfied. / Your brother dies to-morrow" (II, ii, 71-72, 80, 104-105).

Escalus, however, in his remark that "Some rise by sin, and some by virtue fall" (II, i, 38), has spoken more truthfully than he realized.[22] And Angelo's fall is all the harder for his smug self-confidence. The primary signal comes through the asides; as he listens to Isabella's exhortations, "She speaks, and 'tis / Such sense, that my sense breeds with it" (II, ii, 141-142);[23] "I am that way going to temptation, / Where prayers cross" (158-159). The trip is a painful one, for he full well realizes the agony of a passion which good sense and his reputation cannot accommodate. Amazed that woman's "modesty" is more powerful a temptation than "lightness," he reproaches himself for lusting after a nun just this side of her vows and for lacking the moral courage to "let her brother live."

The first complete statement of Angelo's passion takes the form of a soliloquy following Isabella's departure. Shakespeare dramatically emphasizes this crucial moment by carrying this soliloquy into his next appearance, two scenes later, at which time Isabella is returning one day later for the final decision concerning her brother's life. In this manner, the playwright underscores the intensity of the spiritual struggle. Here Angelo mocks himself for the empty words he sends to Heaven, for the "Heaven in my mouth"; he admits to the sin of pride in his grave and prudent public demeanor. But, as Isabella enters, it is clear that soul has lost the struggle to body: "Blood, thou art blood. / Let's write good angel on the devil's horn" (II, iv, 15-16). First by subtle, then by overt and prurient means, Angelo propositions the astounded Isabella. When his declarations of love fail, he proffers Claudio's life for her virginity, threatening painful torture for her brother should she refuse:

> And now I give my sensual race the rein . . .
> Lay by all nicety . . .
>   redeem thy brother
> By yielding up thy body to my will;
> Or else he must not only die the death,
> But thy unkindness shall his death draw out
> To ling'ring sufferance.
>   (160, 162, 163-167)

Through the first half of the play, then, Shakespeare has depicted in stark detail the extremes of innocence and corruption. The very qualities for which Angelo was preeminent in Vienna and for which he respected himself have privately proved the means to his downfall.

While Angelo himself does not appear in the mid-portion of the play (III, i–IV, iii), the playwright reveals in the deputy a degradation of increasing intensity through the comments of others as his public reputation for integrity and respectability begins to crumble. As Isabella reports to her brother, Angelo wears "the cunning livery of hell":

> This outward-sainted deputy,
> Whose settled visage and deliberate word
> Nips youth i' th' head and follies doth [enew]
> As falcon doth the fowl, is yet a devil;
> His filth within being cast, he would appear
> A pond as deep as hell.
>   (III, i, 89-94)

Similarly Lucio, like the other citizens of Vienna unaware of the depths of Angelo's villainy, nevertheless begins to sense in the duke's representative a relentlessness and obduracy which betoken the true tyrant:[24] "Some report a sea-maid spawn'd him; some, that he was begot between two stock-fishes. But it is certain that when he makes water his urine is congeal'd ice; that I know to be true: and he is a motion generative; that's infallible . . . Why, what a ruthless thing is this in him, for the rebellion of a codpiece to take away the life of a man!" (III, ii, 115-119, 121-123). And, it is at this point in the play that the duke, who, of course, has staked the most on Angelo's honesty by delegating the full power of his office, confirms his worst suspicions concerning the young puritan:

> Twice treble shame on Angelo,
> To weed my vice and let his grow!
> O, what may man within him hide,
> Though angel on the outward side!
>   (III, ii, 283-286)

Moreover, the spectator learns for the first time that Angelo some years past had revealed the vicious side of his nature. Betrothed to Mariana, he refused to honor the marriage contract when her dowry was lost at sea in a shipwreck which also cost her the life of her brother Frederick. Even more despicable, he was willing to sacrifice her honor and reputation to his avarice, basing his refusal on fabricated charges concerning her morality: "Left her in tears, and dried not one of them with his comfort; swallowed his vows whole, pretending in her discoveries of dishonour; in few, bestow'd her on her own lamentation, which she yet wears for his sake; and he, a marble to her tears, is washed with them, but relents not" (III, i, 234-239). Shakespeare has, of course, been much criticized for introducing Mariana to the audience so late in the play, and, as we will shortly describe, it undoubtedly poses difficulties for an effective comic perspective.[25] It is nonetheless true, however, that only by withholding such information could the playwright effectively establish Angelo's innocence at the beginning of the drama and thus create the striking contrast with the corruption which destroys both his private and public integrity by the middle of the play.

Angelo again appears in person in the climactic moments of the action, his heart hardened to his duplicity. With what appears to be a bold arrogance, he acts to cover his evil deeds, even if necessary by implicating others in guilt in order to divert suspicion from himself, a ploy in which he had gained experience in his earlier relationship with Mariana. Hence, when Vincentio sends word of his return and of his desire that any subjects who "crave redress of injustice, / . . . should exhibit their petitions in the street," Angelo, though horrified that a charge might be made against him publicly, manages to hide his fear through his snide insinuations concerning the duke's sanity; the letters reflect a "most uneven and distracted manner. His actions show much like to madness; pray Heaven his wisdom be not tainted!" (IV, iv, 3-5). Similarly, when Isabella does accuse him before Vincentio of sexual blackmail for the life of Claudio, Angelo exclaims, "My lord, her wits, I fear me, are not firm . . . she will speak most bitterly and strange" (V, i, 33, 36). In reaching perhaps the nadir of his moral cowardice, he maintains an amazing silence while the duke, who knows better and obviously is more interested in watching the deputy than the maiden, assassinates her character and turns all the blame against her. And, in order to sharpen the portrait of ultimate desperation to maintain a facade no matter whom it destroys, his pride claims a second victim. As Mariana confronts him with further charges, he subjects to public calumny the woman whom he presumably loved at one point enough to marry:

> My lord, I must confess I know this woman;
> And five years since there was some speech of marriage
> Betwixt myself and her; which was broke off,
> Partly for that her promised proportions
> Came short of composition, but in chief
> For that her reputation was disvalued
> In levity.
>
> (V, i, 216-222)

Hard pressed, however, to explain the multiple charges against him, Angelo exclaims that his patience is touched and audaciously declares that he is the victim of a conspiracy.

> These poor informal women are no more
> But instruments of some more mightier member
> That sets them on. Let me have my way, my lord,
> To find this practice out.
>
> (236-238)

Assuming that Friar Lodowick is involved, the deputy demands that he be brought forth, and later accuses him of "treasonable abuses" and commands Lucio to seize him forcibly, an order which leads directly to the recognition of Vincentio beneath the cowl. Thus Angelo, by virtue of his brazen attempts to support his own lies, unwittingly plays the major role in setting the stage for his own exposure.

Beneath this cover, however, lies the anguish of a stricken conscience. With the first reports of Vincentio's return, Angelo is poignantly reminded of his guilt and the inevitable consequences:

This deed unshapes me quite, makes me unpregnant
And dull to all proceedings. A deflow'red maid!
And by an eminent body that enforc'd
The law against it! . . .
　　　　　[Her brother] should have liv'd.
　. . . Would yet he had liv'd!
Alack, when once our grace we have forgot,
Nothing goes right; we would, and we would not.
　　　　　　　　　(IV, iv, 23-26, 31, 35-37)

When Vincentio identifies himself and the deputy realizes that his
deeds are by no means private, this shame and humility assume
full control. Angelo, speaking only twice in the remaining moments
of the play, offers no excuse, no defense, no rationalization for his
actions. Neither does he beg for mercy; contritely admitting his
full guilt, he frankly assumes the only fitting reward is death:

I should be guiltier than my guiltiness,
To think I can be undiscernible,
When I perceive your Grace, like power divine,
Hath look'd upon my passes. Then, good Prince,
No longer session hold upon my shame,
But let my trial be mine own confession.
Immediate sentence, then, and sequent death
Is all the grace I beg.
　　　　　　　　　(V, i, 372-379)

His final words underscore the misery which his sins have cost him
and his repentance, though again there is no indication that he
expects his contrition to pave the way for his salvation:

I am sorry that such sorrow I procure;
And so deep sticks it in my penitent heart
That I crave more willingly than mercy.
'Tis my deserving, and I do entreat it.
　　　　　　　　　(479-482)

It is, nevertheless, the purgation of pride coupled with Mariana's love which leads to his forgiveness, first by Isabella and finally by the duke in the flurry of events which concludes the action.[26] With the deputy condemned to death by Vincentio—measure for measure, an Angelo for a Claudio—Isabella, who herself has learned something of the grace of mercy, pleads for his life. With the sudden revelation that Claudio still lives, Vincentio offers pardon and reconciliation to all, charging the astonished deputy to love his wife; "your evil quits you well" (501). His sins, in other words, have provided the means by which his egomania and self-blindness could be purged and by which he could come to realize and accept the selflessness of true love.

Shakespeare, then, as in *All's Well That Ends Well*, has chosen to work with a plot which centers on the psychological and spiritual development of a single character. It is true that both Isabella and Claudio also develop to some degree. We see, for example, Claudio's valiant attempts to be courageous dissolve, at least momentarily, as he implores his sister to consider his life more precious than her virginity.[27] Once Friar Lodowick provides him the consolation of philosophy, however, he regains his composure. More extensively, we see Isabella, like Angelo, humanized and presumably permanently changed in the course of the action.[28] Legalistic and selfish at the beginning of the play, proud of her virtue, she, too, learns the selflessness of true love. By pleading for Claudio's life and confronting Angelo's terms, by facing the implorations of a brother who desperately wants to live, by harkening to the prayers of Mariana to spare her new husband, Isabella grows in the wisdom of the value of sacrifice and forgiveness.[29] Certainly she is Angelo's most brutalized victim; hence her decision to spare him is a key factor in the general reconciliation at the conclusion. Isabella's growth, however, has occurred within the bounds of conventional morality; none of her "sins" is overt. Only Angelo experiences the full range of human emotion, shocked into right reason as a result of the spiritual anguish of sin and the grace and forgiveness of love in those whom he has wronged.

As in *All's Well That Ends Well*, Shakespeare's intention is to provide a comic vision for this experience. And again, the devices by which the playwright attempts to achieve comic control are double comic pointers and a subplot which extensively parodies the main action. The roles of the comic pointers, however, are not those of Shakespeare's previous comedy. The secondary pointer, Lucio, a presumptuous fool, is quite unconscious of his structural purpose. On the other hand, Vincentio the primary comic controller is quite aware of his function; a virtual *deus ex machina*, the duke plays a double role as he manipulates and observes the other characters. As comedy, however, this play is not a total success, and for much the same reason as *All's Well That Ends Well*. The flaw, however else it might be described, is structural, and, once again, the major problem is with the primary comic pointer.

As is frequently his practice, Shakespeare strives in *Measure for Measure* to maintain a viable comic perspective by creating a subplot which burlesques the main action.[30] This subplot, involving primarily Pompey, Mistress Overdone, and Elbow, appears in only four scenes, but these scenes are inserted at moments in which apparent villainy on stage or sentimentality in the audience threatens to mar the comic tone. Unlike the secondary action in *All's Well That Ends Well*, in which the activities and fortunes of Parolles comically anticipate the events of Bertram's experience, the subplot here mocks the theme of the play. There is no consistent, single parallel to Angelo; instead, there are various characters involved in events and situations which comment humorously upon the deputy's actions. In I, ii, for instance, immediately following the moment Angelo has assumed total authority in Vienna, the subplot anticipates the relativity of justice, the extremes of which are to lead to his destruction. The opening lines envision a law only so binding as the individual wishes to interpret it. As Lucio and others consider the possibility that the duke is in conference with neighboring rulers, the remark is made that Vienna wants peace but only on its own terms;[31] Lucio retorts that for a soldier to desire peace is as bad as for a pirate to follow the ten commandments—including "Thou shalt not steal." Clearly, so the drift of the dialogue goes, the person must "scrape . . . out of the table" or "raze" any part of the law which does not serve his personal interests. Within a few lines, the conversation has veered abruptly from the application of law which considers nothing but the individual's situation to the application which rigidly refuses to recognize any part of it. Mistress Overdone rushes on stage to make the initial announcement of Claudio's arrest for Juliet's pregnancy (for "groping for trouts in a peculiar river," in Pompey's words) and the peremptory judgment that "within these three days his head . . . be chopp'd off (69-70). But Pompey's news strikes much closer home; with the proclamation that "All houses in the suburbs of Vienna must be pluck'd down" (98-99) and that those in the city "shall stand for seed" (102), the prostitute—albeit with greater justification—feels the same withering heat of autocratic power which Claudio is momentarily to describe. Shakespeare's comic edge is sharp, however. A few moments before Claudio is to lament that the body politic is "a horse whereon the governor doth ride" (164) as a tyrant, Pompey consoles the flustered whore, assuring her there will still be a means of livelihood: "Come, fear not you; good counsellors lack no clients. Though you change your place, you need not change your trade. I'll be your taspter still. Courage! there will be pity taken on you. You that have worn your eyes [another pun the auditor could hardly miss] almost out in the service, you will be considered" (109-115).

The dramatist, then, has broached the serious problem of the play through the filter of bawdy comedy. And, a few scenes later, he utilizes the secondary action to reinforce the comic tone through parody by juxtaposing Angelo's legalistic judgment on Claudio with Elbow's fatuous attempts to articulate charges of similar sexual promiscuity against Froth and Pompey. Angelo has just condemned Claudio, adamantly refusing to listen to others and denying the trial which not only would provide an opportunity for the prisoner to proclaim his innocence, but also would display the evidence, or lack of it, on which he was judged. Six lines later, the bumbling constable drags his prisoners before Escalus and Angelo, the latter after a few moments growing impatient and leaving the disposition of the case to Escalus. Ironically, the known bawd, accused of abetting Froth in his improper advances to Elbow's pregnant wife, receives far fairer treatment than Claudio, for the elderly magistrate refuses to condemn without reasonable proof of guilt. Between Elbow's malapropian inability to say what he means and Pompey's loquacious efforts to lead the judge into digression, the truth is indeed difficult to find! Pompey rambles incessantly about the last dish of stewed prunes in the inn, ironically the colloquial phrase for a prostitute, developed from the fact that they were the staple refreshment in brothels—served no doubt to avoid the regulation of 1546 prohibiting the sale of conventional foods. According to Pompey, the woman desired them, and Froth generously agreed to share them with her. Elbow, meanwhile, proclaims that he is the "poor Duke's constable" (the duke's poor constable) and that he brings "before your honour two notorious benefactors" (malefactors). Before he is through misusing and confusing the King's English, he has averred that he "destest[s]" (protests) his wife, that she is not a woman "cardinally" (carnally) given, that she has never been "respected [suspected] with man, woman, or child." His prisoners are "void of all profanation," Pompey an "honourable" man, Escalus a "varlet." Criminal charges obviously dissolve into laughter as Escalus delivers the sentence: "Truly, officer, because he [Pompey] hath some offences in him that thou wouldst discover if thou couldst, let him continue in his courses till thou know'st what they are" (II, i, 194-197). Froth is warned against further association with a tapster, and Pompey is advised: "let me not find you before me again upon any complaint whatsoever; no, not for dwelling where you do. If I do, Pompey, I shall beat you to your tent, and prove a shrewd Caesar to you; in plain dealing, Pompey, I shall have you whipt" (260-264). This warning the bawd finds easy to ignore. "I shall follow it as the flesh and fortunes shall better determine" (267-268). Escalus, nevertheless, has exercised mercy rather than run the risk of using the law to punish the innocent. At the same time, the laughter has sharpened the comic flavor.

Despite the humor, however, the wisdom of Escalus' judgment emphasizes Angelo's brash autocracy. A similar thematic relationship is involved in the two remaining subplot scenes; in each case Shakespeare is clearly concerned with maintaining the comic perspective at critical moments. In the mid-portion of the play, when Vincentio has discovered Angelo's lustful blackmail of Isabella and has solicited her help in bringing correction both to Angelo and his erstwhile fiancée, a comic scene is inserted in which both Pompey and Mistress Overdone also face charges of sexual promiscuity. When Elbow insists that unless Pompey is apprehended "all the world [will] drink brown and white bastard," Vincentio, alias Friar Lodowick, commands him to take the bawd to prison: "Correction and instruction must both work / Ere this rude beast will profit" (III, ii, 33-34). Even as he speaks, he draws the spectator's attention to the analogy of Angelo's condition through an aside: "That we were all, as some would seem to be, / [Free] from our faults, as [from faults] seeming free!" (40-41). Clearly there comes a time— for these characters as inevitably for the deputy—when mercy is not the key to correction; as Escalus comments of Mistress Overdone: "This [continued immorality] would make mercy swear and play the tyrant" (206-207).

Finally, just prior to the last phase of the action, Shakespeare again utilizes the secondary action comically to anticipate the theme. Pompey is offered, instead of outright punishment, the opportunity to aid the hangman as redemption "from [his] gyves": "if not, you shall have your full time of imprisonment, and your deliverance with an unpitied whipping, for you have been a notorious bawd" (IV, ii, 11-15). Pompey readily admits his guilt; he has been "an unlawful bawd time out of mind." But, after a fashion, he is willing to learn through his correction, to profit from his past mistakes: "I would be glad to receive some instruction from my fellow partner . . . Sir, I will serve him, for I do find your hangman is a more penitent trade than your bawd; he doth oftener ask forgiveness" (18-19, 52-54). Angelo too, of course, is ultimately to learn from his partner—whether it be Vincentio, Isabella, or Mariana—just as also his lust and its consequences will provide the opportunity for repentance and ultimately for salvation.

Shakespeare, then, has utilized the subplot sporadically to strengthen the comic perspective by burlesquing motifs of potentially serious concern. Lucio is a device of another sort; a veritable comic *Johannes factotum*, this fantastic is in and out of the action at various levels, and, while he has no significant narrative role, he does markedly contribute to the comic tone of the play both by appearance and his deeds.[32] As a fashion monger, his garrish dress is a constant source of amusement. On numerous occasions he is the comic butt of the conversation. At one point, for example, when he swears that he is to his companion as velvet is to plain material, he is squelched by a scathing double entendre. He is, as the gentleman retorts, "a three-pil'd piece . . . I had as lief be a list of an English kersey as be pil'd, as thou art pil'd, for a French velvet" (I, ii, 32-35). On other occasions he is able to turn the joke to another's expense. For instance, he introduces Mistress Overdone as Madam Mitigation, under whose roof he has purchased many diseases, and he turns even the report of Claudio's arrest to chuckles. To the prisoner's denunciation of Angelo as a tyrant, Lucio quips: "[T]hy head stands so tickle on thy shoulders that a milkmaid, if she be in love, may sigh it off" (176-178). He readily agrees to seek out Isabella to plead for Claudio's release, lest the restraint from sexual promiscuity should become fashionable and Claudio lose his head "at a game of tick-tack" (196). When the gallant converses with her outside the convent door, he reports that her brother is imprisoned "For that which, if myself might be his judge, / He should receive his punishment in thanks" (I, iv, 27-28). Admitting that his own "familiar sin" is to jest and "play with all virgins so," he assures her that Claudio is indeed the victim of Lord Angelo, "a man whose blood / Is very snow-broth, one who never feels / The wanton stings and motions of the sense" (57-59). And he implores her to teach Angelo the subtle tricks by which a woman gains her desires. So also, when Isabella does appear before the deputy, the quipster performs as a cheering section, urging time and again through straight-faced aside comments to the audience that she warm to her task: "O, to him, to him, wench! he will relent. / He's coming; I perceive't" (II, ii, 124-125; see also 56, 70, 89, 109, 129, 132, 148, 156). Certainly the artifice of comedy, especially the incongruous observer commenting from the side, precludes the spectator's emotional involvement in Isabella's plight.

Lucio's motives, at least in the first half of the play, are basically creditable. He does, after all, in his first appearance (I, ii) evince honest concern for Claudio, suggesting that the matter be appealed to the duke and later agreeing to seek out Isabella that she might intervene in behalf of her brother. Two scenes later, he speaks with some eloquence in persuading her of the seriousness of the charge and in urging her to her task:

> All hope is gone,
> Unless you have the grace by your fair prayer
> To soften Angelo.
>
> (I, iv, 68-70)

He implores her to "go to Lord Angelo, / And let him learn to know, when maidens . . . weep and kneel" (79-81), their petitions are granted. Only when she agrees to go "about it straight" does he desist. And, of course, he prompts her from the side lest she flag in her efforts.

Lucio's most significant moments, though, find him the comic butt of Vincentio and his disguise in the latter half of the play. In this manner, as the plot builds to its melodramatic climax, Shakespeare expands the gallant's comic role to support the comic perspective. A flagrant time-server, Lucio has supplied the information leading to the arrest of Pompey and Mistress Overdone—simply because the repression of their trade in sex is fashionable. As Mistress Overdone laments, "this is one Lucio's information against me" (III, ii, 210-211); as for Pompey's bail, Lucio will not provide it, for "it is not the wear. I will pray, Pompey, to increase your bondage" (77-79). While serving the fashion of the present, however, he is not above condemning that of the past. Hence, he remarks to Friar Lodowick, "It was a mad fantastical trick of [the duke] to steal from the state, and usurp the beggary he was never born to" (98-100). Unlike Angelo, the duke "had some feeling of the sport"; even " your beggar of fifty" was not beyond his interest: "The Duke had crotchets in him. He would be drunk too; that let me inform you . . . The Duke, I say to thee again, would eat mutton on Fridays. He's now past it; yet (and I say to thee) he would mouth with a beggar, though she smelt brown bread and garlic" (135-136, 191-194). Moreover, while most of the populace think the duke to be wise, he is actually "A very superficial, ignorant, unweighing fellow" (147-148). All of these slanderous comments the duke and the spectators covertly enjoy, Vincentio retorting that "He [the duke] shall know you better, sir, if I may live to report you" (171-172).

The comic forewarning achieves full fruition in the final act. With the duke's return, Lucio once more shifts his values with politic ease, attempting time and again to ingratiate himself with the ruler by relating his version of the events of past days. Vincentio, however, with the audience fully cognizant of the parasite's duplicity, has little patience as he awaits the perfect moment for exposure. As Lucio tosses in comments like an irrepressible jack-in-the-box while Isabella describes her wrongs, Vincentio methodically squelches his every attempt to become involved in the conversation. The comic possibilities of these sharp retorts are limited only by the inability of the duke to convey to the spectators his obvious delight at the expense of Lucio's hypocrisy. And this hypocrisy becomes more richly humorous as Lucio relates how bravely he defended the duke's honor against Friar Lodowick's slanders:

> 'tis a meddling friar.
> I do not like the man. Had he been lay, my lord,
> For certain words he spake against your Grace
> In your retirement, I had swing'd him soundly.
> (V, i, 127-130)

Branding the man "A saucy friar, / A very scurvy fellow . . . honest in nothing but in his clothes; and one that hath spoke most villanous speeches of the Duke" (135-136, 263-265), Lucio senses his opportunity to grasp favor and prestige from Vincentio. When Lodowick makes a final appearance on stage, Lucio exclaims: "O thou damable fellow! Did not I pluck thee by the nose for thy speeches?" (342-343). His presumption and audacity at the prime, he rushes to assault Lodowick only to discover that a cowl indeed does not make a friar! Thus, at the precise moment at which the serious theme of the play reaches its climax with the exposure of Angelo's villainy, the comic qualities of Lucio's antics also reach their height and thus intensify the comic perspective. To Vincentio's exclamation "Thou art the first knave that e'er mad'st a duke" (361), the abashed gallant—like Angelo, exposed for the hypocrite which he is—can only respond feebly: "This may prove worse than hanging" (365).

In a delightful sense it does. As among the major characters forgiveness and reconciliation produce three happy marriages (either accomplished or forthcoming) and the consequent dangers of emotional treacle, Shakespeare carefully labors to maintain a detached tone through Lucio. Forced to marry Kate Keepdown, whose child by him is the irrefutable evidence of their liaison, the deflated ass begs for whipping or hanging in preference to this union: "I beseech your Highness do not marry me to a whore. Your Highness said even now, I made you a duke; good my lord, do not recompense me in making me a cuckold" (520-523). And, even as the duke is pronouncing his final words of consolation to Angelo and proposing marriage to Isabella, a last sardonic chuckle is raised as Lucio quips while being dragged forcibly offstage: "Marrying a punk, my lord, is pressing to death, whipping, and hanging" (528-529).

Two minor characters are surely worthy of note: the hangman Abhorson, for example, who takes such pride in the mysteries of his trade; and the prisoner Barnardine, who flatly refuses to be hanged because he is suffering from a hangover.[33] Certainly, however, the gull, Lucio, and the subplot (Pompey, Mistress Overdone, Froth, Elbow) are significant devices by which the dramatist controls and reinforces the spectator's comic perspective for a narrative of near-tragic events.

The fundamental structural device in the play is, of course, Vincentio, the primary comic pointer. Through him—as through Helena, Viola, or Prospero—the spectator fully perceives the issues and the scale of values operative in the play, and through him, as the basic manipulator or practicer, the emotional distance necessary for comedy is established as a result of the spectator's awareness of his function in disguise, or his extensive controlling power, or his ultimate benevolent intentions.[34] As stated earlier, delineation of character on the level of transformation entails a powerful tendency for the spectator to become involved in the moral and ethical crises of the play. Consequently, if the spectator is to be blocked from emotional involvement, the comic perspective must be firm. Vincentio, as the ruler who observes in disguise behind the scenes, is a far more powerful character than Helena; his virtual omniscience and omnipotence could well provide the security vital to the spectator for a clear and unobstructed comic experience.

From the first, however, Shakespeare undermines the spectator's confidence in the character.[35] In the first place, the duke does not in his early appearances provide even a nominal moral justification for temporarily abdicating his authority. When he explains to Friar Thomas his desire for anonymity under a friar's cloak, he describes Angelo's "absolute power" as a method by which the city may be purged. For many years certain laws have gone unenforced, and "liberty plucks justice by the nose" (I, iii, 29). To Thomas' observation that the means for correction lie with the duke himself, Vincentio retorts:

> I do fear, too dreadful.
> Sith 'twas my fault to give the people scope,
> 'Twould be my tyranny to strike and gall them
> For what I bid them do."
>
> (34-37)

Easier and safer is it for Angelo "in th' ambush of my name" to "strike home" and thus bring no slander on Vincentio. Obviously, such duplicity suggests a moral cowardice and irresponsibility which, delineated in the early scenes, tends to erode any confidence which the spectator might develop in him.

In the second place, the duke's *deus ex machina* function is not signaled to the spectator until the scene after Angelo autocratically exercises his power by condemning a young man to execution as an example for all Vienna of the law's newfound teeth. Such an arrangement is admittedly highly dramatic, but the tension is achieved at the expense of an effective comic perspective. And one tends to be naturally suspicious of the duke's insistence on the immediacy and the unobtrusiveness of his departure:

> Our haste from hence is of so quick condition
> That it prefers itself and leaves unquestion'd
> Matters of needful value . . .
> I'll privily away. I love the people,
> But do not like to stage me to their eyes.
> (54-56, 68-69)

In any event, the spectator is for the moment as convinced as the citizens of Vienna that Vincentio is leaving, whether to Poland, Rome, Russia, or a political conference. Consequently, when Angelo, as the "demigod Authority," peremptorily arrests Claudio for violating laws concerning fornication—though Claudio asserts his innocence and his honorable intentions concerning Juliet, our emotional reaction is not blocked or comically controlled by knowledge of the duke's actual intentions, revealed later to Friar Thomas:

> to behold his [Angelo's] sway,
> I will, as 'twere a brother of your order,
> Visit both prince and people; therefore, I prithee,
> Supply me with the habit and instruct me
> How I may formally in person bear [me]
> Like a true friar.
> (I, iii, 43-48)

Through this disguise, he on several occasions underscores the dominant theme of the play through sharp rebukes upon the Viennese society, with ironic references to the hypocrisy of civil authorities: "there is so great a fever on goodness, that the dissolution of it must cure it . . . There is scarce truth enough alive to make societies secure; but security enough to make fellowships accurst" (III, ii, 235-236, 239-241). Moments prior to the discovery of his true identity in the final act, he exclaims:

> My business in this state
> Made me a looker on here in Vienna,
> Where I have seen corruption boil and bubble
> Till it o'er-run the stew; laws for all faults,
> But faults so countenanc'd, that the strong statutes
> Stand like the forfeits in a barber's shop,
> As much in mock as mark.
>
> (V, i, 318-324)

As Friar Lodowick, Vincentio is also able to comfort those who are victimized by the deputy's actions and, at the same time, to use their punishment for spiritual therapy. "Bound by my charity and my blest order, / I come to visit the afflicted spirits" (II, iii, 3-4). His visit to Juliet in prison, during which he offers to "teach you how you shall arraign your conscience, / And try your penitence, if it be sound. / Or hollowly put on" (II, iii, 21-23), results in her open confession of sin. In like manner he goes "with instruction" to her mate who is condemned to death. At some length, he urges upon Claudio the consolation of philosophy: "Be absolute for death; either death or life / Shall thereby be the sweeter" (III, i, 5-6). Life it is to be, as later events will determine, but Claudio is made to experience the fear which will give him a greater respect for the law. So also the friar offers spiritual advice to both Pompey and Barnardine, though neither is able to muster enough interest to respond. In effect, Vincentio's concern for the moral welfare of those involved in sin leads him to attempt to manipulate the action to the point of highest tension, and presumably the greatest spiritual efficacy, for each concerned.

Here again, since we observe the action from his level of awareness, the friar-duke is in a position to provide a clear comic perspective. Yet, there are moments of self-contradiction; more serious, there are moments when he appears painfully without the authority needed to contain the evil of this play-world within harmless bounds. A part of the contradiction is implicit in his character; it is somehow incongruous that a man of such benevolent and altruistic intentions should be so utterly devious in his methods, hedging coyly about the reason for his departure and his destination, and on several occasions lying outright—albeit in a "good cause." Other contradictions are more explicit. In IV, ii, for instance, the duke states that Angelo "this very day receives letters of strange tenour, perchance of the Duke's death, perchance entering into some monastery" (214-216); in the next scene—clearly the same morning (as the ordered execution of Barnardine "this morning" in IV, ii, and the attempted execution in IV, iii, indicates)—the duke informs us that he will "write letters to Angelo . . . whose contents / Shall witness to him I am near at home" (97-99). In another instance, Vincentio brands Barnardine "Unfit to live or die" and orders him brought "to the block" (68-69). Three lines later he exclaims that the prisoner is unprepared for death; "to transport him in the mind he is / Were damnable" (72-73).[36] Then there is our assumption that the disguise of Friar Lodowick is a unique experience for Vincentio, an assumption hardly supported by Mariana's initial comment: "Here comes a man of comfort, whose advice / Hath often still'd my brawling discontent" (IV, i, 8-9).

Admittedly, such minor inconsistencies can be explained away as textual problems arising from the rewriting or revising of an older play. The apparent lack of control on occasion, however, more insidiously erodes our confidence in the duke as a comic controller. It is quite true, of course, that Shakespeare with artistry must spin out the narrative yarn to the moment the duke will openly assume control in the final act; to have Vincentio reveal his true identity (something he is admittedly capable of doing at any given moment) would be to foreshorten the play. Even so, the fact that things do not work out precisely according to his master plan does force him to improvise if he is to retain his disguise. As he, for instance, by trickery gratifies Angelo's lust in order to gain Mariana a husband and, of course, to provide a situation conducive to Claudio's pardon,[37] he is foiled by the deputy's second mandate for the execution. At the prison on the appointed morning, he quite confidently awaits Angelo's countermand, assuring the provost of the deputy's integrity:

> his life is parallel'd
> Even with the stroke and line of his great justice.
> He doth with holy abstinence subdue
> That in himself which he spurs on his power
> To qualify in others.
>
> (IV, ii, 82-86)

Hearing a knocking from without, he remarks in an aside, "Now are they come" (88). When the messenger, however, informs the provost that he is to "swerve not from the smallest article" of Claudio's execution and that he is to verify it by sending the prisoner's head to Angelo, the friar-duke is understandably incensed:

> This is his pardon, purchas'd by such sin
> For which the pardoner himself is in . . .
> When vice makes mercy, mercy's so extended,
> That for the fault's love is the offender friended.
>
> (111-112, 115-116)

By enigmatically revealing the duke's signet to the apprehensive provost and requesting a four-day respite for Claudio, Vincentio is able to buy the time necessary to develop the counter-plan by which Angelo's guilt—and Claudio's safety—will be revealed in the final act. While such difficulties indeed render him more human than a more immediately efficient *deus ex machina* would be, the spectator does become increasingly suspicious of how well Vincentio actually understands Angelo's nature and, thus, of the wisdom of the scheme in the first place.

Perhaps the most serious problem concerning the duke as the single character who most significantly controls our comic perspective is the ambiguity of his motive. What, precisely, is he about? Is he a practical jokester, an introverted maker-of-law, a Christ-like meter of justice, a puppet of the dramatist only peripherally related to the plot? Is he a wilful liar, a hopeless weakling, a pitiless tyrant, or a decadent panderer? We have earlier noted that in his initial appearance as the manipulator Vincentio states that Angelo is to be an agent through whom moral law, inoperative for fourteen years, can be re-established in the city. Yet, by the conclusion of the same scene, Angelo's rule would seem to be a test of his personality:

> Lord Angelo is precise,
> . . . scarce confesses
> That his blood flows, or that his appetite
> Is more to bread than stone; hence shall we see,
> If power change purpose, what our seemers be.
> (I, iii, 50-54)

In II, iii, he appears as spiritual minister to Claudio, shoring up his spirit with Stoic philosophy. Still later (III, i, 204-281), describing Angelo's cruelly broken betrothal to Mariana as a result of the lost dowry, he tells Isabella (in suggesting the trick of bed-switching), "you may most uprighteously do a poor wronged lady a merited benefit." Mariana's immediate recognition of him as Friar Lodowick —"Here comes a man of comfort, whose advice / Hath often still'd my brawling discontent" (IV, i, 8-9)—suggests either that Vincentio has previously made use of the friar's cloak or that Mariana is in on the disguise from the first and that perhaps this complex affair has been directed to this end from the outset. One cannot deny that these lines might simply be the result of a lapse on Shakespeare's part—or, for that matter, that the entire portion of the narrative concerning Mariana might have been an afterthought. Certainly the assumption does conveniently solve such inconsistencies as Vincentio's confident choice of Angelo to rule Vienna in spite of what he knows to be the deputy's despicable treatment of his fiancée antecedent to the action of the play. But the results are hardly worth the risks of such guesswork; Vincentio's character remains enigmatic on other counts, his motivation ambiguous. In short, with no evidence to the contrary, one must ultimately account for the play and the author's intention from the available text.

With the spectator uncertain of Vincentio's motivations or goals, with the duke's control (benevolent or otherwise) seriously in question on several occasions, and with various inconsistencies in action, the comic perspective is blurred. As a result, despite the pleasant conclusion, the spectator experiences moments of profound, almost tragic, disturbance as hypocrisy, lust, avarice, and the threat of imminent death plague the stage-world.

When the total impact of the various comic devices in *All's Well That Ends Well* and *Measure for Measure* is considered, there can be little real doubt that, while Shakespeare in both plays was striving to widen the scope of comedy, he was nonetheless concerned that the perspective and the resultant dramatic experience be comic. Certainly the plays raise profound and powerful issues which are never dramatically reconciled. And, as comedies, they are at best only partial successes. The failure, however, is not *ipso facto* thematic—an incongruous mixture of "realistic" and "romantic" material or a narrative "incompatible with comedy." The failure, instead, is structural—the result of a blurring of the comic perspective and consequently a temporary loss of comic control arising from an unintentional ambiguity in the major comic pointer. Any assumption, on the other hand, that Shakespeare's intention was to create satiric or ironic or enigmatic humor seems dangerously to disregard not only the carefully constructed structure of the individual play, firm except for the single pointer, but also the general direction of

Shakespeare's comic evolution, a direction which is ultimately to produce a perspective which will successfully control for comedy the spectator's relationship with characters and issues, reflecting on the one hand the spiritual atrophy of distrust, hate, and avarice, and on the other the regenerative and restorative human values of contrition, love, and forgiveness.

"This affliction has a taste as sweet as any cordial comfort"

5 The Comedies of Transformation

Shakespeare's first attempts at characterization on the level of transformation, Bertram and Angelo are at the outset spiritual innocents. In each instance the character possesses a basic integrity; yet in the course of the action, his experiences require decisions which reveal his base and animalistic nature to himself and others despite his desperate efforts to maintain his public reputation. Eventually, some act of love and forgiveness permits him to be resorbed into normal society. In other words, as the social posers of Shakespeare's comedies of identity are mocked from their abnormal attitudes, so these young men, exposed to temptation and stained by corruption, are ultimately forgiven by a selfless love which only then they are able to comprehend.

In *All's Well That Ends Well* and *Measure for Measure*, however, as we have observed, the playwright has neither clearly established nor consistently maintained a comic perspective which insulates the spectator from emotional involvement. Because Vincentio's motivation is at best ambiguous and at times the spectator must question his ability to control the situation he has provoked, Angelo temporarily assumes the role of villain, and the play a tragic tone. Because of the ambiguous nature of Helena in the early scenes of the play, we react sympathetically to Bertram in his determination to make his own marital decisions, only to find ourselves confusedly committed to an arrant knave bent on lustful and egocentric gratification. The "problem" in these comedies, in short, is the perspective; once the spectator loses his comic detachment from action which involves characters existing on a truly human plane and making fundamental moral decisions which endanger the spiritual and physical well-being of themselves and others, then the dramatic experience is—for the moment at least—no longer a comic one.

In contrast, the characters of the late comedies do not attempt to hide their actions behind a facade of respectability. They either firmly assert the justice of their deeds, or openly and flagrantly disregard the consequences of the opinions of others. Certainly, the evil of man's nature in these plays is no less viable and destructive than in *All's Well* and *Measure for Measure*—the decisions, the consequences, and the eventual transformation of Leontes, for example, no less realistic. Yet *The Winter's Tale* succeeds where the previous works have at least partially failed. The key factor is that Shakespeare in this play has provided a perspective sufficient to control the deeper vision of character, primarily through stylization and through the use of a comic pointer or comic controller who is himself involved in the action and yet whose relationships with the other characters, or whose actions and comments, by reminding us that the artifice is always at work, abstract the spectator from emotional commitment. As a result, the play is successful as comedy, albeit vastly dissimilar in narrative from his earlier comedies of action and identity.

Leontes is the single character developed on the level of transformation. We observe him in the second scene as the gracious host, inveigling Polixenes to prolong his visit in Sicilia. Impulsive and stubborn in his insistence, he is a manifestly intense person, and the passion of jealousy, once he becomes suspicious of his wife's fidelity and his friend's integrity, grows through the first half of the play to overwhelming and frightening proportions. His mind leaps wildly from one fantastic assumption to another while his jealousy feeds entirely on emotional and circumstantial, not logical and tangible, evidence. Shakespeare, not choosing, as in *Othello*, to delineate the slow emergence of the green-eyed monster, presents in Leontes a wrath and fury which suddenly burst forth like searing heat.[1] Indeed, he further underscores the abrupt and pathological nature of this emotion through the comments of shock and amazement from the characters who observe it. Camillo, when Leontes first tells him of Hermione's infidelity, warns the king to "be cur'd / Of this diseas'd opinion, and betimes; / For 'tis most dangerous . . . I cannot / Believe this crack to be in my dread mistress" (I, ii, 296-298, 321-322) and later, in soliloquy, speaks of Leontes as one "Who, in rebellion with himself, will have / All that are his so too . . . There is a sickness / Which puts some of us in distemper" (355-356, 384-385); the lords in attendance at court flatly assert that the "Queen is spotless" (II, i, 131), and Antigonus proclaims that "every dram of woman's flesh is false, / If she be" (138-139). In Leontes' blurred vision, with Hermione swollen to the last stages of pregnancy, her friendly courtesies to Polixenes he sees as lechery, the Bohemian King's nine-months' visit as an odious explanation for the queen's conception.

With astounding rapidity, Leontes' jealousy assumes awesome proportions. The least civility between his wife and friend becomes conclusive proof of his cuckoldry:

> Too hot, too hot!
> To mingle friendship far is mingling bloods.
> I have *tremor cordis* on me; my heart dances,
> But not for joy; not joy.
>
> > (I, ii, 108-111)

The images of decadency and corruption which permeate Leontes' asides and his comments to his young son reflect the depths of his diseased passion. He speaks of his "brows" growing "shoots" (I, ii, 119, 128), of the "hardening of my brows" (146), of himself as "Inch-thick, knee-deep, o'er head and ears a fork'd one" (186), of his "cuckold's horn" (269). No longer certain of his son's legitimacy, he calls him "my bawcock" (121), a "wanton calf" (126), "[s]weet villain" (136), and brands his wife "slippery" (273), "a hobby-horse . . . / As rank as any flax-wench that puts to / Before her troth-plight" (276-278). He observes what he assumes to be palpable guilt in actions of his wife and Polixenes—their "paddling palms" (115), "pinching fingers" (115), "practis'd smiles" (116), "virginalling / Upon [the] palm!" (125-126).

> There have been,
> Or I am much deceiv'd, cuckolds ere now;
> And many a man there is, even at this present,
> Now while I speak this, holds his wife by th' arm,
> That little thinks she has been sluic'd in 's absence
> And his pond fish'd by his next neighbour, by
> Sir Smile, his neighbour, Nay, there's comfort in 't

Whiles other men have gates, and those gates open'd,
As mine, against their will . . .
        Be it concluded,
No barricado for a belly; know 't;
It will let in and out the enemy
With bag and baggage.

(190-198, 203-206)

Sensing guilt and duplicity in the smallest gestures, he fears he has
become the laughing stock of the court:

They're here with me already, whispering, rounding,
"Sicilia is a so-forth." 'Tis far gone,
When I shall gust it last.

(217-219)

As his private suspicions grow and he is content to provide his own
answers, Leontes is compelled to make public his charges against
his wife, and his rage becomes ungovernable. Demanding revenge
upon both Hermione and his erstwhile friend, he commissions
Camillo to poison Polixenes, but so uncontrollable has his passion
become that he is unable to "seem friendly" to Bohemia, lest the
scheme be foiled. Later, his worst suspicions apparently confirmed
by the flight of Polixenes and Camillo, he again cannot restrain
himself as he publicly denounces his pregnant wife; no longer content to brand her "an adultress" (II, i, 78) and a "bed-swerver" (93),
he leaps to a broader accusation:

There is a plot against my life, my crown . . .
More, she's a traitor, and Camillo is
A [fedary] with her.

(47, 89-90)

When his shocked courtiers refuse to sanction such charges, the infuriated Leontes, in true tyrannic fashion, rejects his counsellors
out of hand.

        Our prerogative
Calls not your counsels, but our natural goodness

Imparts this; which if you, or stupefied
Or seeming so in skill, cannot or will not
Relish a truth like us, inform yourselves
We need no more of your advice.

(163-168)

Ordering Hermione to prison without providing her an opportunity
for self-defense, he proclaims that "He who shall speak for her is
afar off guilty / But that he speaks" (104-105). In his ultimate act of
defiance, he scoffs at the need of the oracle to confirm his suspicions:

yet shall the oracle
Give rest to th' minds of others . . .
Whose ignorant credulity will not
Come up to th' truth.

(190-193)

His mental perturbations have at this point destroyed his ability
to rule either himself or his kingdom. When Paulina takes the newborn daughter before the King in hopes of moderating his wrath,
she is subjected to name calling and threats and is physically
shoved out of the room. As for the child, Antigonus is ordered, on
pain of death to himself and to Paulina, to "carry / This female
bastard hence" (II, iii, 174-175) to some "remote and desert place"
and to abandon it without mercy. In effect, so convinced is he that
the oracle will affirm the truth of his suspicions that he peremptorily
sentences the child before the message from Apollo has been delivered. In so doing, he of course gives the lie to his claim mere
moments later that he "proceed[s] in justice." Informed that messengers from the oracle have returned, Leontes summons a session
and aserts that Hermione shall have "just and open trial":

Let us be clear'd
Of being tyrannous, since we so openly
Proceed in justice.

(III, ii, 4-6)

But the words become mockery as he formally arraigns and sentences her. Judge and jury, he maintains that just as she is past all shame, so she is past all truth; to deny the charges is futile: "Look for no less than death" (92). Having delivered his ultimatum, he is mentally unable to accept the oracular statement which clears Hermione, and can only thunder: "There is no truth at all i' th' oracle. / The sessions shall proceed; this is mere falsehood" (141-142).

The immediate flurry of events, capped by Mamillius' actual and Hermione's apparent death, brings Leontes quickly to his knees. From his first statement of his folly ("Apollo's angry; and the heavens themselves /Do strike at my injustice" [III, ii, 147-148]), which immediately precedes Hermione's fainting, there follows through the remainder of the play a succession of progressively contrite confessions of guilt as the king becomes painfully aware of his folly and stupidity. Indeed, his repentance is no less intense than his previous passion. His initial intention is to woo his Queen anew, to recall Camillo, and to reconcile himself with Polixenes. This plan the reported death of the Queen annuls, and in utter despair, Leontes calls for all tongues to punish him through bitter talk and promises, in penance, to visit once a day the chapel where lie his son and wife; "tears shed there / Shall be my recreation" (240-241).

Sixteen years later, in Act V, he is no less contrite: his passion has made his kingdom heirless and "Destroy'd the sweet'st companion that e'er man / Bred his hopes out of" (i, 11-12); had he taken counsel from Paulina,

> even now,
> I might have look'd upon my queen's full eyes,
> Have taken treasure from her lips.
>
> (52-54)

His repentance confirmed, he can now say with utter sincerity that the destruction was "All mine own folly" (135). "I have done sin" (172). Equally significant, motivated by love, he is able in two instances in this scene to act in behalf of another. On the one hand, he comforts Paulina by subjecting himself to her as a living memorial to his wife; as he had earlier implicated her in Hermione's corruption (I, ii, 130 ff.), so now as a token of repentance he agrees that she shall decide whether he shall ever marry again. On the other hand, confronted by Florizel as an exile from father and country, he agrees to attempt to mediate the differences between the young prince and Polixenes and to effect a happy union between the youth and Perdita. The incidents are not unimportant; the first selfless acts of which Leontes has been capable, they reflect a stage of spiritual growth more advanced than contrition. In the final scene, facing what he assumes to be Hermione's statue, he is

> pierc[ed] to my soul . . .
> There's magic in thy majesty, which has
> My evils conjur'd to remembrance.
> (34, 39-40)

As he envisions the life-like statue, his love for Hermione is poignantly rekindled: "this affliction has a taste as sweet / As any cordial comfort" (76-77). The crowning achievement of his love is articulated by Paulina, who commands the statue to "descend; be stone no more"; "from [death] / Dear life redeems you" (99, 102-103).

Hardly the normal material for comedy, Leontes' experience—as in Shakespeare's tragedies—reflects both the worst and the best of humanity.[2] In effect, the playwright has sketched a character who, in fully human terms, must face problems involving the ultimate values of life, of faith itself. Consequently, his fundamental challenge is to create a dramatic structure by which to maintain a comic vision for the spectator. Unlike *The Tempest*, there is here no *deus ex machina* character to explain that the evil is only apparent or to anticipate certain events and thereby suggest that the unhappiness is merely temporary. Indeed, whereas Shakespeare's normal procedure is to capitalize on dramatic irony by keeping the spectator one step ahead of the character, in this play he deliberately conceals information from his audience and thereby creates a situation which would ordinarily stifle the potential comic tone by forcing the spectator to assume the reality of certain tragic events.

Nevertheless, the play does establish a successful comic tone through the device of stylization of both character and action and through the function of Paulina and Autolycus as comic pointers. While we observe Leontes' initial happiness turn to suspicion, its consequences, and his repentance and eventual forgiveness, we remain at a safe emotional distance because of the heightened tone of improbability which surrounds the stage-world and the characters who inhabit it.[3] Nothing is burlesqued through caricature, as, for example, in *The Two Gentlemen of Verona*, and nothing which occurs is palpably impossible. But the tone is unequivocally fictional, and Shakespeare takes pains that his spectators never forget they are observing actions on a stage, and consequently that they never become totally emotionally involved with Leontes and his suffering. The title itself suggests an entertaining fiction for passing time; Mamillius' comment that "A sad tale's best for winter" sets the stage for a narrative he never lives to enjoy.

More specifically, most of the characters surrounding Leontes are highly stylized; they are "flat" or one-dimensional and, consequently, artificial. Hermione, in her Griselda-like patience, utterly lacking the very quality of passion which in excess virtually destroys her husband, is perhaps the most striking illustration. To Leontes' charge that she should help him convince Polixenes to prolong his visit, the queen submissively replies: "I had thought, sir, to have held my peace until / You had drawn oaths from him not to stay" (I, ii, 28-29), after which she does her husband's bidding. At another point, she banters lovingly with Leontes concerning the two occasions on which, according to him, she has spoken to good purpose. Later, her incredible self-control results in a serene and gracious dignity which contrasts graphically with her husband's bilious irascibility. When she is charged, without forewarning, with marital infidelity and treason, she replies to Leontes with apparent placidity:

> How will this grieve you,
> When you shall come to clearer knowledge, that
> You must have publish'd me!
>   (II, i, 96-98)

Assuming that some "ill planet reigns" as she is hauled off to prison, she exclaims:

> I must be patient till the heavens look
> With an aspect more favourable . . .
> The King's will be perform'd!
>   (106-107, 115)

In the courtroom scene, denied even a semblance of a fair trial, she shows no sign of vindictiveness, though again with her serenity and dignity she certainly steals the scene and virtually controls Leontes through her refusal to be denigrated by his preposterous charges. She remarks, for instance, that were her father (the emperor of Russia) alive, she would want him to look upon this scene with "pity, not revenge" (III, ii, 124). In her final appearance, following her "resurrection" after sixteen years, she speaks an incredibly brief seven lines—not even mentioning Leontes, who stands before her in penitent shock.

Appearing in only four scenes, Hermione, although a character of infinite dignity, is frankly a passive pawn who is acted upon but who exerts no positive force.[4] And, in effect, the same is true of the other principals. Polixenes has never outgrown the innocence of his boyhood friendship with Leontes. When Camillo informs him of Leontes' suspicions, there is not the least word of rancor or retribution. In like manner, the argument which later develops between Florizel and his father is presented as more apparent than real. Polixenes, through his disguise, tricks his son into proclaiming a greater love for Perdita than for his father or the throne. Even so, Florizel does not verbally strike back at his father; he simply makes plans to abandon father, kingdom, and land for the sake of his love. Even Camillo, twice branded a traitor—by Leontes and by Florizel

—faces the charge without rancor; there are occasional expressions of pity for Leontes, but never does he describe the King's folly in terms which would suggest total alienation; as for his motivations for treason, rather than ambition or lust, they are an antipathy to murder and homesickness. Actually, he functions in the first act as a manipulator of the action and thus helps to establish the comic tone. With his sudden shifts in allegiance and the geographic displacement which results, he is a constant reminder of the artifice at work in this stageworld. Later, the Bohemian shepherd and his clown-son suggest a rustic innocence worthy of prelapsarian man! Theirs is the simple life filled with hard work, broken on occasion by a period of festivity and merrymaking. Although they hold a rather naive respect for their social betters, their hearts are outgoing, as evinced in the father's immediate desire to care for the abandoned child and in the son's ready determination to aid one he assumes to be an injured traveler. Indeed, just such innocence makes them ready prey for the comic cozenage of the rogue, Autolycus.

With Paulina and Autolycus reserved for special comment, most of the characters surrounding Leontes are simply not human; as a direct result of their idealization or superficial development, the spectator views them as stage pawns. The result is that Leontes' human experience takes place in a stylized environment; the play hovers, so to speak, between playful make-believe and the reality of human experience. And, consequently, while the spectator observes Leontes' agony and transformation, he is forced to do so through a heavy veil of stage fiction.

As for the action of the play, the general alterations from Robert Greene's novel, *Pandosto: The Triumph of Time*, while they provide for the comic resolution by keeping Hermione (Bellaria) secretly alive and eliminating Leontes' (Pandosto's) suicide, at the same time heighten the fictional tone.[5] Bellaria, for example, is a more credible character than Hermione; her reaction to her husband's unfounded jealousy is forthright and vocal, and their alienation builds more slowly and predictably. Then, too, the transfer of the action from one kingdom to another is less contrived in Greene. When

Dorastus (Florizel) has infuriated his father Egistus (Polixenes) by doting upon a common shepherdess, Fawnia (Perdita), Capnio (Camillo) befriends him and accompanies the young lovers in their flight. Bound for Italy, they arrive at Pandosto's kingdom only by accident when a violent storm blows them off course. In Shakespeare's version, Camillo fondly yearns to return to his homeland after sixteen years and "frames" Florizel and Perdita "to serve [his] own turn," urging them to flee to Sicilia and meanwhile secretly informing Polixenes so that the inevitable pursuit will get him home.

The hyperbolic tone is set (by the conversation between Camillo of the Sicilian court and Archidamus of the Bohemian court) before the spectator meets any of the principals of the play. Both the entertainment provided the Bohemian royal visitors and the long-lived and powerful bond of friendship between the two kings are described in terms so extravagant as to suggest artificiality. Archidamus fears Leontes' return visit to Bohemia "shall shame us." "We cannot with such magnificence—in so rare—I know not what to say. We will give you sleepy drinks, that your senses, unintelligent of our insufficience, may, though they cannot praise us, as little accuse us" (I, i, 13-17). As for the renowned friendship, Leontes and Polixenes "were train'd together in their childhoods; and there rooted betwixt them then such an affection, which cannot choose but branch now . . . I think there is not in the world either malice or matter to alter it" (24-27, 36-37).

Throughout the story, one device after another confirms this fictional tone for the spectator: the Oracle from Delphos, Antigonus' premonition through a dream as he prepares to abandon Perdita, the old shepherd's conviction that the fairies have marked him for special favor when he discovers the abandoned child, the elaborate disguises and counter-disguises of the last two acts and, in the midst of them, a masque at the shepherd's cottage, the spectacular "resurrection" of Hermione after sixteen years, and the contrived reunion of "lost" daughter with "dead" mother—all of these presided over by Time as a choral figure who bridges the two generations.

Granted, many of these devices are straight from the "romance" material of medieval prose fiction. This does not alter the fact that Shakespeare has amassed them in such fashion as to create a chimerical narrative to serve as a comic backdrop for an all too credible human passion. The Oracle of Delphos is mentioned early in Act II following Polixenes' flight and Leontes' charge of infidelity against Hermione. Though he personally needs no confirmation of her guilt, Leontes asserts that he has "dispatch'd in post / To sacred Delphos, to Apollo's temple, / Cleomenes and Dion" (II, i, 182-184). Two scenes and twenty-three days later, the messengers have returned with Apollo's fateful decree, by which the spectator is to assume that divinity has corresponded directly with human society and has dictated the terms of its harmony. Similarly, Antigonus, when he dreams Hermione's spirit appears before him to name the infant Perdita ("lost one") and to inform him to abandon the child in Bohemia, believes that "the spirits o' th' dead / May walk again" (III, iii, 16-17), that it is Apollo's behest that the child "here be laid, / Either for life or death." Even Antigonus' death is related in such a bizarre fashion that the incident, while it reminds us again of the inescapable consequences of immoderate passion, seems unreal and grotesquely humorous.[6] The final act capitalizes on the *coup de theatre* of Hermione's statue coming to life.[7] So as to provide maximum dramatic focus on this event, Shakespeare does not dramatize the reunion of the two kings and the reunion of father and daughter (Leontes and Perdita).[8] Instead, Autolycus and several gentlemen, in a lengthy conversation, describe the moment as "a sight which was to be seen, cannot be spoken of. There might you have beheld one joy crown another, so and in such manner that it seem'd sorrow wept to take leave of them, for their joy waded in tears" (V, ii, 46-50). As for the resurrection scene itself, Paulina directs it with great flourish. Both Perdita and Leontes are so struck with the lifelikeness of the statue that they must kiss it. And for Leontes, it is a painful remembrance of things past: "this affliction has a taste as sweet / As any cordial comfort" (V, iii, 76-77). The action delayed to its fullest effect, the statue is then resurrected to the amazement of characters and spectators alike.

The fourth act, with its incredible parade of disguises and musical divertissements, deserves more specific consideration.[9] The scenes are perhaps the most fantastic Shakespeare ever composed. Certainly not since the elaborate confusions of mistaken identity in *The Comedy of Errors* has he so extensively utilized structural devices—rather than character incongruity or hypocrisy—to maintain the comic perspective.

A cursory glance at the activities in scenes three and four boggles the imagination. Autolycus, a clownish and unprincipled knave who has just entered the play, disguises himself as a citizen robbed by one "settled only in rogue. Some call him Autolycus" (IV, iii, 106-107). This ploy he utilizes to pick the pocket of the clown (the son of the old shepherd) who attempts to help him. As we move to the shepherd's cottage, we see Perdita decked as Flora, the Goddess of flowers, for the sheep-shearing feast, and Florizel, the Prince, as Doricles, a young swain. To this feast come Polixenes and Camillo, both disguised as rustics for the festival. Next in appearance is Autolycus, now disguised as a peddler vending the newest ballads. In the closing moments of the act, Florizel, determined to win Perdita even if it means defying his father and the throne, disguises himself by exchanging clothes with the peddler (Autolycus), and Perdita dresses herself as a country wench. Autolycus, in his court finery now, in turn displays his authority to the terror of the shepherd and the clown. Amidst this veritable charade, the spectator has enjoyed a village dance of shepherds and shepherdesses, a round of ballad singing, and an elaborate masque of satyrs (three carters, three shepherds, three neatherds, three swineherds).

The stage, then, is replete with improbabilities which create a detached perspective for the spectator. Aside from this stylization of character and action, Shakespeare utilizes Paulina (in Sicilia) and Autolycus (primarily in Bohemia) to heighten the comic tone of the play. As a variation of the comic pointer, Paulina serves both to provoke laughter (even during Leontes' bitterest moments) and to manipulate and direct—almost like a play within the play—the final climactic moments of the action;[10] Autolycus, through mockery, intensifies the fictive nature of the society through his assertions that honesty is a foregone impossibility so long as he is surrounded by such naive gulls.[11]

For Paulina's first appearance on stage, in which, child in hand, she bursts in upon Leontes and subjects him to a furious tongue lashing, much depends upon the skill of the actor/actress interpreting the role. Surely Shakespeare intended her to be angry and indignant, profoundly concerned for the welfare of her Queen and newborn Princess. But just as surely she should be a termagant, infuriated by the masculine tyrant who dispenses judgment with such preposterous casuistry. The result is a character totally functional in the narrative itself, but also one who, by her loquacity, provides for the spectator a release from tension in the midst of Leontes' wrath. As she prepares to see the king, she asserts that only a woman willing to use a harsh tongue will fit the occasion:

> He must be told on 't, and he shall. The office
> Becomes a woman best; I'll take 't upon me.
> If I prove honey-mouth'd, let my tongue blister
> And never to my red-look'd anger be
> The trumpet any more.
> (II, ii, 31-35)

Her performance does justice to her overture! Successfully breaking through her husband, Antigonus, and several lords who attempt to restrain her, she assaults Leontes unmercifully with a verbal barrage. When Antigonus is unable to silence her, the king exclaims:

> thou art woman-tir'd, unroosted
> By thy dame Partlet here . . .
> lozel, thou art worthy to hang'd,
> That wilt not stay her tongue.
> (II, iii, 74-75, 109-110)

Despite the context, Antigonus' reply can hardly fail to raise a chuckle:

> Hang all the husbands
> That cannot do that feat, you'll leave yourself
> Hardly one subject.
>
> (110-112)

Branding her a "gross hag," "Lady Margery," "A callat / Of boundless tongue," a "lewd-tongu'd wife," Leontes implores his companions to get rid of her by any means whatever. The dramatic moment is powerful: Leontes, at the height of his fury, commands first that the infant be "consum'd with fire," later that it be abandoned in a remote place; clearly, though, through Paulina's garrulousness, Shakespeare is strengthening the comic perspective for the spectator at a moment when the tragic overtones most seriously impinge upon it.

So also in the final act, Paulina prepares Leontes for the reunion with Hermione by providing the final test of his love—his agreement never to marry again except by her permission. Her reply, "That / Shall be when your first queen's again in breath" (V, i, 82-83), anticipates Hermione's resurrection. From the unveiling of the statue, to the first touch, to the command that it descend and take life, Paulina dramatically forces Leontes to recreate the experience of his repentance and thus to reiterate the major statement of the drama. Again, however, Shakespeare creates emotional distance by forcing us to observe these emotions through Paulina, as she, like a puppet-master, stages her greatest scene.

Whereas Paulina is utilized to bolster the comic perspective in the two most powerfully dramatic scenes, Autolycus provides vital comedy in the lengthy fourth act which delineates the romantic interests of the second generation. Certainly the most conventionally comic character in the play, this rogue blandly announces his lineage at his first appearance: "My traffic is sheets . . . My father nam'd me Autolycus, who being, as I am, litter'd under Mercury, was likewise a snapper-up of unconsidered trifles" (IV, iii, 23, 24-

26). With callous disregard of those whose honesty makes them susceptible, he tricks the clown into a merciful act, during which he picks the pocket of his Samaritan, disguises himself as a peddler, to his good profit vocalizes sensationalistic ballads for Mopsa and Dorcas, and finally, exchanges his peddler's rags for Florizel's court finery—again to his good profit. The opportunity for dishonest profit arises at every turn, as Autolycus tells the audience in his private conversation carried on through asides:[12] "I see this is the time that the unjust man doth thrive . . . Sure the gods do this year connive at us, and we may do anything extempore . . . If I had a mind to be honest, I see Fortune would not suffer me" (IV, iv, 687-688, 690-691, 861-862). Among his antics, he seems to delight most keenly in masking as a courtier in Florizel's apparel, allowing the clown and the shepherd to bribe him to speak a good word for them at court. Just so, in the best of comic traditions, the duper is victimized by his own trickery in the final act when, reconciliations accomplished and the shepherd and the clown established as gentlemen, Autolycus must beg their favor at court: "I humbly beseech you, sir, to pardon me all the faults I have committed to your worship, and to give me your good report to the Prince my master" (V, ii, 160-162). But, no doubt, his promise to amend his life is the rogue's most profitable move!

Paulina, then, is an integral part of the narrative, Autolycus entirely peripheral. But to the story as drama, the two serve the same function as comic pointers. Combined with the general stylization, these characters help to create a perspective through which Shakespeare presents a comic, yet profound, observation of human nature. It is true that the play contains a "comic" resolution—a general reconciliation of characters and a solution of all problems. But the comic experience represents more than the final moments; the transformed character is what he is not because he has lived through, escaped, and forgotten his past experiences, but because he has been molded and transfigured by them. His past suffering has provided a kind of wisdom by purging his vision and by making him aware of true values, especially of redemptive and forgiving love. Even so, the values of life itself, and the love which makes it worthwhile, are inexpressible and, once lost or neglected, not totally recoverable. The Sicilian ruler cannot recapture totally what his folly has cost him. He might regain his wife, his daughter, and his friendship with Polixenes. But Hermione is now old, their marriage wasted in the green years; Perdita is grown, the joys of parenthood sacrificed to his withering wrath; Polixenes, like him, is willing to articulate his friendship, but in actuality is capable only of crawling toward the grave; Mamillius, his son, and Antigonus, his courtier, are dead. Through his irascible passion, he has made himself fortune's fool; the consequences have been inescapable, and he faces a future tinged with the waste of past years. Shakespeare finds the most effective statement of this comic ambivalence through depicting a new generation which, without the waste of past years, can presumably profit from the lessons which the parents have so painfully learned.

The dramatic situation in *The Tempest* is similar, as Shakespeare involves several of his characters in realistic decisions and actions which touch the very foundations of man's moral nature. Alonso for years has exploited Prospero personally and Milan publicly by invading the city under cover of darkness, establishing a puppet duke, and extracting annual tribute from the citizens. Antonio, with Alonso's support, has usurped the position of the rightful duke and —to make it even more despicable—of his brother. False to the trust which had led Prospero to relegate significant political authority to him, he has used his position and his power to seize tyrannical control of the city. Fearful of doing public harm to Prospero because of his popularity with the people, Alonso and Antonio have nonetheless committed murder in intent—and for all they know, in fact—by putting him to sea, along with the young child Miranda, in a "rotten carcass of a butt, not rigg'd, / Nor tackle, sail, nor mast" (I, ii, 146-147). The fruit of these past sins, which they have never acknowledged, let alone repented of, extends, of course, to the present.

Now, as if to underscore the fecund and insatiable nature of unrestrained ambition, Shakespeare creates the contemporary opportunity for the pattern of usurpation and murder to repeat itself. Antonio's evil ambition has been in evidence, of course, since his unlawful seizure of the dukedom of Milan. At his earliest opportunity on the island, he feeds Sebastian's dreams: "My strong imagination sees a crown / Dropping upon thy head" (II, i, 208-209); for his companion, he sees "so high a hope that even / Ambition cannot pierce a wink beyond" (241-242). As for the slumbering Alonso, "[W]hat a sleep were this / For your advancement! Do you understand me?" (267-268). Sebastian, perceiving in Antonio what he assumes to be the advantageous fruits of such crime, is persuaded to seize the opportunity:

> Thy case, dear friend,
> Shall be my precedent; as thou got'st Milan,
> I'll come by Naples. Draw thy sword. One stroke
> Shall free thee from the tribute which thou payest,
> And I the King shall love thee.
>
> (II, i, 290-294)

Antonio, then, who has depended upon Alonzo as the ladder and prop of his political existence and who stands to profit directly from Sebastian's political fortunes, plants and nurtures the seeds of ambition until the two have agreed to a conspiracy in which Antonio is to kill Alonso; Sebastian, Gonzalo. Since Shakespeare does not depict a specific transformation in these conspirators, their "conversion" is open to question.[13] Prospero certainly suggests their transformation with his comment in the final act that "They being penitent / The sole drift of my purpose doth extend / Not a frown further" (V, i, 28-30). But a few lines later, the issue is apparently in doubt as the duke forgives Antonio although he is a "wicked sir, whom to call brother / Would even infect my mouth" (130-131). But in any case, their evil is blunted by Prospero's power, they are pointedly included in each of the purgational experiences which the magician arranges, and Antonio is ultimately forgiven for even his "rankest fault" (V, i, 132), perhaps the supreme form of love in that he is forgiven before he requests it.

The action in the play provides for Alonso, at least, a purgative experience through which he is restored to right reason before he is allowed to return to his European society.[14] For the king of Naples, the trip has produced a devastating shock—his daughter Claribel "lost" to a marriage with the King of Tunis, a union which many of his advisors had cautioned him against (II, i, 120-121, 124-127), and his son and heir apparent, Ferdinand, lost, he assumes, to the storm which has destroyed their ship (II, i, 102 ff.). From despair, to fear, to humility and repentance—Alonso runs the emotional gamut of transformation. Frustrated by exhaustion and the fruitless search for Ferdinand (III, iii, 8-10), he is primed for the spectacular appearance of the banquet which Ariel directs:

> I cannot too much muse
> Such shapes, such gesture, and such sound, expressing,
> Although they want the use of tongue, a kind
> Of excellent dumb discourse.
> (III, iii, 36-39)

When Ariel, as a harpy, has scattered the food and, as a minister of Fate, has specifically designated the punishment forthcoming for the past sins against Prospero, Alonso's wheel of fire turns yet further:

> O, it is monstrous, monstrous!
> Methought the billows spoke and told me of it;
> The winds did sing it to me, and the thunder,
> That deep and dreadful organ-pipe, pronounc'd
> The name of Prosper; it did bass my trespass.
> (III, iii, 95-99)

Alonso is "distracted" as contemplation and conscience strike at his guilt, and later, vis-a-vis Prospero, he is subjected to a reiteration of his sins (IV, i, 71 ff.). Eventually he humbles himself completely, admitting his guilt to both Prospero and his daughter:

> Whe'er thou be'st he or no,
> Or some enchanted trifle to abuse me,
> As late I have been, I not know. Thy pulse
> Beats as of flesh and blood; and, since I saw thee,
> Th' affliction of my mind amends, with which,
> I fear, a madness held me. This must crave,
> An if this be at all, a most strange story.
> Thy dukedom I resign and do entreat
> Thou pardon me my wrongs.
>
> (V, i, 111-119)

This transformation he later confirms in the remark that, because Miranda is his daughter-in-law, he "Must ask [his] child forgiveness" (V, i, 198).

The major statements by which the attention of all three men is turned inward upon their guilt are timed most effectively to produce the fear and the humility which must precede repentance. In III, iii, following the sudden appearance and disappearance of the banquet table,[15] they first confront their faults directly and the price which they must pay for them through Ariel, harpy-minister of Fate:

> You are three men of sin, whom Destiny,
> That hath to instrument this lower world
> And what is in't, the never-surfeited sea
> Hath caus'd to belch up you; and on this island
> Where man doth not inhabit; you 'mongst men
> Being most unfit to live. I have made you mad . . .
> I and my fellows
> Are ministers of Fate . . .
> But remember—
> For that's my business to you—that you three

From Milan did supplant good Prospero;
Expos'd unto the sea, which hath requit it,
Him and his innocent child; for which foul deed
The powers, delaying, not forgetting, have
Incens'd the seas and shores, yea, all the creatures,
Against your peace.

(53-58, 60-61, 68-75)

They are told that, unregenerate, a lingering perdition and heart-sorrow will step by step attend their ways. In the final act, moments before Alonso's abject confession, Prospero reiterates their sins as they stand purgatorially dumfounded within a charmed circle:

Most cruelly
Did thou, Alonso, use me and my daughter.
Thy brother was a furtherer in the act.
Thou art pinch'd for 't now, Sebastian. Flesh and blood,
You, brother mine, that entertain'd ambition,
Expell'd remorse and nature, [who], with Sebastian,
Whose inward pinches therefore are most strong,
Would here have kill'd your king.

(V, i, 71-78)

Like Leontes, then, Alonso, Antonio, and Sebastian are delineated as realistic characters motivated to uncontrollable passion—jealousy, murder, ambition and avarice condoning political usurpation.[16] Again, if the dramatic experience involving such potentially tragic events is to be "comic," the spectator must remain emotionally detached; his perspective must be conditioned by the recognition that ultimately benevolent forces control the action. Whereas the comic perspective in *The Winter's Tale* is implicit, largely effected through stylization, the perspective in this play is direct; the fundamental perspective is provided by Prospero as a *deus ex machina* figure.[17]

More specifically, Prospero's control of the action insures the viewer the security and vantage of superiority necessary for a comic perspective. His virtual omniscience is suggested by his knowledge of the island, the magical power provided by his books, the cloak of invisibility, his attendant spirit Ariel, and Caliban's disgruntled dependence upon him. From the initial storm to the magic spell by which he freezes Ferdinand, from the sleep he imposes upon Miranda to the charm he casts upon the entire ship's crew, from the mysterious banquet which he directs through Ariel to the circle of charm by which he dumbfounds Alonzo, Antonio, and Sebastian, from the strange music and the glittering apparel which confound the comic crew to the elaborate masque by which he honors the betrothal of Miranda and Ferdinand, the auditor is firmly convinced of Prospero's control of what is essentially his own private world.

So total, indeed, is the magician's control that the spectator's primary interest is in Prospero's attitude toward and ultimate intentions concerning his captives. Here, too, the comic perspective is firm and unambiguous. Whether the critic envisions Prospero as Destiny, as God, as Shakespeare in his farewell to the stage, as the composite of many Shakespearean heroes, or as a personification of poetry itself, and whether he believes the protagonist to have experienced a transformation either before or in the course of the action of the play,[18] Prospero is, in any case, omnipotent in his limited world. He is never specifically depicted as vindictive; to the contrary, early in the play it becomes clear that his intention is to forgive his enemies and to introduce his daughter to normal society and the bliss of marital love. In the lengthy exposition scene of the first act, he informs Miranda that he has "done nothing but in care of thee" and that "There's no harm done"; aided by "bountiful providence," he later leads his daughter and Ferdinand to a love of mutual concern (I, ii, 494-495). There is really no difference in the tone of his action in Act V when, as his "project gather[s] to a head," he insists on applying noble reason to his enemies, "Though with their high wrongs I am struck to th' quick."

> I do forgive thee,
> Unnatural though thou art.—Their understanding
> Begins to swell, and the approaching tide
> Will shortly fill the reasonable shore
> That now [lies] foul and muddy.
>
> (V, i, 78-82)

Even so, Shakespeare, without blurring Prospero's function or minimizing his power, does humanize his protagonist through several small touches throughout the play. In the long conversation with Miranda, for instance, Prospero, on nine occasions within one hundred thirty-two lines, charges Miranda to pay close attention. Critics have provided ingenious explanations for these lines, and, of course, just as a skilled actor is bound to no single interpretation of a role, so each of these explanations is as correct as the context of the scene and the credibility of the character will allow. The duke may indeed be experiencing his own agonies in first admitting to his daughter his previous failures in Milan; or he may be assuming the role of a stern schoolmaster demanding close attention as he presents significant information; or he may be providing comic moments as an aging father who prattles rather freely, time and again prompting Miranda to attend him during what—despite her best efforts to conceal it—becomes a somewhat tedious monologue. Whatever the interpretation, the fact that he experiences some degree of difficulty in conveying this information not only makes dramatically more interesting a lengthy scene of exposition, but also suggests a convincingly human quality which his wizardry and virtual omnipotence would otherwise disallow.

On occasion, Prospero's passion is all too human as he lashes out in bitterness at a Caliban who has spurned all of his best efforts, or as he at the conclusion of the nuptial masque is suddenly struck with anger when he recalls that "foul conspiracy / Of the beast Caliban and his confederates / Against my life" (IV, i, 139-141). At other moments, his mortality is reflected in his recognition of life as unsubstantial and transitory, soon to melt "into thin air," to "dissolve" and "fade" leaving "not a rack behind":

> We are such stuff
> As dreams are made on, and our little life
> Is rounded with a sleep.
>
> (156-158)

Again later, in the closing moments of the play, Prospero anticipates being able to "abjure" "This rough magic" and "drown my book" (V, i, 50-51, 57), to return to normal humanity "where / Every third thought shall be my grave" (310-311).

Clearly, then, Shakespeare attempts to make the deposed duke dramatically interesting. But whatever the added touches in the characterization, the spectator is essentially never in doubt concerning either the extent of Prospero's control or the benevolent intentions with which he will, following a period of trial and expiation, release his prisoners through forgiveness. Indeed, the fundamental comic perspective of the play, established and maintained by this *deus ex machina,* is perhaps best described in Prospero's words to Ariel just preceding the final judgment scene:

> Though with their high wrongs I am struck to th' quick,
> Yet with my nobler reason 'gainst my fury
> Do I take part. The rarer action is
> In virtue than in vengeance.
>
> (V, i, 24-28)

Prospero, then, provides information directly to the spectator vital to a controlled perspective on the potentially tragic events. Moreover, in this rigidly structured plot with its improbable setting,[19] Shakespeare bolsters the comic perspective by providing a parodic subplot which prevents the action from becoming melodramatic. As Sebastian plots with Antonio to kill Alonso and thus become King of Naples, so, in the scene immediately following, the drunk Stephano unites the coward Trinculo and the naive Caliban in the similarly unholy plan of slaying Prospero and ruling the island: "Monster, I will kill this man. His daughter and I will be king and queen,—save our Graces!—and Trinculo and thyself [Caliban] shall be viceroys" (III, ii, 114-116). Stephano, the "brave god" with his "celestial liquor," forces Caliban to "Swear by this bottle" and "kiss the book." Caliban's "god" is obviously inept and false, just as the "god" of Antonio (who knows not where conscience lies and "feel[s] not the deity in [his] bosom") is characterized by avarice and lust. In Act III, as the plot to kill Alonso progresses, so does that of the comic characters to kill Prospero. The attack upon Sebastian, Antonio, and Alonso by Ariel in the form of a harpy, followed by Prospero's full statement of charges in the final act, is paralleled in the subplot by the attack upon Stephano's crew by spirits in the form of dogs and hounds. And, as Prospero forgives Antonio and Alonso, so he tolerates Stephano and Trinculo. Providing a comic quip in what otherwise might have been a scene of trying sentiment, Caliban swears to be wise hereafter and curses himself for taking a drunkard for a god and for worshipping a fool.

The motivation for Caliban's hatred of Prospero is provided, of course, before Stephano and Trinculo enter. Caliban, who invokes "All the charms / Of Sycorax, toads, beetles, bats" to light on Prospero, "first was mine own king" (I, ii, 339-340, 342) but now

> you sty me
> In this hard rock, whiles you do keep from me
> The rest o' th' island.

> (342-344)

At Prospero's commandment and in fear of his wrath, Caliban has gone into the forest to fetch fuel when a thunderstorm provokes the most unlikely of confrontations with those who will become his fellow rebels. The storm itself is obviously a realistic parallel to the tempest which has created Sebastian's and Antonio's opportunity for conspiracy. But for the conspiracy itself, it is hard to imagine a more farcical travesty—the timorous Trinculo beset with logorrhea, who crawls beneath the cloak of the prostrate Caliban, equally terrified; the staggering Stephano, bottle in hand, belching out his lusty song as he discovers a monster with four legs and two mouths, each of which he fills with his "celestial liquor." Caliban's assumption that Stephano and his nectar have "dropp'd from heaven" ("I prithee, be my god" [II, ii, 152]) mocks the love-at-first-sight of Miranda and Ferdinand ("I might call him / A thing divine; for nothing natural / I ever saw so noble . . . Most sure, the goddess / On whom these airs attend!" [I, ii, 417-418, 421-422]). The antics of Ariel (speaking in Trinculo's voice) which lead to Stephano's beating his disobedient subject add vigorous physical humor to the subplot, as do their parade through the filthy mire in which they lose their treasured bottle and their fascination with the glittering wardrobe which scuttles their entire plan of attack with their appearance in the final act. With their skin caked with grime from the stagnant pool but their bodies cloaked in the flamboyant finery which they have stolen, Shakespeare provides one of the finest comic moments of the play.

In addition to this elaborate comic parallel, Shakespeare clearly strives to maintain a viable comic tone through the development of Gonzalo as a kind of comic pointer. At times consciously the author of risible observations or unconsciously the butt of the conversation and at times pointedly the thematic commentator on scene, in all instances he is a character through whom the playwright controls and modulates the spectator's view of the action. For instance, in the opening scene, before the spectator is aware of Prospero's control of the apparent chaos in nature, it is Gonzalo who first signals the comic nature of the plot. Amidst the screams of royalty and commoner alike in the face of death at sea, the old advisor on three occasions quips to a boatswain that his surliness is their best insurance against drowning: "I have great comfort from this fellow. Methinks he hath no drowning mark upon him; his complexion is perfect gallows. Stand fast, good Fate, to his hanging . . . I'll warrant him for drowning though the ship were no stronger than a nut-shell and as leaky as an unstanched wench" (I, i, 30-33, 49-51).

And he returns to this same reference at the conclusion of the play, when, Prospero having released them from a magical spell, the boatswain and his companions rejoin the group:

> Oh, look, sir, look, sir! here is more of us.
> I prophesi'd, if a gallows were on land,
> This fellow could not drown.
>
> (V, i, 216-218)

Similarly, the conclusion of the storm scene can hardly be taken in high seriousness with Gonzalo moaning that he would give a thousand furlongs of sea for an acre of any kind of ground. "The wills above be done! but I would fain die a dry death" (I, i, 71-72).

Later, it is Gonzalo who again prevents a scene from becoming tedious. For almost two hundred lines, Alonso bemoans the loss of his children, providing through his comments expository information which explains the nature of the voyage; as Gonzalo prattles words intended more for comfort than for sense, he is mocked extensively in asides by Sebastian and Antonio. What appears superficially to be merely ridicule of an old man's senility is obviously dramatically significant to the tone of this lengthy scene. For that matter, Gonzalo is neither totally oblivious to their comments nor defenseless in the face of them. When Alonso, his despondency alleviated, tells his companion that the speech is nonsense, Gonzalo retorts, "I do well believe your Highness; and did it to minister occasion to these gentlemen, who are of such sensible and nimble lungs that they always use to laugh at nothing" (II, i, 172-175).

In the mid-portion of the play, Gonzalo is equally important in pointing the spectator to the significant developments in the transformation of character. During the banquet scene, as the purgation of Alonso, Antonio, and Sebastian is set in motion, the old counsellor who had befriended Prospero observes:

> For, certes, these are people of the island—
> Who, though they are of monstrous shape, yet, note,

Their manners are more gentle, kind than of
Our human generation.

(III, iii, 30-33)

When Ariel as a harpy denounces the villains for their specific sins,
Gonzalo, himself unaffected by Prospero's spell, describes their
spiritual agony:

All three of them are desperate: their great guilt,
Like poison given to work a great time after,
Now gins to bite the spirits.

(III, iii, 104-106)

As his comments signal their spiritual guilt, so his tears of com-
passion later signal their contrition (V, i, 15-19). And, appropriately,
it is Gonzalo, following Prospero's forgiveness of his enemies and
the acknowledgement of their contrition, who gives final articulation
to the theme of redemption and self-knowledge:

O, rejoice
Beyond a common joy, and set it down
With gold on lasting pillars: in one voyage
Did Claribel her husband find at Tunis,
And Ferdinand, her brother, found a wife
Where he himself was lost, Prospero his dukedom
In a poor isle, and all of us ourselves
When no man was his own.

(V, i, 206-213)

In sum, both *The Winter's Tale* and *The Tempest* successfully
depict character on the level of transformation, but there are significant differences in the means by which Shakespeare establishes
and maintains the comic perspective and in the nature of the perspective itself. In a sense, *The Tempest* maintains a more carefully
controlled comic vision of evil. To be sure, the stage-world of this
final comedy is populated with a greater number of characters involved in ultimate moral decisions; but, whereas the intensity of

Leontes' passion is presented in meticulous and graphic detail, the experiences of Alonso, Sebastian, and Antonio are sketched rather lightly. Moreover, *The Winter's Tale* literally portrays the sins of the one generation which must be atoned for in the second; *The Tempest*, through a long expository scene, describes the sins antecedent to the play which Prospero intends to correct through his magical powers. Hence the evils of Milan to which Prospero was victim are related through the filter of time. The conspiracy of Antonio and Sebastian, which serves to maintain the dramatic tension, also shifts the focus of danger away from the protagonist, unlike the constant focus on Leontes in *The Winter's Tale*. Then too, Leontes, following his repentance, spends virtually three acts in a penitential search for forgiveness. Alonso, by contrast, is given only ten lines to articulate his sorrow; Prospero, forgiving him virtually in the same breath, informs Ariel and the spectators that the repentance has been accomplished.

Both plays make sensationalistic use of apparent death, but the actual deaths of Mamillius and Antigonus and the presumed death of Hermione darken further the action of *The Winter's Tale*. As we have noted, both plays make use of variations of a comic pointer—Paulina, Autolycus, Gonzalo. Finally, whereas Shakespeare in *The Winter's Tale* depends largely on stylization of character and action for aesthetic distancing, he in *The Tempest*, for the first time since *Twelfth Night*, provides a subplot which fully and extensively parodies the main plot. And above all, the playwright provides a benign *deus ex machina* as the presiding figure who specifically informs us of the safety of each of the characters and reveals his powers to contain the potential danger of their activities.

Shakespeare's last decade in London was, to be sure, an era of shifting dramatic fashion. In the first years of the century, the humor character was popularized as a vehicle for satiric attacks upon the follies and abuses of late Elizabethan London in the plays of Jonson, Marston, and Chapman—or in the *Parnassus* trilogy. And in the later years, the pastoral tragicomedy was developed to cater to changing tastes and in part at least to utilize the more elaborate scenic possibilities of the private stage. Obviously, as a practical playwright, Shakespeare reflects the popular fashions in his work. Numerous commentators have observed that the melancholy Jaques, the puritanical Malvolio, and the fantastic Lucio—to name only a few—are characters in the mold of typical humors which strutted across Jonson's stage; and Shakespeare, at least in *Troilus and Cressida*, apparently creates the sardonic comedy so fashionable in the early years of James' reign. Yet, except for *Troilus*, he reflects the popular fashion even as he adapts it to his own comic purposes; his plays do not become caustic diatribes against specific social or moral values or ironic exposures of man's basically immoral nature. So also, in his final plays, Shakespeare is not merely returning to the popular romance motifs of his youth; nor is he merely imitating the seriocomic fashion of, for example, Day, Beaumont, or Fletcher.[20] In the works of the latter, such as *Philaster, The Loyal Subject,* or *The Island Princess,* there is no attempt either for credible characterization or for a comically controlled perspective. Indeed, the aim of the consciously extravagant plot is presumably to create for the spectator the hybrid aesthetic experience described by Beaumont in the prologue to *The Woman Hater* (1607): "I dare not call it comedy or tragedy; 'tis perfectly neither"; or by Fletcher in his well-known definition of the new dramatic form: "A tragicomedy is not so called in respect of mirth and killing, but in respect it wants deaths, which is enough to make it no tragedy, yet brings some near it, which is enough to make it no comedy." Actually, Guarini, in his formal theory of tragicomedy, described a controlled tone as crucial to the form. The events of the play throughout must guide the reader and lead him to anticipate the surprise reversal. The spectator must be allowed to fall neither "into an excess . . . of tragic melancholy or of comic relaxation. From this results a poem of the most excellent form and harmonious composition."[21] Again, except for *Pericles*—if indeed it is his—Shakespeare is demonstrably concerned with such comic control even as he utilizes the dramatic motifs popular to his age.

In conclusion, Shakespeare's structural approach to comedy is consistent throughout his career. In the last comedies, characterization has reached realistic depths; Shakespeare has involved his characters in issues and events which force decisions literally touching the emotional strings of tragedy. Yet in both *The Winter's Tale* and *The Tempest*, he has maintained the spectator's detachment, or withheld the spectator's total emotional commitment, thus producing an art form which on occasion resembles tragedy in terms of narrative but is quite distinct from it in terms of the relationship between the character and the spectator.

The result is Shakespeare's most profound comic artistry. But it is nonetheless drama of a piece with his earlier comedy of action and identity, in which, albeit with less complex characterization, his concern for comic control through a carefully regulated perspective for the spectator is equally firm. Through the evolution of his comic vision, that which he and his age inherited from Plautus and Terence as well as from the village green becomes significant not for action alone, but also for character growth and transformation resulting from an exposure to love and forgiveness. Ben Jonson spoke of himself as a vatic poet when, through his satiric comedy, he took therapeutic aim on the human race. Despite their vast differences, Shakespeare in his final characterizations on the level of transformation has utilized comedy for no lesser purpose.

Notes

Index

Abbreviations

CE	*College English*
ELN	*English Language Notes*
Forum	*Ball State University Forum*
HLQ	*Huntington Library Quarterly*
JEGP	*Journal of English and Germanic Philology*
MLN	*Modern Language Notes*
MLQ	*Modern Language Quarterly*
MLR	*Modern Language Review*
N&Q	*Notes and Queries*
PQ	*Philological Quarterly*
RES	*Review of English Studies*
SAB	*Shakespeare Association Bulletin*
SAQ	*South Atlantic Quarterly*
SP	*Studies in Philology*
SQ	*Shakespeare Quarterly*
UTQ	*University of Toronto Quarterly*

Notes

1. Introduction

1. *Shakespeare and His Comedies* (London, 1957), p. 28.
2. Page 43.
3. *The Growth and Structure of Elizabethan Comedy* (London, 1955).
4. *Shakespeare and the Rival Traditions* (New York, 1952).
5. "The Basis of Shakespearean Comedy," *Essays and Studies by Members of the English Association* (1950).
6. *Shakespeare's Satire* (Hamden, Conn., 1943); *Comicall Satyre and Shakespeare's Troilus and Cressida* (San Marino, 1938).
7. *Shakespearian Comedy* (London, 1938), pp. 17, 281.
8. P. G. Phialas, "Comic Truth in Shakespeare and Jonson," *SAQ*, LXII (1963), 85; see also his *Shakespeare's Romantic Comedies* (Chapel Hill, 1966).
9. *An Essay on Shakespeare's Relation to Tradition* (Oxford, 1916).
10. *Anatomy of Criticism* (Princeton, 1957).
11. Northrop Frye, *A Natural Perspective* (New York, 1965), p. 74.
12. *Shakespeare's Festive Comedy* (Princeton, 1959), p. 7.
13. *Shakespere's Five-Act Structure* (Urbana, 1947).
14. *Shakespeare's Comedies* (London, 1960).
15. Page 241.
16. Northrop Frye, "The Argument of Comedy," *English Institute Essays, 1948* (New York, 1949), p. 67.
17. Bradbrook, p. 78.
18. *The Mirror Up to Nature: The Technique of Shakespeare's Tragedies* (San Marino, 1965), p. 10.
19. Northrop Frye, in "Characterization in Shakespeare's Comedy," *SQ*, IV (1953), 271-277, points out that character depends upon function, function in turn upon structure, and structure in turn upon the category of the play. See also *A Natural Perspective*, p. 14. Josephine Waters Bennett (*Measure for Measure as Royal Entertainment* [New York, 1966], p. 5) has flatly stated that to discuss character in Shakespearean comedy is to beg the question, and J. Lawlor ("On Historical Scholarship and the Interpretation of Shakespeare," *Sewanee Review*, LXIV [1956], 193) has warned that "preoccupation with character" may be "disastrous to disciplined attention." Nevertheless, as J. H. P. Pafford (ed., *The Winter's Tale*, The Arden Shakespeare [London, 1963], p.

lxxi) has observed, Shakespeare's characters "have individuality . . . The personality of each character has importance whatever its other functions may be." Since above all it is Shakespeare's characterization which reflects his greater artistry than that of his fellow playwrights, an examination of his concept of dramatic character—as a vehicle for setting forth his increasingly complex comic narratives—hardly seems irrelevant.

20. Sidney L. Gulick, Jr., "More Ado about Much Ado," *SAB*, XXIII (1948), 56.

21. "The Argument of Comedy," p. 70. Such characters are "people who are in some kind of mental bondage, who are helplessly driven by ruling passions, neurotic compulsions, social rituals and selfishness. The miser, the hypochondriac, the hypocrite, the pedant, the snob: these are humours; people who do not fully know what they are doing, who are slaves to a predictable self-imposed pattern of behavior."

22. Robert G. Hunter, in a recent study (*Shakespeare and the Comedy of Forgiveness* [New York, 1965]), has described the form of these comedies as a secularized pattern of the medieval morality involving sin, contrition, and forgiveness.

23. Concerning the late comedies, Joseph Summers expressed something of this general idea in his comment that "after *Twelfth Night* the so-called comedies require for their happy resolution more radical characters and devices—omniscient and omnipresent dukes, magic, and resurrection. More obvious miracles are needed for comedy to exist in a world in which evil also exists, not merely incipiently but with power" ("The Masks of *Twelfth Night*," *The University of Kansas City Review*, XXII [1955], 32).

24. Page 208.

2. The Comedies of Action

1. As his title suggests, he considers "happy" an apposite description for Shakespeare's "first ten comedies." *Shakespeare's Happy Comedies* (Evanston, 1962), pp. 35-36.

2. Critics generally speak of Shakespeare's theatrical competency evinced in the contrived complexities of plot. Those who disagree attack the incredibility of the narrative: "A play supposed to be reenacted by real persons exempt from magic must hold some claim of credence in its postulates, even though it call itself farce" (Arthur Quiller-Couch and J. Dover Wilson, eds., *The Comedy of Errors* [Cambridge, 1922], p. xix). More pertinent is the point made by Peter Alexander (*Introductions to Shakespeare* [New York, 1964]) that it is absurd to speak of Shake-

speare's making his plot more improbable; the important thing is that as a comic device it works!

3. Comments are commonplace concerning the comedy of "physical predicament" (Mark Van Doren, *Shakespeare* [New York, 1939], p. 34), the farcical effects (E. M. W. Tillyard, *Shakespeare's Early Comedies* [New York, 1965], p. 46; E. K. Chambers, *Shakespeare: A Survey* [London, 1925], p. 29; Harold C. Goddard, *The Meaning of Shakespeare* [Chicago, 1951], I, 25). The comedy creates the "plautine atmosphere" of "conventionality and make believe" (Hardin Craig, ed., *The Complete Works of Shakespeare* [Chicago, 1951], p. 81). The situation comedy (Thomas M. Parrott, *Shakespearean Comedy* [New York, 1949], p. 105) is a "self confident and successful attempt to outdo Plautine farce in complexity and swiftness of intrigue" (Sidney Thomas, "The Date of *The Comedy of Errors*," *SQ*, VII [1956], 381).

4. All line reference to Shakespeare's plays throughout this study are to the edition of William A. Neilson and Charles J. Hill, *The Complete Plays and Poems of William Shakespeare* (Boston, 1942).

5. Derek A. Traversi (*Shakespeare: The Early Comedies* [London, 1960]) takes a serious view of the play as a study in the problems of human relationships. R. A. Foakes, in the New Arden edition (London, 1962), sees "a playwright already beginning to generate, out of clashes between suffering and joy, disorder and order, appearance and reality, the peculiar character and strength that is found in his mature works" (p. li).

6. Certain critics, by insisting on the significance of character, make the comedy more than farce. Thus, for example, Craig (p. 82) remarks that, in contrast with the Plautine sources, "Shakespeare's people are real people whose destinies matter." Harold Brooks ("Theme and Structure in *The Comedy of Errors*," *Early Shakespeare*, ed. J. R. Brown and B. Harris [New York, 1966], p. 70) says that the characters' "attitudes of mind develop, so that each is felt to have an inner self." And Parrott (*Shakesperean Comedy*, p. 106) observes that Shakespeare is more skillful in character portrayal than most give him credit for. The "play deepens from farce, touching on the relations of husbands and wives, parents and children" (Geoffrey Bullough, ed., *Narrative and Dramatic Sources of Shakespeare* [London, 1957], I, 8). According to B. O. Bonazza (*Shakespeare's Early Comedies* [The Hague, 1966], p. 20), Shakespeare attempts to shift emphasis from situation to character by creating more subtle characters than Plautus, while to John Munro "emphasis on plot prevailed and characterisation suffered" (ed., *The London Shakespeare* [New York, 1957], p. 4). As others have noted,

Shakespeare has done much to moralize the narrative; "Shakespeare ethically cleanses and remotivates Plautus" (Allison Gaw, "The Evolution of *The Comedy of Errors*," *PMLA*, XLI [1926], 626): Antipholus of Ephesus is not a lecher; Antipholus of Syracuse is not a thief. But for Shakespeare to bring his characters into moral accord with his age is not *ipso facto* to humanize them. And to create the two Antipholuses and the two sisters as character foils is not to develop them within the play or involve them emotionally with the spectators. The characters remain puppets, humorous because of what and where they are, not who they are. The Antipholuses and Dromios are twins, not men; they exist to be mistaken. As Bertrand Evans remarks, "comic effect emerges *not once* from character as such" (*Shakespeare's Comedies* [London, 1960], p. 1).

7. In Plautus the setting was Epidamnum; Shakespeare's change was evidently quite deliberate for the potential comic effects. As Parrott remarks, Ephesus was a city famous for the cult of Diana, who, in the form of Hecate, was goddess of witches (*Shakespearean Comedy*, p. 104). Elizabethans knew the city was noted for its magic arts (Tillyard, p. 48). Also Shakespeare's audience would recognize the comic irony in the confused relationships of wife, master, and servant and the fact that Paul's Epistle to the Ephesians exhorts wives to be obedient to their husbands, children to their parents and servants to their masters (Bullough, I, 9-10). See also: G. R. Elliott, "Weirdness in *The Comedy of Errors*," *UTQ*, IX (1939), 95-106. Harold Brooks' assertion that the references to sorcery and witchcraft "seize the imagination of the audience at the deep level where the ancient dread of losing the self or soul is very much alive" is simply not plausible in this dramatic context of broad comedy (in Brown and Harris, p. 60). By the same analogy, one would assume there could be no humor in *Mankind* or even Jonson's *The Devil Is an Ass* because the spectators would be aware of the ultimate potential for Satan's destroying the soul.

8. Bonazza (p. 37) maintains that Shakespeare attempts to humanize her by revealing that her shrewishness is motivated by love for her husband. Critics are, of course, predictably contradictory in their opinions; Charles Brookes ("Shakespeare's Romantic Shrews," *SQ*, XI [1960]), for example, describes her as strong willed and "admirably intelligent," while Tillyard (p. 58) flatly brands her as stupid.

9. It is true, of course, that Shakespeare, by adding Luciana to the plot, avoids the unpleasant problem of adultery—incest to some—for Antipholus of Ephesus. And she does serve "as a univocal chorus to echo the mores of society" (Bonazza, p. 39). But, in dramatic context, her

major importance is to furnish the ironic and incredible romantic interest for Antipholus of Syracuse.

10. Critics have labored to describe this effect at length. In such fashion, says Edward Dowden (*Introduction to Shakespeare* [London, n.d.], p. 57), Shakespeare rises from mirth to pathos and thus humanizes Plautus' farce; "for all his bad poetry [Aegeon] wrings a few drops of pathos" (Van Doren, p. 36); the frame of pathos envelops and humanizes the farce (Bonazza, p. 17). The Aegeon story offsets the farce (Munro, p. 4) and prevents us from "weary[ing] of a play wholly made up of surprises and mistakes" (W. J. Craig, ed., *The Comedies of Shakespeare* [London, 1946], pp. 301-302). Shakespeare's addition was intended to satisfy his audience's craving for romance (H. B. Charlton, *Shakespearian Comedy* [London, 1938], p. 20; O. J. Campbell, ed., *The Living Shakespeare* [New York, 1958], p. 80). The framing scenes have even given rise to conjecture concerning the philosophy and personal motives of the playwright. T. W. Baldwin (*On the Compositional Genetics of The Comedy of Errors* [Urbana, 1965], p. 145) examines at length Aegeon's Job-like attitude toward life, concluding that the playwright was not a Calvinist; Aegeon is not "an *exemplum* . . . but a hopeless, if not completely broken, old man, appealing to our sympathies." Even more astounding, A. Bronson Feldman examines the frame as a revelation of Shakespeare's mind: the play was written to save his sanity, and the framing events "to gratify his wish to fall together with his father and mother into destruction, to return to the womb of his mother as a tomb" ("Shakespeare's Early Errors," *The International Journal of Psycho-Analysis and Bulletin of the International Psycho-Analytical Association*, XXVI [1955], 114-133). These latter critics, however, are in the study, not the playhouse. As Professor Tillyard has commented, "the romantic frame does not go beyond arousing our simple feelings of wonder" (p. 53). More than that, these framing scenes, effectively played, can arouse humor. To actors commanding a wide range of grim facial expressions, the roles of Aegeon and the duke offer excellent comic roles. Bertrand Evans is correct in asserting that this play exploits the gap between the participants' understanding and ours without an active "practiser" (p. 3), but in effect the framing scenes, while adding a human element, create the gap through which we enjoy the play.

11. Tillyard (p. 57) calls her sudden appearance "the great moment" of the play, providing a sudden check to the wild fancy. Bullough (p. 11) is perhaps closer to the hyperbolic comic spirit in his observation that the appearance of the mother as abbess is humorous—piling wonder upon wonder at an accelerated rate.

12. O. J. Campbell (*Studies in Shakespeare, Milton, and Donne* [New York, 1925]) suggests that *The Two Gentlemen of Verona* is seminal to the English drama of romance. Greene, Lyly, Peele, and Nash were, of course, making dramatic use of similar motifs. See, for instance, Joseph L. Tyson, "The Influence of Greene on Shakespeare's Early Romance," *PMLA*, XX (1912), 246-264.

13. Some critics become so intent upon analyzing the romantic motifs and the courtly love tradition that they tend to neglect Shakespeare's use of the material for situation comedy. Hence, we read that the playwright employs all the conventions of English courtly love, standards of life and conduct which he and his audience took for granted (Ralph M. Sargent, "Sir Thomas Elyot and the Integrity of *The Two Gentlemen of Verona*," *PMLA*, LXV [1950], 1167-1168); of these conventions, the most significant was "that honor is an essential part of love, that the two cannot exist independently" (Karl F. Thompson, "Shakespeare's Romantic Comedies," *PMLA*, LXVII [1952], 1087). Since Shakespeare is "fitting a play into the pattern of the ancient debate of chivalry and the Court of Love, of Friendship against Love" (C. J. Sisson, ed., *The Complete Works of William Shakespeare* [New York, 1953], p. 28), it is impossible to read the play except in light of the sonnets (Chambers, *Shakespeare: A Survey*, p. 54). John Vyvyan (*Shakespeare and the Rose of Love* [London, 1960], pp. 98-135) sees the play as an allegory of principles that should govern love and friendship in man's mind, while John Masefield (*William Shakespeare* [New York, 1911], p. 36) interprets it as an exploration of the moral blindness that leads to vow breaking, and Geoffrey Bullough (I, 210) as "a sympathetic exploration of the difficulties of young people in love." To be sure, critics who assume that Shakespeare is taking his plot seriously are not universally happy with the results. Samuel A. Tannenbaum ("The New Cambridge Shakespeare and *The Two Gentlemen of Verona*," *Shakespeare Association Bulletin*, XIII [1938], 151), for example, brands the story "preposterous," the dramatic technique "puerile," the characters "inconsistent," the dialogue "unnatural," its ethics "pernicious"; the play is not without crudity and unreasonable motivation (Munro, p. 263).

14. "Shakespeare tells a story that stylizes his characters and may force them to do quite unreasonable things" (Frye, *A Natural Perspective*, p. 14). Many who condemn the play assume that Shakespeare was attempting to make his characters credible and failed to do so. The characters are not welded into plot (Arthur Quiller-Couch and J. Dover Wilson, eds., *The Two Gentlemen of Verona* [Cambridge, 1921], p. xii); changes in character are never lived through, only announced (John F. Danby, "Shakespeare Criticism and *The Two Gentlemen of Verona*,"

Critical Quarterly, II [1960], 316). The comedy is a failure because Shakespeare plays it straight; we are unable to develop a rapport with the protagonist—the upholder of the faith—simply because he is "ridiculous" (Charlton, p. 35). "Had [Shakespeare] been content to make them [the characters] mere puppets controlled by supernatural urges beyond their control instead of people presumably motivated by rational considerations" (Bonazza, p. 101), they would have been credible as creatures "created to carry out preconceived actions" (Parrott, *Shakespearean Comedy*, p. 115).

15. G. B. Harrison (ed., *Shakespeare, The Complete Works* [New York, 1948], p. 366) has suggested that Shakespeare is "quietly mocking the whole convention of romantic love" and Hardin Craig (p. 132) that the playwright's attitude toward love mocks the levity of such high school infatuation. Hereward T. Price ("Shakespeare as Critic," *PQ*, XX [1941], 390, 397) maintains that Shakespeare, keenly sensitive to the absurdities and vices of Elizabethan literature, was in this play gunning for the literary convention which sets friendship between men above the love of man for woman. More extensively, H. C. Goddard (I, 46) suggests a Horatian attack upon the Petrarchan code: "Either this is excellent burlesque of 'gentlemanly' manners and morals, or else the young author fooled himself as well as the rest of us by swallowing such silliness because it was sweetened by melodious verse."

16. The critics' determination to create credible characterization has led to weird contradictions concerning the principals of the play. On the one hand, Valentine is the "perfect friend and perfect lover" (Wilson, p. 45), capable of noble sacrifice (Sargent, p. 1177); gentleman to the core (Quiller-Couch and Wilson, *Two Gentlemen*, p. xii), he is the "personification of the ideal courtly friend for whom no sacrifice or surrender is too great as long as it be in the sacred name of friendship" (Bonazza, p. 82). On the other hand, he is the vehicle for Shakespeare's attack on the courtly lover (Price, p. 397), insulting his rival in his lady's presence, lying to the duke, betraying the confidence of his host, writing smutty love sonnets, and offering his sweetheart to be raped (Tannenbaum, p. 152), a puppet who resorts to perjury and forgery, a nincompoop (Charlton, pp. 36-37).

17. Taken at face value, Valentine's offer of Silvia to Proteus has been more than most critics have been willing to digest. Sargent (p. 1177), Thompson (p. 1088), Alwin Thaler ("The Unhappy Happy Ending of *The Two Gentlemen of Verona*," *PMLA*, XLII [1927], 744), and G. G. Gervinus (*Shakespeare Commentaries* [London, 1883], p. 162) rather unconvincingly maintain that such action is in the tradition of friendship's

superiority over love. Tannenbaum (p. 154), exploiting any avenue to disagreement with Quiller-Couch, claims the resolution too clever for a fake adapter, and Bertrand Evans (p. 19) notes that at least Shakespeare does not allow Silvia to be endangered until we know salvation is at hand. More outspoken are Quiller-Couch and Wilson (pp. vii, 102), who would blame the "dammed spot" on an adapter, E. M. W. Tillyard (p. 112), who asserts that the scene is "morally and dramatically monstrous," and John Russell Brown (*Shakespeare and His Comedies* [London, 1957], p. 17), who calls it "precipitous, heartless, and possibly cynical." Bonazza (pp. 85, 98) brands the action as a "precipitous concatenation of absurd events" which is better termed a "retreat" than a "resolution." See further: W. J. Craig, p. 73; John Drinkwater, *Shakespeare* (London, 1933), p. 73; Masefield, p. 41; M. R. Ridley, *William Shakespeare, A Commentary* (London, 1936), p. 26; Samuel Asa Small, "The Ending of *The Two Gentlemen of Verona*," *PMLA*, XLVIII (1933), 776.

18. Proteus, to Chambers (*Shakespeare: A Survey*, p. 56), is the image of the false friend of the sonnets; he, to Tannenbaum (p. 164), is the "villain of an Elizabethan play." Artistically incredible to Tillyard (p. 128), he is "the Italianated youth in whom false friendship and false love accompany the attempts of the youth to acquire sophistication" (Thomas A. Perry, "Proteus, Wry-Transformed Traveller," *SQ*, V [1954], 40). Sargent (pp. 1173, 1176), on the other hand, does not consider him as morally lost, but as receptive to fidelity in love and friendship.

19. Evans (p. 17) sees her as a sympathetic creature, so fully aware of Proteus' confused plight as to be able to pity her prodigal lover, and Parrott (*Shakespearean Comedy*, p. 116) as "the first of Shakespeare's loving girls." On the contrary, Sir George Young, in *The Reading University College Review* (III, No. 19), calls her an "ordinary wench" with "all her quick and rather vulgar wits" about her.

20. Launce and Speed, aside from being recognized as early examples of Shakespeare's masterful creation of comic clowns, have received scant attention. Goddard (I, 44) ironically calls Launce the one gentleman in the play, while both Charlton (p. 36) and Parrott (p. 116) admit the play would be duller without them but perceive no intrinsic relationship between them and the main plot. C. L. Barber (*Shakespeare's Festive Comedy* [Princeton, 1959], p. 14) sees Launce's romance with his dog as a parody of the extravagant romantic postures of the two gentlemen of Verona, and S. Sen Gupta (*Shakespearian Comedy* [Calcutta, 1950]) comments that the clowns alone have imagination, whereas the others merely have roles. But, more recently, Bonazza (p. 83) has maintained

that Launce and Speed are not sufficiently developed to serve as sustained ironic parody.

21 "The abstract Hes and Shes of the conventional love story" (Chambers, p. 83), the Athenian lovers must be played with "a touch of the burlesque" (Harrison, p. 515). They "remain to the end four automatic creatures whose artificial and pretty fate it is to fall in and out of love like dolls" (Van Doren, p. 61), significant not as individuals but in "the whole movement of the farce" (Barber, p. 128). "The four lovers, after all, are puppets while they are in the woods, the helpless victims of supernatural enchantments" (D. P. Young, *Something of Great Constancy* [New Haven, 1966], p. 68). An actor must above all not attempt to suggest real feelings in the lovers (W. Oechelhaüser, *Einführungen in Shakespeare's Bühnen-Dramen* [Minden, 1885], II, 279).

22. Thomas M. Parrott praises the general advance in Shakespeare's characterization (ed., *Shakespeare: Twenty-Three Plays and the Sonnets* [New York, 1938], p. 133); see also Alexander, p. 68. Nevertheless, if in the mind or on the stage the play becomes more than situation comedy with one-dimensional characters, strange distortions follow: Hartley Coleridge, for example, speaks of "the distress of Hermia and Helena" as "too serious, too real for so fantastic a source" (*Essays and Marginalia* [London, 1851], II, 138). Providing the sixth act which the imagination demands if these are to be characters with which we become emotionally involved, W. Modwyn Merchant asserts that there is growth for the lovers and for Bottom; "after their nightmare confusion, vision in the waking world 'grows to something of great constancy' " ("*A Midsummer-Night's Dream*: A Visual Recreation," in Brown and Harris, p. 185).

23. Only rarely does one encounter a negative view, such as Samuel Pepys' charge that it is "a most ridiculous insipid play" (entry for September 29, 1668), or J. M. Robertson's that it is "juvenile, fantastic, unvital" (*Montaigne and Shakespeare* [London, 1909], p. 237), lacking structural unity (R. A. Law, "The Preconceived Pattern of *A Midsummer Night's Dream*," *Texas University Studies in English*, XXII [1943], 5-14). To most critics the drama displays Shakespeare's genius at full glow (F. J. Furnivall, ed., *Leopold Shakespeare* [London, 1877], p. xxvi), "a continued revelry and jollification of soul" (H. N. Hudson, ed., *The Works of William Shakespeare* [New York, 1880], p. 15), the purest of comedies (S. P. Zitner, "The Worlds of *A Midsummer Night's Dream*," SAQ, LIX [1960], 402). To some, the play is a "tenuous" piece of "decoration" (Derek A. Traversi, *An Approach to Shakespeare* [London, 1957], p. 17), a play not for all time but for an age (Zitner, p. 398), a burlesque of romance (Ernest Schanzer, "The Central Theme of *A Midsummer Night's*

Dream," UTQ, XX [1951], 233-238) which is too exquisite to be dulled by the infliction of philosophic analysis (J. O. Halliwell-Phillips, *Memoranda on the Midsummer Night's Dream* [Brighton, 1879], p. 13). To others, there is "marked intellectual content" (Frank Kermode, "The Mature Comedies," in Brown and Harris, p. 214), an allegory of love (P. Fisher, "The Argument of *A Midsummer Night's Dream*," *SQ*, VIII [1957], 307-310) exploring the higher possibilities of a passion usually restrained by necessity (P. Olsen, "*A Midsummer Night's Dream* and the Meaning of Court Marriage," *ELH*, XXIV [1957], 95-119). Reflecting "that perennial human quest for harmony" (J. A. Bryant, "The Importance of *A Midsummer Night's Dream*," *Forum*, V [1964], 3), the play is "one phase of Shakespeare's continuing exploration of the nature, function, and value of art" (James L. Calderwood, "*A Midsummer Night's Dream*: The Illusion of Drama," *MLQ*, XXVI [1965], 507). We witness the spiritual escalation of love toward the recognition of heavenly beauty and virtue (John Vyvyan, *Shakespeare and Platonic Beauty* [New York, 1961], pp. 77-91) in a play which prophesies the constant theme of his mature work—"that this world of sense in which we live is but the surface of a vaster unseen world by which the actions of men are affected or overruled" (Goddard, I, 74).

24. D. P. Young, who would have us "stop speaking of plot and subplot in Shakespearean comedy," describes "the uniqueness of its form" in the manner in which he is able "spatially" to "mirror" his primary theme and characters in other strands of action (pp. 97-106). Whatever the terminology, the results are irrefutable: Shakespeare has created a stage-world in which all lines of subordinate action focus comically and thematically upon the major characters and their experiences.

25. Editor, with J. Dover Wilson, *A Midsummer Night's Dream* (Cambridge, 1949), p. xviii.

26. See, for example, Edward Capell, ed., *The Works of William Shakespeare* (London, 1767), I, 64; George Steevens, ed., *The Works of William Shakespeare* (London, 1773), II, 102; R. J. Ritson, *Remarks, Critical and Illustrative, on the Texts and Notes of the Last Edition of Shakespeare* (London, 1783), p. 47; J. P. Collier, *A Bibliographical and Critical Account of the Rarest Books in English* (London, 1865), II, 43; Charles Knight, ed., *A Midsummer Night's Dream* (London, 1840), p. 343; F. G. Fleay, *Biographical Chronicle of the English Drama* (London, 1891), p. 186; J. O. Halliwell, *An Introduction to "A Midsummer Night's Dream"* (London, 1841), p. 11; W. W. Skeat, *Shakespeare's Plutarch* (London, 1875), pp. 278-279, 284, 286, 288; F. S. Sidgwick, *Sources and Analogues of "A Midsummer Night's Dream"* (London,

1908) *passim*; Quiller-Couch and Wilson, *Midsummer Night's Dream*, p. xiii; and, more recently, E. K. Chambers, *William Shakespeare: Facts and Problems* (Oxford, 1930), I, 363; E. I. Fripp, *Shakespeare, Man and Artist* (London, 1938), p. 394; Bullough, I, 368-371; Kenneth Muir, *Shakespeare's Sources* (London, 1957), pp. 31 ff.; Walter F. Staton, Jr., "Ovidian Elements in *A Midsummer Night's Dream*," *HLQ*, XXVI [1962-63], 165-178. Even more labored discussions include Sister M. Generosa, "Apuleius and *A Midsummer Night's Dream*: Analogue or Source, Which?" *SP*, XLII (1945), 198-204; Michael Poirer, "Sidney's Influence upon *A Midsummer Night's Dream*," *SP*, XLIV (1947), 483-489. To the contrary, Sir Ifor Evans asserts the play to be "one of [Shakespeare's] most original" (*The Language of Shakespeare's Plays* [Bloomington, 1952], pp. 49-50).

27. Page 46. These are "separate figures" and "separate worlds" which give evidence of Shakespeare's "skillful blending" in bringing "together divergent tendencies in the theater" (D. P. Young, pp. 15, 58). "Properly speaking there is no source for *A Midsummer Night's Dream* ... The pattern ... is composed of varied threads drawn by Shakespeare from his reading and observations and woven into the lovely tapestry of his play" (Parrott, *Twenty-Three Plays*, p. 132). The argument has grown circular by the time one describes the playwright as "select[ing] a part here and a part there ... combin[ing] these with ideas from other sources, chang[ing] their location ... and greatly modif[ying] the borrowed thought" (Generosa, p. 200).

28. Horace H. Furness, ed., *A Variorum Edition of Shakespeare: A Midsummer Night's Dream* (Philadelphia, 1895), p. xxii.

29. Israel Gollancz, ed., *A Midsummer Night's Dream*, The University Society of New York (New York, 1901), p. 3; Staunton, "On Shakespeare's *A Midsummer Night's Dream*," *The Athenaeum* (June 27, 1874), p. 476. Staunton continues: "The persistence [of the commentators] in assigning the groundwork of the fable to Chaucer's 'The Knight's Tale' is a remarkable instance of the docility with which succeeding writers will adopt, one after another, an assertion that has really little or no foundation in fact." Furness (p. xxvi) concurs that there is only a superficial similarity between Shakespeare's play and Chaucer's tale, a resemblance limited essentially to the names Theseus and Philostrate. See further: Capell, I, 64; Steevens, II, 102; Ritson, p. 47; Collier, II, 43; Fleay, *Biographical Chronicle*, p. 186; Halliwell, p. 11; Sidgwick, pp. 39 ff.; Quiller-Couch and Wilson, *Midsummer Night's Dream*, p. xiii; Fripp, pp. 394-395; Bullough, I, 368 ff.; Muir, *Shakespeare's Sources*, p. 32; Harrison, p. 512; D. P. Young, pp. 16 ff.

30. "The Knight's Tale," *The Poetical Works of Chaucer* (Cambridge, Mass., 1933), 11. 3040-3041, 2987.

31. Campbell (*Living Shakespeare*, pp. 225-226) perceives topical political satire in Oberon's determination to secure the changeling boy. He suggests that the situation reflects the efforts of the Earl of Hertford to have his children legitimized, an attempt to which Queen Elizabeth was inalterably opposed.

32. As K. M. Briggs writes, "When the fear of heresy lifted and the fairies became less formidable they became available [in literature] for ornament and delight" (*The Anatomy of Puck* [London, 1959], p. 6). This "mad-cap sprite, full of wantonness and mischief" (William Hazlitt, *Characters of Shakespeare's Plays* [London, 1817], p. 128) provides "a sense of reality" and furnishes the audience "the immediate assurance of boisterous gayety and a harmless fun" (Minor White Latham, *The Elizabethan Fairies* [New York, 1930], p. 221).

33. See, for instance, Chambers, *William Shakespeare*, I, 358-359; *Shakespeare: A Survey*, p. 79; Neilson and Hill, p. 88; Hardin Craig, pp. 182-183; Enid Welsford, *The Court Masque* (Cambridge, 1927), pp. 331-332.

34. The name, as critics have frequently noted, is obviously from Chaucer's Egeus, father of Theseus; the name Philostrate, the May Day observance, and the hunting scene are similar incidental borrowings. See, for example: Bullough, I, 369; Muir, p. 32; Harrison, p. 512; Parrott, *Twenty-Three Plays*, p. 132; Quiller-Couch and Wilson, *Midsummer Night's Dream*, p. xiii.

35. The claims vary: their play ridicules the children's companies' histrionic style (G. E. P. Arkwright, "The Death Songs of Pyramus and Thisbe," *N&Q*, May 5, 1906, 341-343; May 26, 1906, 401-403), a mockery of Sussex' men (F. G. Fleay, *Life and Work of Shakespeare* [London, 1886], p. 18), of Hertford's men (E. K. Chambers, *The Elizabethan Stage* [Oxford, 1923], II, 117), of the theatrical heroines of an earlier age (Kenneth Muir, "Pyramus and Thisbe: A Study in Shakespeare's Method," *SQ*, V [1954], 141-153), of early amateur player-poets (J. Macmillan Brown, "An Early Rival of Shakespeare," *New Zealand Magazine* [April 1877], p. 102), of the Elizabethan playwrights who plotted without decorum (Muir, "Shakespeare as Parodyist," *N&Q*, CXCIX [1954], 467-468), of the hybrid or transitional plays "performed at court and on tour" by the small groups which were to become the major companies (J. W. Robinson, "Palpable Hot Ice: Dramatic Burlesque in *A Midsummer Night's Dream*," *SP*, LXI [1964], 203-204). "In the bickerings, jealousies, and contemptible conceits which [Shakespeare] has

represented we are furnished with a picture of the greenroom politics of the Globe" (Augustine Skottowe, *Life of Shakespeare* [London, 1824], I, 255).

36. "The translation of a metaphor in its literal sense" (A. W. Schlegal, quoted in Hudson, p. 20), "he is the very embodiment of that self-esteem which is a human virtue by no means to be dispensed with, though it needs some strong counterpoise in the well-balanced mind" (D. Wilson, *Caliban, The Missing Link* [London, 1873], p. 262). His presence "has the effect of short circuiting attempts to draw a moral from the play" (John A. Allen, "Bottom and Titania," *SQ*, XVIII [1967], 113) by providing the "sober man by whom we judge the intoxicated" (J. R. Brown, p. 84).

37. "A satirical comment on the exaggerated love of . . . Lysander and Hermia" (John P. Cutts, "The Fierce Vexation of A [Midsummer Night's] Dreame," *SQ*, XIV [1963], 183), Pyramus and Thisbe "might be said to be a representation in little of *A Midsummer Night's Dream* as it would be seen through a distorting medium" (Paul N. Siegel, "A Midsummer Night's Dream and the Wedding Guests," *SQ*, IV [1953], 142). "An integral part of the main theme of the play" (A. Brown, "The Play Within a Play: An Elizabethan Dramatic Device," *Essays and Studies*, XIII [1960], 47), reflecting "the headie force of frentick love" (Olsen, p. 118), the Pyramus and Thisbe playlet provides a foil for the entire play (R. W. Dent, "Imagination in *A Midsummer Night's Dream*," *SQ*, XV [1964], 124). See also: Madeleine Doran, "Pyramus and Thisbe Once More," in *Essays on Shakespeare and Elizabethan Drama in Honor of Hardin Craig*, ed. Richard Hosley (Columbia, Missouri, 1962), pp. 149-161; James V. Holleran, "The Pyramus-Thisbe Theme in *A Midsummer Night's Dream*," *California English Journal*, III (1967), 20-26.

38. "Bottom and his company of 'hempen homespuns' are pure English" (Neilson and Hill, p. 89). "They are of the earth, earthy. Bottom sat at a Stratford loom, Starvling on a Stratford tailoring-board; between them they perhaps made the doublet which captivated the eyes of Richard Hathaway's daughter, or the hose that were torn in the park of the Lucy's" (*The Edinburgh Review* [April 1848], p. 422).

39. The lovers' quarrel is funny because we see it "as a crowd of mortals overwatched by benevolent omnipotence"; this is Shakespeare's only comedy in which the controlling force remains outside; the participants' level is not raised to equal ours at the conclusion (Evans, pp. 40-41). The spectator may agree that the "separate worlds [are] moulded into one by a controlling point of view, by an idea," but for the practical purposes of controlling his comic perspective he is never allowed to forget

that the world of the play "is a land of enchantment, where all between the cold moon and the earth is filled with fairy strains" (Charlton, pp. 103, 111).

40. "The ruinous weather of 1595 that was bringing famine and poverty to England provides the substance of a fancy about Oberon and Queen Titania" (Alfred Harbage, *As They Liked It* [New York, 1947], p. 47). Even so, it seems strained to insist upon the "potentially dangerous" quality of these fairy rulers (D. P. Young, p. 29; Merchant, p. 182). One need not assume them to be incipiently malevolent in order to accept them as powerful.

41. Hardin Craig, p. 183; Bullough, I, 367.

3. The Comedies of Identity

1. Critics of *Much Ado about Nothing* are far from agreement in their assumptions concerning the original date of composition and any subsequent revision before the play appeared in quarto in 1600. Well over a century ago, the play was suggested as a revision of *Love's Labor's Won* (A. E. Brae, *Collier, Coleridge, and Shakespeare* [London, 1860]; F. J. Fleay, *Biographical Chronicle of the English Drama* [London, 1891]); this assumption was essentially disproved several years ago by T. W. Baldwin's discovery of a leaf of manuscript indicating that a play entitled *Love's Labor's Won* was in print as late as 1603 (*Shakespere's "Love's Labor's Won": New Evidence from the Accounts of an Elizabethan Bookseller* [Carbondale, 1957], pp. 3, 13-15). Horace H. Furness (ed., *A New Variorum Edition of Shakespeare* [Philadelphia, 1899], p. xxi) believes Shakespeare's work to be a revision of a lost play entitled *Benedicte and Betteris*. The general question of revision has been one of the most volatile issues of the play. Arthur Quiller-Couch and J. Dover Wilson (eds., *Much Ado about Nothing* [Cambridge, 1923]) maintain that Shakespeare constructed the play in 1600 on the groundwork of his own earlier comedy (pp. ix, 102 ff.), a view rigorously denied by E. K. Chambers (*William Shakespeare: Facts and Problems* [Oxford, 1930], I, 386) and Allison Gaw, who can find no grounds either for "believing in an early Shakespearean version of the play" or for "believing that there was an earlier English dramatic version contributory to that of Shakespeare" ("Is Shakespeare's *Much Ado* a Revised Earlier Play?" *PMLA*, L [1935], 737). Hardin Craig asserts that whatever revision there was took place, not upon an old play, but shortly after the composition of the play in the late 1590's, before copy came into the printer's hands (*An Introduction to Shakespeare* [Chicago, 1952], p.

283), a conclusion supported by John Hazel Smith's meticulous study of the problems of composition in Q_1 ("The Composition of the Quarto in *Much Ado about Nothing*," *Studies in Bibliography*, XVI [1963], 9-26).

2. The traditional view that Shakespeare, having decided on his "main" plot, "cast . . . about for something bright to enliven it" (Mary A. Scott, "*The Book of the Courtyer*: A Possible Source of Benedick and Beatrice," *PMLA*, XVI [1901], 490)—though possibly an apt comment on the original draft of an earlier play—simply does not describe the play as we now have it. This fact is implicitly acknowledged by numerous critics, though they almost apologetically continue to speak of Hero and Claudio as the main plot: the Hero-Claudio material is but the "casual framework" for the play (Francis Fergusson, *The Human Image in Dramatic Literature* [Garden City, 1957], p. 151), "little more than a background" (Thomas M. Parrott, *Shakespearean Comedy* [New York, 1949], p. 162), "sacrificed . . . for the sake of Benedick and Beatrice" (Peter Alexander, *Introductions to Shakespeare* [New York, 1964], p. 63); "the sub-plot is much more significant than the main plot" (H. B. Charlton, *Shakespearian Comedy* [London, 1938], p. 277); Benedick and Beatrice are the "salt of life" for the plot (Parrott, ed., *Shakespeare: Twenty-Three Plays and Sonnets* [New York, 1938], p. 480); the persons of the "central action grow to be puppets, while the puppets of wit grow to be characters" (Mark Van Doren, *Shakespeare* [New York, 1939], p. 123). Brander Matthews flatly terms the Hero-Claudio material a "dark subplot" (*Shakespeare as a Playwright* [New York, 1923], p. 152). "It is the affair of Benedick and Beatrice, though suspended and almost unexploited for two acts, that best sustains the comic spirit" (Bertrand Evans, *Shakespeare's Comedies* [London, 1960], p. 86). Various critics find an adequate solution in a statement of theme to which the two plot strands are equally contributory: both the wise (Benedick and Beatrice) and the foolish (Hero and Claudio) must learn "love's truth," the inward trust which results from true love (John Russell Brown, *Shakespeare and His Comedies* [London, 1957], p. 118); the center of the play lies in the self-justifying process of courtship as viewed from two angles (D. L. Stevenson, *The Love-Game Comedy* [New York, 1946]); the play is a study in the egotism of youth—romantic egotism in Claudio, intellectual egotism in Benedick (Harold C. Goddard, *The Meaning of Shakespeare* [Chicago, 1951], I, 277); the characters reflect various types of *hybris*, resulting from their living in a Philistine matchmaking society which brings out the worst in men (J. Smith, "*Much Ado about Nothing*," *Scrutiny*, XIII [1946], 242-257); from two perspectives courtship is presented as an imminent threat to masculine honor, a view which sees

the play as more "ironic" and "reflective" than "gay" (P. and M. Mueschke, "Illusion and Metamorphosis in *Much Ado about Nothing*," *SQ*, XVIII [1967], 53).

3. Mrs. Inchbald brands Benedick and Beatrice nosey for being so willing to eavesdrop (*British Theatre* [London, 1822]; Shaw has compared them to a coster and a flower girl; Beatrice has been accused of being obscene (E. J. West, "Much Ado about an Unpleasant Play," *SAB*, XXII [1947], 31) and odious (T. Campbell, *Dramatic Works of Shakespeare* [London, 1838], p. xlvi). But these are indeed not the majority opinion. They are the "seeded players" in the game of wit (A. P. Rossiter, *Angel with Horns* [New York, 1961], p. 69); there would be no pleasure in their deception "were [they] not so admirable in all their more important actions" (Muriel C. Bradbrook, *Shakespeare and Elizabethan Poetry* [New York, 1952], p. 183). The "free" woman of the Renaissance (Nadine Page, "My Lady Disdain," *MLN*, L [1935], 498), she is the "soul of loyalty" as Benedick is the "mirror of honor" (Sidney L. Gulick, Jr., "More Ado about *Much Ado*," *SAB*, XXIII [1948], 57). The complete wit (Henry Giles, *Human Life in Shakespeare* [Boston, 1868], p. 189), a fine lady (Anna Jameson, *Characteristics of Women* [London, 1833], I, 128), a true Elizabethan (Andrew Lang, *Harper's Magazine*, September 1891, p. 492), Beatrice is "poetic, scintillating" (H. A. Taine, *Histoire de la littérature anglaise* [Paris, 1866], II, 215), a "generous-hearted lady of the latter chivalric time" (George Fletcher, *Studies of Shakespeare* [London, 1847], p. 282), "a gallant creature and complete in mind and feature" (Ellen Terry, quoted in George Gordon, *Shakespearian Comedy* [London, 1944], p. 57). Together, the couple mock the dreary conventions of romantic love (C. T. Prouty, *The Sources of "Much Ado about Nothing"* [New Haven, 1950], p. 63); they are destroyers of convention (W. Sypher, "Nietzsche and Socrates in Messina," *Partisan Review*, XVI [1949], 710 ff.) in their merciless railing against marriage and Petrarchan blarney" (W. N. King, "Much Ado about *Something*," *SQ*, XV [1964], 148).

4. "In love with each other without knowing it" (Goddard, I, 276), Benedick and Beatrice are flirting from the beginning (Bradbrook, p. 181).

5. Benedick must justify his "inconsistency" on "the highest moral grounds" (G. B. Harrison, ed., *Shakespeare: The Complete Works* [New York, 1948], p. 699). The development of both Benedick and Beatrice is "highly natural and humorous" (Augustine Skottowe, *Life of Shakespeare* [London, 1824], I, 354), proof that "no human being exists . . . who cannot be thrown off his balance if assailed through his temperament"

(E. W. Sievers, *William Shakespeare* [Gotha, 1866], p. 304; see also: Charles Gildon, *Remarks* [London, 1710], p. 304). The characters "exhibit the growth of [Shakespeare's] dramatic power in the years following the creation of their prototypes Rosaline and Berowne" (C. F. Tucker Brooke, J. W. Cunliffe, and H. N. MacCracken, eds., *Shakespeare's Principal Plays* [New York, 1935], p. 373). Our vantage point from the outset is secure for comedy; as B. Evans remarks, no play builds so exclusively and so fully on "exploitable differences in awareness" (*Shakespeare's Comedies*, p. 69); "we, who are in on the secret, know that the whole rests within that sphere where comedy finds its nurture" (*Edinburgh Review*, July 1840, p. 493).

6. Benedick is now ready to trust his "love-inspired belief in the decency of Beatrice and [to trust] her instinctive belief (also love-inspired) in Hero" (Robert G. Hunter, *Shakespeare and the Comedy of Forgiveness* [New York, 1965], p. 97). The command shows the lovers less selfish and more serious (Denezell S. Smith, "The Command 'Kill Claudio' in *Much Ado about Nothing*," *ELN*, IV [1966-67], 181-182).

7. There has been much effort to explain Shakespeare's intentions through an examination of his sources. The most exhaustive is that of C. T. Prouty (*The Sources of "Much Ado about Nothing"* and his article "George Whetstone, Peter Beverly, and The Sources of *Much Ado about Nothing*," *SP*, XXXVIII [1941], 211-220). See also: D. A. Evans, "Some Notes on Shakespeare and *The Mirror of Knighthood*," *SAB*, XXI (1946), 161-167; D. J. Gordon, "*Much Ado about Nothing*: A Possible Source for the Hero-Claudio Plot," *SP*, XXXIX (1942), 279-290. Quite recently, John Wain has blamed the partial failure of the play on the Hero-Claudio plot. Caught up with Benedick and Beatrice in his "drive toward three-dimensional characterization," Shakespeare simply could not muster sufficient interest in Hero and Claudio to make them interesting, consistent, or credible. "The Shakespearean Lie-Detector: Thoughts on *Much Ado about Nothing*," *Critical Quarterly*, IX (1967), 27-28, 31-38.

8. Claudio has been found both noble and ignoble, consistent and inconsistent. On the one hand, justifiable in terms of Elizabethan expectancy (W. Meader, *Courtship in Shakespeare* [New York, 1954]), a "slandered groom" without self-conceit (Kirby Neill, "More Ado About Claudio: An Acquittal for the Slandered Groom," *SQ*, III [1952], 101, 107), Claudio is "a man of noble mind" (W. Wetz, *Shakespeare von Standpunkte der Vergleichenden Literatur* [Worms, 1890], p. 156), a consistent character acting more like soldier than lover (L. C. Hartley, "Claudio and the Unmerry War," *College English*, XXVI [1964-65], 614). On the other hand, Claudio is conceited (Lang, p. 492), "vain,

arrogant, inconsiderate, and fickle" (F. Kreyssig, *Vorlesungen ueber Shakespeare* [Berlin, 1862], p. 217), a "generic character" who is "never more than the typical lover of the romances" (O. J. Campbell, *The Living Shakespeare* [New York, 1958], pp. 519-520), a "badly plot-ridden character" (Hardin Craig, ed., *The Complete Works of Shakespeare* [Chicago, 1951], p. 531), a perverted reflection of Calidore (Abbie Findlay Potts, "Spenserian 'Courtesy' and Temperance in *Much Ado*," *SAB*, XVII [1942], 103-111, 126-133), a blot on the play (M. R. Ridley, ed., *Much Ado about Nothing* [London, 1935], p. ix), "a worm" (E. K. Chambers, *Shakespeare: A Survey* [London, 1925], p. 134).

9. As William A. Neilson and Charles J. Hill write, Don John "is so lacking in subtlety as to seem . . . funny . . . the proper kind of villain for a comedy" (eds., *The Complete Plays and Poems of William Shakespeare* [Boston, 1942], p. 180).

10. Graham Storey has touched the central nerve of the critics' disagreement in his assertion that the greatest difficulty is from those who respond to this play as though the protagonists (Hero and Claudio) were psychologically real (*More Talking of Shakespeare* [New York, 1959]).

11. Richard Grant White (ed., *The Works of William Shakespeare* [Boston, 1857], III, 226-227) was the first to suggest a pun on eavesdropping in the title, based on the Elizabethan pronunciation of *Nothing*. Both Helge Kökeritz (*Shakespeare's Prounuciation* [New Haven, 1953], p. 132) and Paul Jorgensen ("Much Ado about *Nothing*," *SQ*, V [1954], 287-295) deny this pun, though Kökeritz admits the Elizabethan *nothing* could mean observation or overhearing. Certainly Jorgensen's attack is overstated, as Dorothy C. Hockey reveals in her discussion of the significance of misnoting or misobserving as central to the play ("Notes, Notes, Forsooth . . ." *SQ*, VIII [1957], 353-358).

12. This scene has drawn the special ire of numerous critics. "A repulsive scene" (Stopford Brooke, *Ten More Plays of Shakespeare* [New York, 1913], p. 21), "Hero's dishonoring is very badly managed" (M. Messiaen, *Shakespeare, Les Comedies*, trans. Pierre Messiaen [Paris, 1937], p. 777); it "enfeebles the plot" (Robert Bridges, *The Influence of the Audience on Shakespeare's Drama* [London, 1927], pp. 5-6). Others attempt to make the altar-rejection plausible to the Elizabethan viewer in terms of "the convention of the slanderer believed" (E. E. Stoll, *Shakespeare Studies* [New York, 1927], p. 94) or the age's religious and social views of female weakness (Nadine Page, "The Public Repudiation of Hero," *PMLA*, L [1935], 739-744). Certainly more pertinent is D. J. Gordon's observation (p. 289) that the playwright provides us just "enough for dramatic illusion." Or, more directly, "the whole scene's

deliberate *theatricality* lessens our involvement and distances our emotions . . . It is highly exaggerated and hovers on the edge of caricature" (Storey, p. 118).

13. D. J. Gordon and Alwin Thaler explain the enigma through a source, Gordon (p. 284) through *Gli duoi fratelle rivale* and Thaler through Spenser ("Spenser and *Much Ado about Nothing*," *SP*, XXXVII [1940], 225-235), while Allan Gilbert explains it through revision: "The discrepancy . . . may be explained by assuming that the playwright first wrote the play without Margaret's disguise, then revised the manuscript to include the disguise. But in his revision he failed to change Don John's promise so that the window entered would become the window of Hero's room, occupied by Margaret in disguise" ("Two Margarets: The Composition of *Much Ado about Nothing*," *PQ*, XLI [1962], 65).

14. The critics' delight, Dogberry and Verges are "inimitable specimens of quaint blunderings and misprisions of meaning" (William Hazlitt, *Characters of Shakespeare's Plays* [London, 1817], p. 303), a "coarse tallow candle burning near the center, and keeping the comic peace" (Van Doren, p. 123); displaying "genial pomposity, suspicious complacency, [and] racy muddle-headedness" (J. C. Smith, ed., *Much Ado about Nothing* [Boston, n.d.], p. xviii), Dogberry is suffering from delusions of vanity and uncontrolled verbosity (Fergusson, *The Human Image*, p. 152). The bumbling constables function to preserve the comic perspective by letting the audience in on Don John's villainy (O. J. Campbell, p. 521), to provide a "parody or, in musical analogy, an undersong" (Bradbrook, p. 188)—the "apposite farce-fool for a play in which all three plots turn on understandings and misunderstandings" (Rossiter, p. 70). "Dogberry personifies . . . the spirit and meaning of the whole, and, therefore, plays essentially the same part as . . . the majority of the clowns in Shakespeare's comedies" (Hermann Ulrici, *Shakespeare's Dramatic Art* [Leipzig, 1839], II, 101).

15. The structure of the play has received both praise and condemnation. For example, "Here is no stuff for a comedy. A girl slandered and ill-treated to an unutterable extent is not an object to awaken merriment" (Roderich Benedix, *Die Shakespearomanie* [Stuttgart, 1873], p. 319); "the unsatisfactory final scene . . . is the inevitable consequence of the faulty method of construction" (W. Oechelhauser, *Einführungen in Shakespeare's Bühnen-Dramen* [Minden, 1885], p. 355); the pain in the plot cuts too deep (J. C. Smith, p. xxiv) in its mixture of comedy and tragicomedy (Chambers, *Shakespeare: A Survey*, p. 133); "Shakespeare made the mistake of choosing a romantic story that could never be assimilated to the spirit of comedy" (E. C. Pettet, *Shakespeare and the*

Romance Tradition [London, 1949], p. 132). To the contrary, according to other critics, the play makes "excellent sense as it stands . . . [It] is not a tragicomedy . . . [We watch] with callous detachment" (T. W. Craik, "*Much Ado about Nothing,*" *Scrutiny,* XIX [1953], 298, 316). The play "should rank, in point of dramatic construction and development of character, with the best of Shakespeare's works" (Lady Martin, *On Some of Shakespeare's Female Characters* [Edinburgh, 1891], p. 290). The structural skill, a "wedding of love and humor" (Donald Stauffer, *Shakespeare's World of Images* [New York, 1949], p. 68), is in the combination of three tones—the highly romantic, the gayer comedy of manners, the low comedy (Hazleton Spencer, *The Life and Art of William Shakespeare* [New York, 1940], p. 251). "For absolute power of composition, for faultless balance and blameless rectitude of design, there is unquestionably no creation of [Shakespeare's] hand that will bear comparison with *Much Ado about Nothing*" (A. C. Swinburne, *A Study of Shakespeare* [London, 1880], p. 152).

16. "With the writing of *Twelfth Night* Shakespeare reached perhaps his highest achievement in sheer comedy" (Louis B. Wright, ed., *Twelfth Night* [New York, 1960], p. vii). Such statements concerning this play are commonplace in Shakespearean criticism. Both the dramatist and his characters appear at ease (C. Bathurst, *Differences of Shakespeare's Versification* [London, 1857], p. 89) in this "most perfect of his comedies" in which Shakespeare has "set himself the task to show, within the limit of one treatment, like a recapitulation, every combination of comedies in one single comedy" (Kreyssig, III, 268). J. O. Halliwell-Phillips describes the work as "the most perfect composition of the kind in the English or in any other language" (*Outlines of the Life of Shakespeare* [Brighton, 1882], p. 247).

17. Viola's importance in the plot has been frequently described. Bertrand Evans, for instance, comments that in *Twelfth Night* "the spirit of the practiser prevails. Seven of the principal persons are active practisers, and they operate six devices. All action turns on these, and the effects of the play arise from exploitation of the gaps they open" (*Shakespeare's Comedies,* p. 118). Of these devices, "Viola's is truly a practice on the whole world of Illyria" (p. 120). John Russell Brown, who explains the theme of the play as "love's truth," sees Viola and her disguise as central to the development of the action (p. 168). H. B. Charlton calls her "the peculiar embodiment in personality of those traits of human nature which render human beings most lovable, most loving, and most serviceable to the general good" (p. 288). Viola "represents a genuineness

of feeling against which the illusory can be measured" (Harold Jenkins, "Shakespeare's *Twelfth Night*," *Rice Institute Pamphlet*, XLV [1959], 30). In effect, she "teaches others the true meaning of love" (Porter Williams, "Mistakes in *Twelfth Night* and Their Resolution," *PMLA*, LXXVI [1961], 197). She, since Orsino will marry her and Olivia will marry Sebastian, is allegorically the spirit of love, which functions to redeem the disordered society (William B. Bache, "Levels of Perception in *Twelfth Night*," *Ball State Teachers College Forum*, V [1964], 56). To the contrary, Clifford Leech recently described her importance to the plot "exaggerated by the critic"; she is by no means "a reformer of the Illyrian emotional condition" (*"Twelfth Night" and Shakespearean Comedy* [Toronto, 1965], p. 36).

18. "In *Twelfth Night*, affectation is everywhere—among the heroic as among the foolish, among the central characters as among the marginal . . . Olivia cannot bear to be known for what she is—a healthy and nubile woman; Viola cannot permit herself to be known for what she is, a girl; Orsino cannot bear to be known for what he is—a lover in love with the idea of love; Sir Toby cannot bear to be known for a parasite, Sir Andrew for a fool, Malvolio for a steward" (G. K. Hunter, *Shakespeare: The Late Comedies* [London, 1962], p. 36). Jenkins (p. 21) describes the action as "the education of a man or woman," a plot fundamental to comedy. The characters, wearing psychological masks (Williams, p. 193), are "caught up by delusions or misapprehensions which take them out of themselves, bringing out what they would keep hidden or did not know was there" (C. L. Barber, *Shakespeare's Festive Comedy* [Princeton, 1959], p. 242).

19. Irving Ribner has suggested that Shakespeare's critical attitude toward the affectations of Petrarchan love was influenced by Barnabe Riche's puritanical attack on the convention in "Apolonius and Silla" (ed., *Twelfth Night*, The Kittredge Shakespeares [Waltham, Mass., 1966], pp. xv-xvi).

20. If Aguecheek is intelligent enough to boast of his prowess in pressing a duel with one whom he assumes to be a coward and then to recoil in terror when his adversary appears to have a backbone, he is intelligent enough to be the object of satiric humor since he can learn something from his comic experience. Any assumption that, in *this* aspect of his character, he is not the proper prey of a satirist—and the charge is as old as the editorial commentary of Samuel Johnson—is surely missing the point.

21. Esquire of Worden, steward until 1594 to Lord Fernando Strange,

Earl of Derby and patron of Shakespeare's company (Alwin Thaler, "The Original Malvolio," *The Shakespeare Association Bulletin*, VII [1932], 57).

22. Queen Elizabeth's chief steward and Squire of the Presence (Israel Gollancz, *A Book of Homage to Shakespeare* [London, 1953], pp. 177-178).

23. The Comptroller of the Royal Household, first suggested by E. K. Chambers (*Shakespeare: A Survey*, p. 178) and extensively supported by Leslie Hotson (*The First Night of "Twelfth Night"* [London, 1955], pp. 93-118).

24. Malvolio has been of particular interest to commentators on the play. He has been described as Shakespeare's grand attack upon Puritanism (Joseph Hunter, *New Illustrations of Shakespeare* [London, 1845], I, 381), as a Philistine (William Archer, "Twelfth Night," *Macmillan's Magazine* [August, 1884], p. 275), as "an excellent specimen of the sentimental fool . . . the *fool-part* of masculine vanity exposed" (Giles, p. 177), as "a spoil-sport, a fussy, pompous upper servant" (David Cecil, "Malvolio, Sir Andrew, and Feste," *The Fine Art of Reading*, ed. R. M. Ritchie and R. A. James [London, 1957], p. 52), as an illustration of "overstretched morality" (Charles Lamb, "On Some of the Old Actors," *The Essays of Elia*, ed. Saxe Commins [New York, 1935], p. 119), as a narcissist suffering from an inferiority complex (Norman N. Holland, *Psychoanalysis and Shakespeare* [New York, 1964], p. 278; Theodore Reik, *The Need to Be Loved* [New York, 1963], pp. 53-54), as a reflection of the large number of malcontents in London in the early seventeenth century, unemployed university-trained men (L. C. Knights, *Drama and Society in the Age of Jonson* [Manchester, 1936], pp. 315-332). M. Seiden ("Malvolio Reconsidered," *The University of Kansas City Review*, XXVIII [1961], 105-114) finds the steward a form of scapegoat who undergoes sacrificial comic death so that comedy itself may live.

25. Francis Fergusson says that Feste, "keep[ing] his sanity better than any of the other characters" and "mov[ing] through the play like a modern master of ceremonies, commenting on the characters with elaborate mockery," seems to represent Shakespeare himself ("Introduction to *Twelfth Night*," *Shakespeare's Comedies of Romance* [New York, 1963], p. 304). As a ringleader (Enid Welsford, *The Fool* [London, 1935], p. 253) who remains outside the action with telling remarks (John Hollander, "*Twelfth Night* and the Morality of Indulgence," *The Sewanee Review*, LXVII [1959], 226), Feste plays a "role as observer [which] is analogous to Viola's role as 'actor'" (Joseph H. Summers, "The Masks of

Twelfth Night," University of Kansas City Review, XXII [1955], 27).
"If the Fool be cleverly played, it can be a guide through the most important points of this comedy" (G. G. Gervinus, *Shakespeare* [Leipzig, 1862], p. 438). "*Twelfth Night* is Feste's night . . . It is [his] function in both parts of the action to make plain to the audience the artificial, foolish attitudes of the principal figures" (Alan S. Downer, "Feste's Night," *CE,* XIII [1951-1952], 261, 264).

26. Certainly the role of Malvolio is a dramatic highlight of the play. In fact, a court performance of February 2, 1623, is recorded as *Malvolio.* Nevertheless, I cannot agree with those critics who would make him the central figure in the play. See, for example, Milton Crane, *"Twelfth Night* and Shakespearean Comedy," *Shakespeare Quarterly,* VI (1955), 4. Cf. also Van Doren, p. 169: "The center is Malvolio. The drama is between his mind and the music of old manners." Morris P. Tilley ("The Organic Unity of *Twelfth Night," PMLA,* XXIX [1914], 554-556) sees Malvolio and the forces to whom he is opposed as reflective of the parting of the ways of the Renaissance and the Reformation in England: "Shakespeare composed *Twelfth Night* in praise of the much-needed, well-balanced nature, to extoll that happy union of judgment and of feeling which is the basis of a higher sanity." With greater restraint, Harold C. Goddard speaks of *Twelfth Night* as—in retrospect—Shakespeare's "farewell to comedy . . . It marks the end of Merry England, of the day of the great Tudor houses where hospitality and entertainment were so long dispersed . . . It seems like an imitation of the Puritan revolution with its rebuke to revelry" (I, 295).

27. It is impossible to conclude within the context of the drama, for instance, that Viola is "Shakespeare's ideal of the patient idolatry and devoted, silent self-sacrifice of perfect love" (W. Winter, *Shadows of the Stage* [New York, 1895], III, 24) or that Orsino is a man of "deep sentiments of the most sacred tenderness and truth" displaying a "firm constancy in his love" (Gervinus, p. 429). And it borders on the ridiculous to describe Orsino as doting on Olivia as a mother substitute because he suffers from a mother fixation and Olivia as frigid, sexually terrified of men in positions of power (W. I. D. Scott, *Shakespeare's Melancholics* [London, 1962], pp. 57-60; Holland, pp. 278-279).

4. The Problem Comedies

1. Shakespeare's authorship of this play—or his possible collaboration with Rowley, Heywood, Wilkins, or Day—is an issue of long-standing contention. Since the eighteenth century, however, critics have assumed

the presence of Shakespeare's hand in Acts III–V. "Two possible alternatives suggest themselves: either *Pericles* was a new play, which for some reason Shakespeare decided to write only in part, assigning the first two acts to other, and certainly minor, dramatists; or the play reached Shakespeare in a complete or nearly complete state, and he decided to rewrite only the second part; perhaps because his imagination was only aroused then, perhaps because the thing had to be done in a hurry—one can only speculate" (F. D. Hoeniger, ed., *Pericles,* The Arden Shakespeare [London, 1963], p. liii).

2. As G. K. Hunter comments, "*Measure for Measure* and *All's Well That Ends Well* are obvious twins. The affinities they share might, of course, be due to nothing more than the chance similarity of their sources; but it is not probable that plot, characterization, themes, vocabulary (see the articles by Alfred Hart in *RES,* XIX [1943]), even the tangles, perplexities, and perversities of treatment should be shared, unless the mind and technique of the author were still at the same stage" (ed., *All's Well That Ends Well,* The Arden Shakespeare [London, 1959], pp. xxiii-xxiv). R. Turner ("Dramatic Conventions in *All's Well That Ends Well,*" *PMLA,* LXXV [1960], 497-502) relates both *Measure for Measure* and *All's Well That Ends Well* to a group of "prodigal son" plays, popular in London from 1601-1604, in which the prime interest is the redemption of the protagonist. Robert Hapgood, in a counter view, maintains the similarities are more apparent than real ("Dramatic Conventions in *All's Well That Ends Well,*" *PMLA,* LXXIX [1964], 177-179).

3. As C. L. Barber remarks, "In both plays, release often leads, not simply to folly, but to the vicious or contemptible" (*Shakespeare's Festive Comedy* [Princeton, 1959], pp. 258-259). If Barrett Wendell's assertion concerning *All's Well That Ends Well* that no work in Shakespeare is "so corrupt . . . so painful . . . less pleasing" (*William Shakespeare* [New York, 1895], p. 250) is extreme, so also is Madeleine Doran's comment that there is no problem in the play, "nothing gloomy or bitter . . . It is a problem in wit, not in manners or morals" (*Endeavours of Art* [Madison, 1954]). However insufficient the label "problem play" (F. S. Boas, *Shakespeare and His Predecessors* [London, 1896], p. 344 ff.) might seem, *All's Well That Ends Well* and *Measure for Measure* do, as A. P. Rossiter observes, "bother us"; the " 'happy ending' . . . makes us neither happy nor comfortable" (*Angel with Horns* [London, 1961], p. 128).

4. Exact dating of either *All's Well That Ends Well* or *Measure for Measure* is impossible. G. B. Harrison, for example, would place the date of composition for *All's Well That Ends Well* at 1608 (ed., *All's Well*

That Ends Well, The Penguin Shakespeare [New York, 1955], p. 16), and John L. Lowes—on the basis of an unpublished metrical analysis in The Harvard University Archives—at 1606-1608. The consensus of critical opinion, however, dates the play in its present form at 1602-1604. Similarly, *Measure for Measure,* assumed to be the later of the two, is assigned to the summer of 1604 (see J. W. Lever, ed., *Measure for Measure,* The Arden Shakespeare [London, 1965], pp. xxxi-xxxv).

5. Critics for the most part have disliked Bertram in varying degrees of intensity. Samuel Johnson, for example, denounced him as "a man noble without generosity and young without truth; who married Helena as a coward and leaves her as a profligate; when she is dead by his unkindness, sneaks home to a second marriage, is accused by a woman he has wronged, defends himself by falsehood, and is dismissed to happiness" (*Johnson on Shakespeare,* ed. Sir Walter Raleigh [London, 1908], p. 103). Harold C. Goddard considered him a "mettlesome animal, and arrogant young count" (*The Meaning of Shakespeare* [Chicago, 1951], II, 40), and E. M. W. Tillyard described him as both mean and repellent, "moral cowardice joined to physical courage" (*Shakespeare's Problem Plays* [London, 1950], p. 114). "[L]ack[ing] the intuition by which the worth of men is measured" (H. B. Charlton, *Shakespearian Comedy* [London, 1938], p. 261), he is "seduced by the appearance of this world" (William B. Toole, *Shakespeare's Problem Plays* [The Hague, 1966], p. 132). Other critics find an explanation in his youth: not really wicked, he is a "thoughtless, petulant boy" (S. Nagarajan, "The Structure of *All's Well That Ends Well,*" *Essays in Criticism,* X [1960], 24); still others in his victimization: "one cannot but feel some sympathy for Bertram" (E. K. Chambers, *Shakespeare: A Survey* [London, 1925], p. 206); "If Bertram is guilty of lies and evasions, so is Helena; if he fails to respect her choice, she will allow him none; if he rejects her, she drives him from her; if he humiliates her by refusing her, she humiliates him by choosing him publicly" (A. H. Carter, "In Defense of Bertram," *SQ,* VII [1956], 24). Sworn to marriage by verbal contract and by church ceremony, the count was seeking the only legal escape from a woman he did not love—refusal to consummate the union; our realization of Elizabethan matrimonial convention, according to Margaret Loftus Ranald, helps to rehabilitate our concept of Bertram ("The Betrothals of *All's Well That Ends Well,*" *Huntington Library Quarterly,* XXVI [1962-63], 186, 192). A valuable clue to his enigmatic quality is Peter Alexander's comment: "In the original it is Giletta's story; Bertram is merely a functionary in the action; we are not to inquire into the nature or motives of his conduct. Translated into drama however a principal

character who is merely a functionary raises questions that cannot be answered satisfactorily by referring us to a scheme for which he is designed" (*Introductions to Shakespeare* [New York, 1964], p. 77).

6. Bertram calls for Parolles to "go with me to my chamber and advise me" (II, i, 311), and a few scenes later he defends the rogue before Lafeu as both courageous and wise: a soldier "of very valiant approof . . . I do assure you, my lord, he is very great in knowledge and accordingly valiant" (II, v, 2, 8-9).

7. *All's Well* is called "a play in which the characterization of the major dramatic persons is at odds with the final tendency of the action, in which a tone of irony and often satire conflicts with the 'all's well' complacency implied by the fairy-tale elements, and in which a concrete, realistic presentation works at cross purposes with the romantic image of experience which the play seems to project" (James L. Calderwood, "Styles of Knowing in *All's Well That Ends Well*," *MLQ*, XXV [1964], 274). See also W. W. Lawrence, *Shakespeare's Problem Comedies* (New York, 1931), pp. 67-72; Mark Van Doren, *Shakespeare* (New York, 1939), pp. 184-185; Harold S. Wilson, "Dramatic Emphasis in *All's Well That Ends Well*," *HLQ*, XIII (1949-50), 217-240; J. M. Murray, *Shakespeare* (New York, 1936), p. 253.

8. See primarily Lawrence, "The Meaning of *All's Well That Ends Well*," *PMLA*, XXXVII (1922), 418-469, and *Problem Comedies*, pp. 38-63. For a further discussion on medieval analogues, see G. Vogt, "Gleanings for the History of a Sentiment: *Generositas Virtus, Non Sanguis*," *JEGP*, XXIV (1925), 102-124.

9. The die was cast by R. W. Chambers' British Academy paper of 1937, *The Jacobean Shakespeare and Measure for Measure* (reprinted in *Man's Unconquerable Mind* [London, 1939]); here the problem plays emerge as anticipations of the final plays in their theme of forgiveness, reflecting Shakespeare's Christian philosophy. E. LaGuardia ("Chastity, Regeneration, and World Order in *All's Well That Ends Well*" in *Myth and Symbol* [Lincoln, 1963]) describes the pattern of initiation, purification, and regeneration; see also *Nature Redeemed: The Imitation of Order in Three Renaissance Poems* (The Hague, 1966). As a mystery moving from pain to begetting, the play sets forth the unborn child as the central symbol, representing the strange commingling of love and lust (J. Arthos, "The Comedy of Generation," *Essays in Criticism*, V [1955], 97-117). Though not written allegorically, *All's Well That Ends Well* is a "moral play" in which the "characters have a symbolic and extra-personal significance" (Muriel C. Bradbrook, "Virtue Is the True Nobility," *RES*, I [1950], 290). "In a world of divided, sin-struck

humanity [Helena] is a redeeming power, a perfect unit" (G. Wilson Knight, *The Sovereign Flower* [London, 1958], p. 145); Helena "supplies the Christological element in the drama. The sacrifice that she makes out of her human love for Bertram reflects the sacrifice that Christ made out of divine love for all humanity, and the pardon that Bertram asks for and receives anticipates or reflects salvation on a metaphysical plane" (Toole, p. 232).

10. *All's Well That Ends Well* as a revision of *Love's Labour's Won*, first suggested by Bishop Percy in a letter to Dr. Farmer dated February 28, 1764, was repeated by Farmer in his *Essay on the Learning of Shakespeare* (1767) (see D. Nichol Smith, *Eighteenth-Century Essays on Shakespeare* [London, 1903], p. 178). Coleridge assumes *All's Well That Ends Well* to be a play written in two layers (T. M. Raysor, ed., *Shakespearean Criticism* [London, 1930], I, 237), and Israel Gollancz agrees that it is "very probable, almost certain" that *Love's Labour's Won* is the first layer (ed., *The Temple Shakespeare* [New York, 1894], p. v). See further: A. H. Tolman, *What Has Become of Shakespeare's Play "Love's Labour's Won?"* (Carbondale, 1957), and Hardin Craig, ed., *The Complete Works of Shakespeare* (Chicago, 1951), p. 803. Arthur Quiller-Couch and J. Dover Wilson predictably champion the view that *All's Well That Ends Well* is Shakespeare's revision of another's work; "a master's hand has obviously scratched over a poor original" (eds., *All's Well That Ends Well*, The New Cambridge Shakespeare [Cambridge, 1955], p. vii).

11. Analyzed in terms of O. J. Campbell's discussion of *Measure for Measure* (*Shakespeare's Satire* [New York, 1943]), *All's Well That Ends Well* is a satiric attack on Bertram and his decadent aristocratic vices. Murray Krieger sees the failure of the play as a result of the attempted fusion of "pastoral romantic comedy" and "neo-classical Jonsonian comedy" ("*Measure for Measure* and Elizabethan Comedy," *PMLA*, LXVI [1951], 775-784).

12. Turner, pp. 497-502.

13. "It is important for us to train ourselves to accept [Shakespeare's] guidance in each play from first to last . . . [to accept] the obvious attitudes he wants us to take toward the characters and what they do" (F. G. Schoff, "Claudio, Bertram, and A Note on Interpretation," *SQ*, X [1959], 23). While such a statement is hardly debatable, it is the height of absurdity *ipso facto* to assert that both Helena and Bertram are noble and that to think otherwise is to pervert Shakespeare's design. Indeed, if Shakespeare did intend for Helena and Bertram to be noble, the necessary guidance breaks down, resulting in what Bertrand Evans describes

as "the inexplicabl[e] un-Shakespearian slippage of focus" (*Shakespeare's Comedies* [London, 1960], p. 159). In this play "our general awareness is sustained falteringly, often by belated injections of information" (p. 145).

14. Certainly he cannot be dismissed as "without function" (Quiller-Couch, p. xxv), one, created to add a dash of comedy to a rather serious plot, who "drifts in and out to crack jokes with whoever happens to be on stage" (Thomas M. Parrott, *Shakespearean Comedy* [New York, 1949], p. 353). As Hazleton Spencer writes, "Lavatche is not among the greatest of the clowns; he is a coarser and less merry, but his wit comes from the same mint" (*The Art and Life of William Shakespeare* [New York, 1940], p. 298). In Lavache, "Feste's wry smile has turned to a leer . . . One may cavil at calling [him] a wise fool, but one must agree that he is a conscious humorist" (Robert H. Goldsmith, *Wise Fools in Shakespeare* [Liverpool, 1955], pp. 58-59). Knight sees the clown as Parolles' foil; "since neither offers us a code to live by, some compromise must be reached" (p. 103). The part of the "philosophic" clown, according to G. K. Hunter (*All's Well*, p. xxi), is obviously in its present form created for Robert Armin some time after 1599. Leslie Hotson (*Shakespeare's Motley* [London, 1952], p. 88) takes the counter view—that the part of the "rustic and boorish" clown was written for Will Kempe, preceding *As You Like It* and *Twelfth Night*.

15. Parolles, on the one hand, has been branded "about the inanest of all Shakespeare's inventions" (Quiller-Couch and Wilson, p. xxiv), a role "given space disproportionate to its significance for the main action" (Evans, p. 159), singularly independent of the main action (Lawrence, *Problem Comedies*, p. 37). On the other hand, he is considered "one of Shakespeare's greatest creations" (G. L. Krapp, *Shakespearian Studies by Members of the Department of English and Comparative Literature in Columbia University* [New York, 1916], p. 43), providing extensive parallels with the main plot in both symbol and action (James L. Calderwood, "The Mingled Yarn of *All's Well That Ends Well*," *JEGP*, LXII [1963], 65-66). To Robert Hapgood, it is the rogue's vitality in opting for life at any cost which provides the driving force for compromise and life at the conclusion of the play ("The Life of Shame: Parolles and *All's Well*," *Essays in Criticism*, XV [1965], 270, 278). With roots in the *Commedia dell'arte* (H. Spencer, p. 298), Parolles is subjected to an exposure in Act IV which is the comic highlight of the play (H. S. Wilson, p. 231). To one he suggests Jonson's Bobadil (Knight, *Sovereign Flower*, p. 118), to another Falstaff (Charlton, pp. 37-39), to another a Lucio or Thersites (G. K. Hunter, *All's*

Well, p. xxxvii), to another Shakespeare's odious portrait of a Renaissance gentleman on the Italian model (Goddard, II, 44), to another the symbolic values of false nobility and lies (Bradbrook, "Virtue," p. 296).

16. The enormous diversity of critical opinion concerning Helena is, more than any other single factor, responsible for the varied interpretations of the play. In general terms she has been described as despicable, as admirable, and as symbolic. A *"crampon"* (Andrew Lang, *Harper's Magazine*, LXXXV [1892], 213) who "overstep[s] all bounds of female decorum" (John C. Dunlop, *History of Prose Fiction* [London, 1888], II, 86), she "put a man into a position of ignominy quite unbearable, and then plot[ted] with other women to keep him in that position" (John Masefield, *William Shakespeare* [New York, 1911], p. 147). Nobility flawed by "virginal passion" (C. H. Herford, *Shakespeare* [London, n.d.], p. 61), she is both ignoble and debased; her diseased ambition is the driving force in the play (Clifford Leech, "The Theme of Ambition in *All's Well That Ends Well*," *ELH*, XXI [1954], 17-29). She is womanhood degraded, a "keen and unswerving huntress of man" (E. K. Chambers, p. 203); her practice is "so darkly designed and so efficiently executed . . . that it borders on witchery" (Evans, p. 166). On the other extreme, one reads that Helena is noble, submissive, and sacrificial (Kenneth Muir, *Shakespeare's Sources* [London, 1957], pp. 100-101), a clever wench (Lawrence, *Problem Comedies*, p. 38) engaged in a practice with which the audience would be familiar (C. J. Sisson, "Shakespeare's Helena and Dr. William Harvey," *Essays and Studies* [London, 1960], p. 17). Shakespeare's "loveliest character" (S. T. Coleridge, *Lectures on Shakespeare* [New York, 1930], p. 83), preserving a most scrupulous female modesty (William Hazlitt, *Characters of Shakespeare's Plays* [Cambridge, 1915], p. 215), "she is utterly without and above feminine artifice (H. Spencer, p. 295); "the beauty of the character is made to triumph over all" (Anna Jameson, *Shakespeare's Heroines* [London, 1913], p. 109). "The providence of the play" (Edward Dowden, *Shakespeare: His Mind and Art* [New York, 1881], p. 76), Helena involves herself in actions which "are admirable proof of her perfect integrity and fidelity" (William A. Neilson and Charles J. Hill, eds., *The Complete Plays and Poems of William Shakespeare* [Boston, 1942], p. 355). Occasional critics have seen in the heroine an intentional ambiguity by which the dramatist "brings to the surface the wavering balance between the virtues and faults of ordinary human nature" (Walter N. King, "Shakespeare's 'Mingled Yarn'," *MLQ*, XXI [1960], 38; Calderwood, "The Mingled Yarn," p. 64; J. F. Adams, "*All's Well That Ends Well*: The Paradox of Procreation," *SQ*, XII [1961], 261-270). Still

others view Helena symbolically, as "the life force" (Edward L. Hart, "A Mixed Consort: Leontes, Angelo, Helena," *SQ*, XV [1964], 81-82), as "true nobility and truth" (Bradbrook, "Virtue," p. 298), as "a channel, or medium, for the divine or cosmic powers" (Knight, *Sovereign Flower*, p. 156).

17. Calderwood ("Styles of Knowing," p. 277) suggests that Shakespeare, in altering the heroines name from Giletta to Helena, may have been mindful of the Venus and Adonis story which he previously treated poetically. In both cases the heroine, offering love and salvation, is the aggressor. Equally possible—*if* Shakespeare intended her to be ambivalent—is his choice of the name Helen because of its social connotations. See my article "Shakespeare's Nell," *Names*, XVI (1968), 357-361.

18. Helena's confronting Bertram in Florence has been called "pure chance" (Nagarajan, "Structure," p. 22), "chance-directing providence" (Toole, p. 145), "fate" (Goddard, II, 42). But it has also been called intentional (E. K. Chambers, p. 206); Helena "cannot resist forming a plan to *enforce* a return," attempting to take what can only be given (John Russell Brown, *Shakespeare and His Comedies* [London, 1957], pp. 186-188).

19. Ernest Schanzer (*The Problem Plays of Shakespeare* [New York, 1963], pp. 92-93) describes Angelo as "a compendium of the human qualities which Shakespeare most disliked . . . cruelty, ingratitude, perfidy, judicial tyranny, calculated cunning, Pharisaism, humourlessness." A "puritan judge" who becomes "*humanum genus*" by the end of the play (Robert G. Hunter, *Shakespeare and the Comedy of Forgiveness* [New York, 1965], pp. 213, 219) and in whom we see ourselves (F. R. Leavis, "The Greatness of *Measure for Measure*," *Scrutiny*, X [1942], 238), the deputy clearly illustrates the intoxicating nature of power (Goddard, II, 59). "The outstanding trait in his character . . . is cruelty . . . [a cruelty] best demonstrated by the fact that [among all the known bawds in Vienna] he selects Claudio as the victim for the renewed enforcement of the laws against profligacy" (Hanns Sachs, "The Measure in *Measure for Measure*," in *The Creative Unconscious* [New York, 1951], quoted in David Daiches, *Critical Approaches to Literature* [Englewood Cliffs, 1956], p. 349). "This psychological picture, the conflict caused by the regression to the sadistic stage of sensuality, would to us moderns who are concerned with the psychic processes in their immediate and intimate experience, constitute an obsessional neurotic" (Daiches, p. 350). "The embodiment of pure evil" (Walter Pater, *Appreciations* [London, 1910], p. 177), Angelo "seems to suggest symbolically the devil in Everyman" (Toole, p. 194). His pardon and marriage "baffles the strong

indignant claim of justice" (S. T. Coleridge, *Shakespearean Criticism*, I, 113-114). O. J. Campbell contends that the deputy was created as a gull, an object of ridicule to be satirically exposed (p. 124), a view enlarged upon by Murray Krieger, who sees in the character a combination of the neo-classical gull and the romantic villain primed for repentance (p. 782). Hoxie N. Fairchild frankly claims there are two Angelos, the cold, harsh prig of I-II from Whetstone, and the "smooth rascal of II-V resulting from Shakespeare's adaptations" ("The Two Angelos," *SAB*, VI [1931], 55). Arthur Sewell explains the character inconsistency in terms of a primary figure who is never allowed the center of the stage and hence is never permitted adequate sympathetic development (*Character and Society in Shakespeare* [Oxford, 1951], p. 68). The counter view is asserted by W. M. T. Dodds, who describes Angelo as a tragic character "imagined intensely in all his complexity and capacity for serving" ("The Character of Angelo in *Measure for Measure*," *MLR*, XLI [1946], 255). A similar tendency to envision the deputy as something more than one who "enjoys tyrannizing over less successful, more decent men" (H. Spencer, p. 302) is reflected in the comment by John Wassen, describing the character as "the incontinent man" who "might do vicious or unjust deeds" but "is at no time convinced that he ought to pursue his evil desire" ("*Measure for Measure*: A Play of Incontinence," *ELH*, XXVII [1960], 269-270).

20. An occasional critic would dispute this point. For instance, to consider the duke a satiric and moral commentator, a Jonsonian intriguer (Campbell, pp. 124, 133-134), is to prejudge his motive for appointing Angelo. Darrell Mansell, Jr. flatly asserts that Vincentio suspects his deputy when he makes the appointment ("'Seemers' in *Measure for Measure*," *MLQ*, XXVII [1966], 271). The same point is implied by Harold S. Wilson ("Action and Symbol in *Measure for Measure* and *The Tempest*," *SQ*, IV [1953], 379), who observes that for the duke to reveal his plan would lessen the sense of conflict for the spectator.

21. G. Wilson Knight's study (*The Wheel of Fire* [London, 1930], p. 106), describing the play as a New Testament parable in which love and mercy are opposed to justice, is the basis for all succeeding Christian intepretations. The "barbarous old story of *Promos and Cassandra*" has been "turn[ed] . . . into a consistent tale of intercession for sin, repentance from and forgiveness of crime" (R. W. Chambers, p. 306). The most elaborate scheme is set forth by Roy W. Battenhouse ("*Measure for Measure* and the Christian Doctrine of Atonement," *PMLA*, LXI [1946], 1029-1059); the play becomes an allegory of the divine atonement, with Vincentio and Mariana obviously in the key symbolic roles.

With a slightly different emphasis, the play "might be named The Contention between Justice and Mercy, or False Authority Unmasked by Truth and Humility" (Muriel C. Bradbrook, "Authority, Truth, and Justice in *Measure for Measure*," *RES*, XVII [1941], 385). To one, *Measure for Measure* reveals Shakespeare's hostility toward Calvinism, his "sympathy with Roman Catholic institutions" (D. J. McGinn, "The Precise Angelo," *Joseph Quincy Adams Memorial Studies* [New York, 1948]), pp. 129-139); to another, grace is the central issue of the play; "the medieval conception of grace is treated as essential to the maintenance of social order and social well-being" as opposed to the separation of social from spiritual grace in Catholic-Protestant controversy of the time (Raymond Southall, "*Measure for Measure* and the Protestant Ethic," *Essays in Criticism*, XI [1961], 32). This story of "human testing, trial, or assay, seen in relation to God and man" is not a "one-stringed morality" but is "in the tradition of the parables of Christ" (Neville Coghill, "Comic Form in *Measure for Measure*," *Shakespeare Survey 8*, VIII [1955], 18-19). Hermann Ulrici in 1846 anticipated the current archetypal criticism in his comment that the Christian message of the play declares "we are sinners, children of wrath and in need of mercy" (*Shakespeare's Dramatic Art* [London], pp. 310 ff.).

22. J. C. Maxwell calls Escalus the drama's "straightforward representative of moderation and commonsense" ("*Measure for Measure*: 'Vain Pity' and 'Compelled Sins,'" *Essays in Criticism*, XVI [1966], 253), and Charlton speaks of his charity, his "tolerance grown of experience" (p. 256). Through him as counterpart to the corrupted Angelo, Shakespeare stresses the theme of equity (John W. Dickinson, "Renaissance Equity and *Measure for Measure*," *SQ*, XIII [1962], 294-297). Along with the provost, he is the leading exponent of the principle of equity in the play (Robert Hapgood, "The Provost and Equity in *Measure for Measure*," *SQ*, XV [1964], 114).

23. William Empson explores the ambiguities of the play through an elaborate analysis of the levels of meaning in the word *sense* as used in various contexts (*The Structure of Complex Words* [London, 1951], pp. 270-284). L. C. Knights sees "sexual instinct" as the dominant force of this cynical play ("The Ambiguity of *Measure for Measure*," *Scrutiny*, X [1941-42], 223), a view countered by F. R. Leavis, who describes the play as distinguished by a high valuation of life and the moral standards which uphold it (pp. 234-247). Virgil K. Whitaker frankly asserts that the source could not bear the burden of philosophy placed on it by Shakespeare (*The Seventeenth Century* [Stanford, 1951], p. 354).

24. Coghill disagrees: "Lucio gives us reason to think that he knows

all the time who the friar-duke is" ("Comic Form," p. 23); similarly, J. A. Bryant argues that if Lucio did not know the friar's identity, "he has half suspected him all along" (*Hippolyta's View* [Lexington, Ky., 1961], p. 103). See also Mansell, p. 275. Christopher Spencer, on the other hand, argues vigorously that the evidence for Lucio's being aware of the disguise is not persuasive ("Lucio and the Friar's Hood," *ELN*, III [1965-66], 17-21), and J. Dover Wilson asserts that any such "evidence" is the result of a "revising botcher" (The Cambridge Shakespeare, p. 99).

25. Mariana's role has been argued as evidence of the corrupt nature of the text. R. K. Wilson, for example, believes that in the original version of the play, Isabella gave herself to Angelo; the substitution of Mariana is a later addition, "a substitute *denouement*, imitated from *All's Well That Ends Well*" ("The Mariana Plot of *Measure for Measure*," PQ, IX [1930], 342). See also S. Musgrove, "Some Composite Scenes in *Measure for Measure*," SQ, XV (1964), 67-74. To the contrary, Lawrence W. Hyman claims that Mariana, far from being an addition, is vital to the theme of the play. Her entrance brings into focus a vitality for life as the dominant motif, a vitality signaled in Isabella's aceptance of sex from this moment ("Mariana and Shakespeare's Theme in *Measure for Measure*," *University Review*, XXXI [1964-65], 125). Mariana's role is also central to W. W. Lawrence's thesis that the play is a composite of realistic and romantic material; the introduction of Mariana is the pivotal scene in which the "archaisms and improbabilities" characteristic of the traditional story begin to predominate (*Problem Comedies*, p. 79; "*Measure for Measure* and Lucio," SQ, IX [1958], 443-444). See also: Tillyard, p. 123; V. K. Whitaker, *Shakespeare's Use of Learning* (San Marino, 1953), p. 221. Her importance is also primary to the Christian apologists, as a symbol or reflection of the vicarious atonement in the bed switch, the same trick which Brander Matthews finds repulsive (*Shakespeare as a Playwright* [New York, 1913], p. 227) and which leads L. L. Schucking to describe her "ready in a moment to entrap the faithless lover by this union in the dark" (*Character Problems in Shakespeare's Plays* [London, 1922], p. 197). Of course, as Joseph Quincy Adams observes, since Shakespeare himself took advantage of such a betrothal with Anne Hathaway, it is unlikely that he would be condemning Mariana (*A Life of Shakespeare* [Boston, 1923], p. 69). "No question of morals would in those days have arisen, or could have been entertained" (J. O. Halliwell-Phillips, quoted in Adams, p. 69).

26. Elizabeth Marie Pope brands the fifth act "clumsy" and "romantic," an attempt "to do something about that disturbing discrepancy between the concepts of religious mercy and secular justice" ("The Renais-

sance Background of *Measure for Measure*," *Shakespeare Survey 2*, II [1949], 79-80). Paul N. Siegel, on the other hand, sees in the conclusion an appropriate meting out of justice, following "not *lex talionis* but the law of comic justice, a retaliation which makes the audience feel that the punishment has been made to fit the crime and yet that justice has been tempered by mercy" ("*Measure for Measure*: The Significance of the Title," *SQ*, IV [1953], 318). Harold Skulsky, in yet another view, describes the ending of the comedy as a ridiculing of every sane concept of law and justice ("Pain, Law, and Conscience in *Measure for Measure*," *Journal of the History of Ideas*, XXV [1964], 168). At least one critic has described the last act as "brilliant," "providing an amazing exhibition of the actor's art for the part of the duke" (Josephine Waters Bennett, "*Measure for Measure*" as *Royal Entertainment* [New York, 1966], p. 131).

27. Claudio, in his fear of legal punishment, helps the spectator to visualize a portion of Angelo's internal struggle (Skulsky, pp. 161-162). To Miss Bradbrook ("Authority," p. 379), he is a symbol of original sin in his guilt with Juliet. Indeed, in Pater's view, "the many veins of thought which render the poetry of this play so weighty and impressive unite in the image of Claudio" (p. 180).

28. The critical dilemma concerning Isabella is well stated by D. L. Stevenson: "Isabella's chastity cannot at once be Griselda-like and archaic to Lawrence, destroy the plot for Tillyard, and rescue it for Battenhouse" ("Design and Structure in *Measure for Measure*," *ELH*, XXIII [1956], 261). At one extreme, "A Vixen in her Virtue" (Charlotte Lennox, *Shakespeare Illustrated* [London, 1753], p. 78), a "virtue sublimely good at another's expense" (Hazlitt, p. 239), "she is something rancid in her chastity" (Quiller-Couch and Wilson, p. xxx), "lend[ing] her countenance to a dubious intrigue" (J. S. P. Tatlock, "The Chief Problem in Shakespeare," *Sewanee Review* [1916], 142) and submitting to a wedding which is a "scandalous proceeding" (A. C. Bradley, *Shakespearean Tragedy* [New York, 1955], p. 78). Condemned by Johnson in the eighteenth century (Raleigh, p. 80), she is still today described as maliciously suggestive in her comments to Angelo, living by a code of "verbal presumption" rather than of "an intense spiritual dedication" (Charlton, pp. 251, 254). At the other extreme, she is "moral grandeur," "saintly grace" (Jameson, p. 55), "simple," "natural," "unskilled purity" (E. C. Morris, ed., *Measure for Measure*, The Tudor Shakespeare [New York, 1912], p. xiv), "melting tenderness" (William Winter, *Shakespeare on the Stage* [New York, 1911], p. 121); "stainless," "incorruptible," "adorable" (Hamilton Mabie, *Heroines* [New York, 1927], p. 58); "the

heavenly purity of her mind is not even stained with one unholy thought"
(A. W. Schlegal, *A Course of Lectures on Dramatic Art and Literature*
[London, 1946], p. 387). "The first of three splendid women who il-
lumine the dark Third Period" (F. J. Furnivall, quoted in Quiller-Couch
and Wilson, p. 29), "she is a young and inexperienced girl with all the
charm of girlish innocence about her" (Bennett, p. 70). She is the
central character, demonstrating the fallacy of attempting to live by
"an absolute moral standard" (William John Roscelli, "Isabella, Sin, and
Civil Law," *University of Kansas City Review*, XXVIII [1962], 221-223),
reflecting the clash between "high ideals and moral problems" and
"human loyalties and affections" (Schanzer, *Problem Plays*, p. 130)—
even reflecting a Protestant audience which would happily observe her
disillusionment with Catholic vows! (Eileen MacKay, "*Measure for Measure*," *SQ*, XIX [1963], 115-119). See further Lawrence Sargent Hall,
"Isabella's Angry Ape," *SQ*, XV (1964), 157-165.

29. G. K. Hunter has pointed out that Shakespeare intended to imply
Isabella's obsession with legalistic religion at the beginning of the play
through her choice of the strict Franciscan Order of St. Clare ("Six Notes
on *Measure for Measure*," *SQ*, XV [1964], 167-168).

30. "This world of Vienna . . . is a weak world, full of little vanities
and stupidities . . . abundantly human" (Raleigh, pp. 78-79); the "atmosphere of Vienna . . . curls like acrid smoke through all the crannies
of the plot" (Van Doren, p. 190). In the subplot, static characters set off
the dynamically developing main characters (Warren D. Smith, "More
Light on *Measure for Measure*," *MLQ*, XXIII [1962], 321); the grimly
comic scenes underscore the seriousness of moral dissolution within the
city (Derek A. Traversi, "*Measure for Measure*," *Scrutiny*, XI [1942-43],
42). The realistic scenes serve to make us forget the improbabilities of
the main plot (Lawrence, *Problem Comedies*, p. 110). Shakespeare
emphasizes the severity of Claudio's punishment "by providing a realistic
background of professional vice and its punishment" (Bennett, p. 19).
The low characters are universals (William Dunkel, "Law and Equity in
Measure for Measure," *SQ*, XIII [1962], 279) who provide a "teasing" of
the central situation (D. L. Stevenson, *The Achievement of Shakespeare's
"Measure for Measure"* [Ithaca, 1966], p. 16). The Elbow-Pompey-Froth
scene is introduced to show ideal justice at work (Schanzer, *Problem
Plays*, p. 116).

31. "Heaven grant us peace, but not the / King of Hungary's!" (I, ii,
4-5). J. Dover Wilson explains the line as a reference to the "disgraceful"
peace signed between the Holy Roman Emperor and the Turks in 1606,
inferring the necessary late revision (The Cambridge Shakespeare, pp.

104-105). J. W. Lever believes the dialogue "turn[s] upon King James' negotiations for a settlement with Spain, the issues being suitably veiled in view of the censor's objection to the discussion of current political affairs on the stage" (p. xxxi). More recently, J. W. Bennett has found a key in a letter from John Chamberlain involving Queen Anne's brother Ulrich, the duke of Holst or Holstein (pp. 10-11).

32. Lucio, described as "the witty spokesman for the point of view of the professional adepts in vice" (Stevenson, *The Achievement*, p. 15), provides "in his dialogue with the Duke . . . a necessary dramatic counterpoint" (Lever, p. li). A "jester, butt, and intermediary, a cold-blooded lecher, and a kindly, sympathetic friend to both Isabella and Claudio" (Lever, p. xcvi), he coaches Isabella from the sidelines so that "her pleading becomes a theatrical performance . . . in which Lucio is the director" (Bennett, p. 32). Lawrence sees his thesis of disparate halves reflected in this character, who is at first bawdy but sympathetic, but later is merely a comic butt ("*Measure for Measure* and Lucio," p. 444), reflecting the image of those who live solely by social grace (Southall, p. 22). His fate permits "the spirit of comedy [to] join forces with clemency" (Lever, p. xxii), at the same time assuring us that law has been restored in the city (Anthony Caputi, "Scenic Design in *Measure for Measure*," JEGP, LX [1961], 433-434).

33. The caliban of Vienna (Hazlitt, p. 240), Barnardine in his indifference to death is a perfect example of the Stoicism which Friar Lodowick tries to teach Claudio (Mansell, p. 282). As the lost sheep whose pardon gives evidence of the "ultimate extent of Divine Mercy" (Bennett, p. 28), he asserts the "major truth" of the play, "that no man's life was as worthless as to be sacrificed to another's convenience" (Lever, p. xc). While Charlton believes Shakespeare became too fond of his character to behead him (pp. 215-217), Mary Lascelles argues forcefully that the playwright never intended him to die ("*Measure for Measure*" [London, 1953], pp. 109-113). To Toole, Barnardine's refusal to die is the funniest scene in the play (p. 173), and Tillyard calls him "comic just this side of gruesome" (p. 125).

34. Polarized interpretations of the play converge on the character of the duke: at one extreme he is "a *deus ex machina* [and] . . . explanatory chorus" (Lawrence, *Problem Comedies*, p. 92), the "incarnate Lord" (Battenhouse, p. 1053), the force of virtue (Charlton, p. 257), "correspondent with Jesus" (Knight, *Wheel of Fire*, p. 82), "Heavenly Justice and Humility" (Bradbrook, "Authority," p. 386), the "*primum mobile* of the play" (Coghill, "Comic Form," p. 21), temperence (Wassen,

p. 262), the God of the New Testament (Toole, p. 184), a humanitarian ruler (Dunkel, p. 285), a power (Murray, p. 310). At the same time other critics see him controlling a "gray craft-against-vice world" (Mansell, p. 278); as a "motiveless malinger[er]" who "alternatively and arbitrarily bares [his] fangs and turns [his] cheek" as through a fictitious journey he sets a "trap . . . for his good friend and highly commended deputy" (Howard C. Cole, "The 'Christian' Context of Measure for Measure," JEGP, LXIV [1965], 428, 429, 436); a machiavellian strategist co-ordinating absolute power with safe public relations (Norman N. Holland, "Measure for Measure: The Duke and the Prince," Comparative Literature, XI [1959], 16-20), he is an excrescence which ruins the play in his attempts to "throw the odium on his subordinates" (Marco Mincoff, "Measure for Measure: A Question of Approach," Shakespeare Studies, II [1966], 147); he is an ironical providence, using the tactics of cat and mouse (E. K. Chambers, pp. 215-216), an "enigmatic providence" (F. P. Wilson, Elizabethan and Jacobean [Oxford, 1945], p. 117), as he attempts to evade responsibility (Raleigh, p. 158); he is, in short, platitudinous and pompous as he "plunges into a vortex of scheming and intrigue" (H. C. Hart, ed., Measure for Measure, The Arden Shakespeare [London, 1905], quoted in Lawrence, Problem Comedies, p. 83). On the one hand, Vincentio is an interested observer in complete control (Roscelli, p. 221), "present to watch over his dangerous representative, and to avert every evil which could possibly be apprehended" (Schlegal, p. 388); "evil has a line drawn around it . . . Vincentio, unseen and unknown, will see all and know all" (Evans, p. 189). On the other hand, "his infallibility is taxed by his own admission of fault" (Lever, p. 1viii); "neither omnipotent nor omniscient" (Bennett, p. 126), the duke frequently permits the machinations of evil to catch him unprepared (Traversi, p. 58). On the one hand, the duke is ambivalent, a contradiction between his human qualities and his dramatic function (Clifford Leech, "The Meaning of Measure for Measure," Shakespeare Survey 3, III [1950], 69), standing for both "comic irresponsibility and ethical responsibility" (W. Sypher, "Shakespeare as Casuist," Sewanee Review, LXIII [1950], 262-280). On the other hand, Vincentio is modeled directly on James I (Lever, p. xlviii); with "deliberate emphasis on early seventeenth-century Jamesian views" (Stevenson, The Achievement, p. 124), "the Duke . . . was no doubt very like the person Shakespeare and his contemporaries had ideally pictured the new king to be" (Stevenson, "The Role of James I in Shakespeare's Measure for Measure," ELH, XXVI [1959], 200). See further: Louis Albrecht, Neve Untersuchungen in *Shakespeare's Mass für Mass* (Berlin, 1914), p. 82; Bennett, pp. 70, 101; Herbert Howarth, "Shakespeare's Flattery in *Measure for Measure*," *SQ*, XVI (1965), 29-37.

35. As a man primarily concerned with his public image and his reputation (William A. Freedman, "The Duke in *Measure for Measure*: Another Interpretation," *Tennessee Studies in Literature*, IX-X [1964-1965], 31), the "Duke provokes our doubts to the very close"; racking our minds with grief and fear, he makes us "suspect the end which is meant to justify such doubtful means" (Brown, pp. 192-193); see also D. R. C. Marsh, "The Mood of *Measure for Measure*," *SQ*, XIV [1963], 31-38.

36. Clifford Leech attacks the duke for such vacillating on a matter of life and death ("Shakespeare's Comic Dukes," *RES*, V [1964], 110-114). Neville Coghill explains the apparent contradiction as a compositor's error ("The Small Points in *Measure for Measure*," *RES*, XVI [1965], 393-395).

37. On Friar Lodowick's role concerning the bed switch between Isabella and Mariana, see D. Harding, "Elizabethan Betrothals and *Measure for Measure*," *JEGP*, XLIX (1950), 139-158; Ernest Schanzer, "The Marriage-Contracts in *Measure for Measure*," *Shakespeare Survey 8*, VIII (1960), 81-89; S. Nagarajan, "*Measure for Measure* and Elizabethan Proposals," *SQ*, XIV (1963), 115-119.

5. The Comedies of Transformation

1. A few critics have objected to the rapidity with which the obsession develops. E. C. Pettet, for instance, who describes the characters of the romances as "thinner" and "half pasteboard," maintains that Leontes as a character is absurd (*Shakespeare and the Romance Tradition* [London, 1949], pp. 166, 177, 179), and A. Thorndike (*The Influence of Beaumont and Fletcher on Shakespeare* [Worcester, 1901], p. 137) and Arthur Quiller-Couch (ed., *The Winter's Tale* [Cambridge, 1950], p. xxiii) emphasize the implausible motivation. The weight of critical opinion, however, affirms Leontes' dramatic credibility. "The jealousy of Leontes, though rash and irrational, is not unnatural in a hasty and wilful man" (T. Campbell, ed., *Dramatic Works of Shakespeare* [London, 1838], p. lxii; see also Hartley Coleridge, *Essays and Marginalia* [London, 1851], II, 148). His mind is "like a fiery furnace at such a temperature that everything introduced into it—combustible or not—becomes fuel" (Harold C. Goddard, *The Meaning of Shakespeare* [Chicago, 1951], II, 262). Leontes is "a powerfully realistic portrait" (Thomas M. Parrott,

ed., *Shakespeare: Twenty-Three Plays and the Sonnets* [New York, 1938], p. 1011), who "infests the first three acts" (Mark Van Doren, *Shakespeare* [New York, 1939], p. 272), a victim of temporary insanity (A. Symons, ed., *The Henry Irving Shakespeare* [New York, 1890], VII, 320), caused—according to John Ellis—by his sublimated love for Polixenes ("Rooted Affection: The Genesis of Jealousy in *The Winter's Tale*," *CE*, XXV [April 1964], 546; see also P. Siegel, "Leontes a Jealous Tyrant," *RES*, I [1950], 302-307; and R. Trienens, "The Inception of Leontes' Jealousy," *SQ*, IV [1953], 321-326).

2. Leontes' repentance has, of course, been of paramount significance to recent critics of the play. Obsessed in the last plays with the idea of reconciliation (Quiller-Couch, p. xix), "Shakespeare's love intuition . . . was close to, if not identical with, the Christian statement" (G. Wilson Knight, *The Christian Renaissance* [New York, 1962], p. 208). The pattern of Leontes' experience is from prosperity through destruction to repentance (E. M. W. Tillyard, *Shakespeare's Last Plays* [London, 1951], p. 25). "As in Mamillius Leontes died to sin, so Perdita in his new life, and Florizel and Perdita recapitulate Leontes and Hermione, but with a difference, for they represent the positive, redeeming principle spontaneously active, whereas Leontes and Hermione must tread a bitter road to the final understanding" (S. L. Bethell, *"The Winter's Tale": A Study* [London, 1947], p. 76). With its theme of "Grace and Graciousness" (F. Tinkler, "*The Winter's Tale*," *Scrutiny*, V [1937], 344), the play sets forth the "association of human growth, decay, and rebirth with the vital rhythms of nature at large" (F. R. Leavis, *The Common Pursuit* [New York, 1964], p. 180; see also F. Hoeniger, "The Meaning of *The Winter's Tale*," *UTQ*, XX [1950], 11-26). The recognition scenes of the romance supply a "sense of an irresistible power, whether of divine or human agency, making for a providential resolution" (Northrop Frye, "Recognition in *The Winter's Tale*," *Essays on Shakespeare and Elizabethan Drama in Honor of Hardin Craig* [Columbia, Mo., 1962], p. 239). Professor Derek A. Traversi describes the play as a kind of parable of resurrection, healing, and unity (*Shakespeare: The Last Phase* [London, 1954], pp. 189-190), and the extreme archetypal view is expressed by Joseph A. Bryant: Leontes and Mamillius = Judaism, Perdita = true church, Polixenes = the Gentiles, Paulina = St. Paul, Hermione = Christ ("Shakespeare's Allegory: *The Winter's Tale*," *Sewanee Review*, LXIII [1955], 202-222). This view is countered by J. H. P. Pafford, who asserts that it is ridiculous to reduce the play to allegory: "The play is in a pre-Christian era and should therefore not refer to an Emperor of Russia, the betrayal of Christ, Whitsun pastorals, a Puritan singing songs to

hornpipes, a Christian burial custom, or Julio Romano" (ed., *The Winter's Tale* [London, 1963], p. li). For similar reservations against resurrection and myth, see Adrian Bonjour, "The Final Scene of *The Winter's Tale*," *English Studies*, XXXIII (1952), 193-208.

3. As Professor Bethell has observed, Shakespeare obtrudes matters of technique upon the audience. "By deliberately drawing the audience's attention to technique Shakespeare was able to distance his story and to convey a continual reminder that his play was after all only a play" (p. 52).

4. Critics, though not addressing themselves to the one-dimensional quality of her character, have implied as much through their praise of her perfection. She is "never betrayed into the least sign of anger or impatience or resentment, but maintains, throughout, perfect order and fitness and proportion in act and speech" (H. N. Hudson, ed., *The Works of Shakespeare* [London, 1880], p. 21). "Dignity without pride, love without passion, and tenderness without weakness" (Anna Jameson, *Characteristics of Women* [London, 1833], II, 2), she is "in sunshine a butterfly, in misery a martyr" (Hartley Coleridge, II, 148). Her serene dignity raises her above pity (William Neilson and Charles Hill, eds., *The Complete Plays and Poems of William Shakespeare* [Boston, 1942], p. 561). Professor Tucker Brooke approaches my present point more directly in his observation that Shakespeare's modifications of Bellario's role tend to stylize the queen (ed., *Shakespeare's Principal Plays* [New York, 1935], p. 855).

5. Shakespeare has been attacked on this very point by critics who fail to see his concern for comic distancing through a stylized plot. Charlotte Lennox, for instance (*Shakespeare Illustrated* [London, 1753], II, 75), asserts that Shakespeare's adaptation of Greene transformed bad to worse; "we shall find the original much less absurd and ridiculous . . . [Shakespeare] entirely destroys the little probability the Novelist had preserved in the relation." The same condemnation is levelled by Heinrich Bulthaupt (*Dramaturgie der Classiker* [Oldenburg, 1884], II, 378). Jerry H. Bryant ("*The Winter's Tale* and the Pastoral Tradition," *SQ*, XIV [Autumn 1963], 394) is more to the point—that Shakespeare creates an artifice as a comic vehicle for serious matter, using the pastoral tradition to comment "seriously upon the theme of reality and experience and its importance to the conduct of a king." On the same point, see John Lawlor, "*Pandosto* and the Nature of Dramatic Romance," *PQ*, XLI (1962), 113. Bertrand Evans (*Shakespeare's Comedies* [London, 1960], p. 298) calls this scene a critical one which determines whether the play will ultimately turn to tragedy or comedy. While Shakespeare's comic

perspective has long since been firmly established, Evans does appreciate the comic momentum of the scene.

6. This scene vividly illustrates the division between those critics on the one hand who, from the disarming perspective of the armchair, take particular aim at those scenes to which they subjectively object or who absorb themselves in the high seriousness of the theme, and those on the other hand who keep at least one eye on the stage and Shakespeare's comic devices. Mrs. Jameson (II, 75) predictably proclaims the bear scene the worst of all, and Sir Walter Raleigh (*Shakespeare* [London, 1907], pp. 137-138) agrees that the incident is handled recklessly and carelessly, merely an expedient for eliminating Antigonus. G. Wilson Knight (*The Crown of Life* [London, 1947], pp. 101 ff.), equally predictably, insists on the profound solemnity of the event, and in like fashion, Dennis Biggins views the scene with symbolic significance: the bear is an instrument of divine wrath; Antigonus himself, pursued and killed by the gods, symbolizes man degenerated to the level of a beast (" 'Exit Pursued by a Bear': A Problem in *The Winter's Tale*," *SQ*, XIII [Winter 1962], 7). Thomas M. Parrott (*Shakespearean Comedy* [New York, 1962], pp. 385-386) reminds us that Shakespeare's company had the use of a tame bear for a production of *Mucedorus* and that Shakespeare might have taken advantage of what he knew would please the audience. Neville Coghill ("Six Points of Stage-Craft in *The Winter's Tale*," *Shakespeare Survey 11* [Cambridge, 1958], pp. 34-35) confronts the issue directly in his description of the scene as "wildly or grotesquely comic," though he is not concerned with a discussion of the overall artifice of the action.

7. This resurrection has been described both as an afterthought in revision (Hardin Craig, ed., *The Complete Works of Shakespeare* [Chicago, 1951], p. 1217) and as "one of the most effective bits of stage business in Shakespeare" (O. J. Campbell, ed., *The Living Shakespeare* [New York, 1949], p. 1105; see also Francis Fergusson, ed., *Shakespeare's Comedies of Romance* [New York, 1959], p. 16).

8. Quiller-Couch (p. xxiii) calls Shakespeare's mishandling of Leontes' recognition of Perdita the "greatest fault in the play," and Van Doren (p. 279) claims Shakespeare was simply "weary of the plot." Most critics, however, agree that the playwright was thereby attempting to gain dramatic focus on the resurrection scene (see, e.g., G. B. Harrison, ed., *Shakespeare: The Complete Works* [New York, 1948], p. 1432).

9. The act has been branded a lengthy interlude for its own sake by E. K. Chambers, "an exercise in pastoral" (*Shakespeare: A Survey* [London, 1925], p. 299). To others, the act is the second movement in the

structure of the play which Goddard (II, 267) describes as thesis (Corruption), antithesis (Innocence), Synthesis (Atonement); Ernest Schanzer ("The Structural Pattern of *The Winter's Tale*," *RES*, V [April 1964], 73) labels Act IV "the grown daughter," as distinguished from "the father" (I-III) and "the reunion" (V); and Inga-Stina Ewbank ("The Triumph of Time in *The Winter's Tale*," *RES*, V [April 1964], 85) sees Act IV as a "vehicle for the exploration of the meaning of time—in a sense of what time does to man." In perhaps the earliest examination of the play's structure, T. R. Price ("The Construction of 'A Winter's Tale,'" *Shakespeariana* [London, 1890], pp. 195-207) describes the play as a diptych—a tragic followed by a comic element, fused into a whole, a romantic play.

10. Apparently only Professor Bethell has clearly recognized Paulina's comic possibilities in his description of her as a shrewish scold (p. 59). Traditionally, critics speak of her vehement temper (Georg Brandes, *William Shakespeare* [Munich, 1896], p. 924), which personifies Leontes' conscience and prepares us for the resurrection (Knight, *Crown of Life*, p. 115). To A. Mezieres (*Shakespeare, ses oeuvres* [Paris, 1865], p. 428) she "fills the most noble role in the play."

11. Evans (pp. 307, 309) calls Autolycus a manipulator who "insinuates into our minds the comforting idea of a controlling force." He is otherwise described as light-hearted irresponsibility (Pafford, p. ix), a "most admirable rascal (Henry Giles, *Human Life in Shakespeare* [Boston, 1868], p. 199), a "true Artist . . . *musically*, as far as his style of song is concerned" (Alfred Roffe, *A Musical Triad* [London, 1872], p. 14). "Knavery sublimated into play . . . he is like the childlike and elfin half of Falstaff come back to a world freed of all ethical complications—and excess fat" (Goddard, II, 275).

12. Of the broad comic possibilities in this melange of theatrical devices, Bethell comments: "Now it is hard to believe that Shakespeare—even if tired, bored, cynical, in despair and dead drunk at the time—could repeat a crudely amateur device like this 'talking aside' or 'walking before' four times in a few minutes and not intend something by it" (p. 49).

13. Frank Kermode (ed., *The Tempest* [London, 1954], p. liii) sees in Antonio "the operation of sin in a world magically purified but still allowing freedom to the will." Rose A. Zimbardo states flatly that Prospero "has not been able to touch the deeply disordered natures of Antonio and Sebastian" ("Form and Disorder in *The Tempest*, *SQ*, XIV [Autumn 1963], 55). To the contrary, Lawrence E. Bowling observes, "The conversion of Sebastian is indicated by the fact that, whereas he had

originally scorned miracles, he now admits that there are powers beyond the grasp of his realistic faculties" ("The Theme of Natural Order in *The Tempest*," *CE*, XII [January 1951], 208). The various adversaries are brought to reconciliation with the "characters who most closely resemble the audience's attitude" (Northrop Frye, "Nature and Nothing," *Essays in Shakespeare*, ed. Gerald W. Chapman [Princeton, 1965], p. 48).

14. This cathartic dramatic experience has invited extravagant symbolic analysis. Francois-Victor Hugo (*Oeuvres complètes de Shakespeare* [Paris, 1865], II, 87), for example, describes the play as "the supreme denouement, dreamed by Shakespeare, for the bloody drama of Genesis. It is the expiation of the primordial crime." To one critic, the play is an allegory of the history of the church (E. B. Wagner, *Shakespeare's Tempest: An Allegorical Interpretation* [Yellow Springs, Ohio, 1933]); to another it depicts the mystery of redemption, the initiation rites of the Eleusinian adepts (Colin Still, *Shakespeare's Mystery Play: A Study of "The Tempest"* [London, 1921]; *The Timeless Theme* [London, 1936]). "[T]he very essence of the hopes and the aspirations of a new epoch" (E. P. Kuhl, "Shakespeare and the Founders of America: *The Tempest*," *PQ*, XLI [1962], 128), *The Tempest* depicts "The glorious supremacy of the righteous human soul over all things by which it is surrounded" (F. A. Kemble, *Notes upon Some of Shakespeare's Plays* [n.p., 1882]). The narrative is "an exposition of the themes of the Fall [Caliban's nature] and the Redemption [Prospero's art]" (Kermode, p. lxxxiii), "a rebirth, a return to life, a heightened, almost symbolic, awareness of the beauty of normal humanity after it has been purged of evil" (Theodore Spencer, *Shakespeare and the Nature of Man* [New York, 1942], p. 201).

15. Elizabeth Marie Pope (*Paradise Regained: The Tradition and the Poem* [Baltimore, 1947], pp. 70-79) describes the exegetical tradition of the banquet as a symbol of sensual and materialistic desire which must be overcome by the soul committed to God. Certainly Shakespeare is putting this religious significance to dramatic use as Ariel spreads the delicacies before Alonso's eyes moments prior to his spiritual purgation. Kermode (p. 86) recalls similar banquet scenes in *Timon of Athens*, Chapman's *Ovid's Banquet of Sense*, Jonson's *Poetaster*, Milton's *Comus*, and, of course, *Paradise Regained*.

16. If one occasionally feels that the symbolic exegetes possess an overactive imagination, it is even more dangerous to take the opposite tack—that Shakespeare, merely using the materials which came to hand, had no artistic aims in the work (Richard Grant White, *Studies in Shakespeare* [Boston, 1886], p. 27). A wrong done and redressed, reconciliation

and forgiveness—the pattern repeated in the last comedies could hardly be mere coincidence. On the other hand, to envision the characters as merely symbols or pawns which are manipulated to form a parable is to destroy them as credible, interesting, indeed even comic, in the broadest sense of the term.

17. What the critic has made of Prospero—a symbol or a dramatic character—has largely determined the individual interpretation of the play. Goddard (II, 279) flatly asserts that there are two Prosperos, the father and the master; Kermode (p. xlvii), that he has two functions, symbolic and magic. As a symbol, he has been described as the embodiment of the Imagination (James Russell Lowell, *Among My Books* [Boston, 1870], p. 199), as pure Intellect (T. Spencer, p. 198), as Art, a "translation of merit into power" (R. H. West, *The Invisible World* [Athens, Georgia, 1939], p. 42), as the Deity (Edward R. Russell, "The Tempest," *Theological Review* [October 1876], p. 482), as the Vicar of God in his own country, a visible providence" (C. J. Sisson, "The Magic of Prospero," *Shakespeare Survey 11* [Cambridge, 1958], p. 76), as "Destiny itself" (Arthur Quiller-Couch and J. Dover Wilson, eds., *The Tempest* by William Shakespeare [Cambridge, 1921], p. lv) as Christ (Knight, *Crown of Life*, pp. 242-253), as Justice (Derek A. Traversi, "*The Tempest*," *Scrutiny*, XVI [1949], 127-157), as White Magic (English Humanism) (J. Hart, "Prospero and Faustus," *Boston University Studies in English*, II [1956], 197-206), as—like Vincentio but refined—the model of the Christian governor (Harold S. Wilson, "Action and Symbol in *Measure for Measure* and *The Tempest*," *SQ*, IV [1953], 381), as an Italian sorcerer (O. J. Campbell, p. 1158), as the masque presenter (Enid Welsford, *The Court Masque* [New York, 1962], pp. 335 ff.), and as Shakespeare—either making his farewell to the stage (Chambers, p. 309) or providing a lesson to Fletcher (Ferdinand) in proper dramaturgy (E. Dowden, *Shakespeare: His Mind and Art* [London, 1875], p. 901). Conversely, G. L. Kittredge asserts his complete credibility as an Elizabethan magician (ed., *The Tempest* [Boston, 1939], p. xviii); both Charles Cowden Clarke (*Shakespeare's Characters* [London, 1873], p. 279) and Mark Van Doren (p. 286) view him as a strict elder, stern and domineering, and Bernard Knox ("The Tempest and the Ancient Comic Tradition," *English Institute Essays* [1954], pp. 61, 64) sees an irritable old man with a touch of the irascible Plautine *senex*. Whatever he is, he functions as the comic pointer-controller for the stage-world; as Evans (p. 319) remarks, his "mantle, staff, and book . . . are ultimate expressions of lowlier means by which his predecessors held advantage."

18. A persistent critical view insists that Prospero is himself guilty of an infraction of natural order and that he grows in wisdom and the spirit of forgiveness during the course of the play. See, e.g., Clifford Leech, "Shakespeare's Comic Dukes," *RES*, V, ii (April 1964), 113. Victim of his own political mismanagement in Milan, even repeating the same error on the island in his initial sentimentality to Caliban, Prospero has experienced a period of suffering and regeneration (Bowling, pp. 204, 207). Like Sycorax, he has been cast upon the island as a result of the misuse of his power (Allan H. Gilbert, "*The Tempest*: Parallelism in Characters and Situations," *JEGP*, XIV [1915], 64). To one critic, he is tempted to forgiveness by Ariel (Goddard, II, 283); to another, his daughter approaching marriage with Ferdinand prompts him to intensive self-examination (Conrad Hillberry, "*The Tempest*: Act IV," *CE*, XXIII [April 1962], 587).

19. The more fantastic the story, the more it must be balanced and disciplined by stringent adherence to the dramatic unities and the Neo-Terentian act structure (Zimbardo, p. 50). Prospero and his subordinates, Ariel and Caliban, suggest the Latin master-slave relationship, the stock classical comic characters (Knox, p. 54). As Peter Alexander observes, the exotic and mysterious Bermudas would lead the audience to expect unusual characters and events, "a wonderful but not incredible plot" (*Introductions to Shakespeare* [New York, 1964], p. 54).

20. David L. Frost (*The School of Shakespeare* [Cambridge, 1968]) has recently observed that Shakespeare's final plays are "regulated by a Divine Providence, which may permit a limited evil or mischance, but which guides events toward human reconciliation and married peace" (p. 212). Beaumont and Fletcher lack such control, "smuggl[ing] in their ragbag of dramatic odds and ends under the cover of Shakespeare's popular stage romances" (p. 227).

21. *Compendio* was first published separately in 1601 and was appended to *Il Pastor Fido* in 1602. The translation is from Madeleine Doran, *Endeavors of Art: A Study of Form in Elizabethan Drama* (Madison, 1954), p. 205.

Index

Charlton, H. B., 3, 11, 193, 195, 196, 202, 203, 208, 213, 216, 220, 222, 224

Chaucer, Geoffrey, 50, 51–54, 57, 58, 59, 199; "The Knight's Tale," 50, 51, 52, 54, 59, 199, 200

Clarke, Charles Cowden, 232

Coghill, Neville, 3, 220, 224, 226, 229

Cole, Howard C., 225

Coleridge, Hartley, 197, 226, 228

Coleridge, S. T., 202, 215, 217, 219

Collier, J. P., 198, 199, 202

Comedy of Errors, The, 3, 4, 5, 9, 11, *13–24*, 25, 38, 39, 41, 43, 45, 47, 48, 61, 94, 167, 191–193; experimental nature of the comic structure, 13, 21, 46–47; framing device as comic pointer, 22–24, 193; level of the characterization, 13–14, 191, 192, 193; stylized action, 17–21, 191, 192, 193

Comic form, the classical and medieval traditions, 3–5, 10–11, 189, 190

Commins, Saxe, 210

Compendio (Guarini), 233

Comus (Milton), 231

Craig, Hardin, 191, 195, 200, 201, 202, 206, 215, 227, 229

Craig, W. J., 193, 196

Craik, T. W., 208

Crane, Milton, 211

Cunliffe, J. W., 205

Cutts, John P., 201

Cymbeline, 97, *98–99*

Daiches, David, 218

Danby, John F., 194

Day, John, 184, 211

Dent, R. W., 201

Devil Is an Ass, The (Jonson), 192

Diana (Montemayor), 51

Dickenson, John W., 220

Dido, Queen of Carthage (Marlowe), 50

Discovery of Witchcraft, The (Scot), 50

Dodds, W. M. T., 219

Donatus, Aelius, 3

Donne, John, 194

Doran, Madeleine, 201, 212, 233

Dowden, Edward, 193, 217, 232

Downer, Alan S., 211

Dramatic characterization, 7–11; in Aristophanes, 5, 6; in Terence and Plautus, 6, 7; in pre-Shakespearean drama, 7

Drayton, Michael, 50; "Nymphidia," 50

Drinkwater, John, 196

Dunkel, William, 223, 225

Dunlop, John C., 217

Dyskolos (Menander), 11

Edinburgh Review, 201, 205

Elliott, G. R., 192

Ellis, John, 227

Elyot, Thomas, 194; *The Book of the Courtyer*, 203

Empson, William, 220

Evans, Bertrand, 4, 192, 193, 196, 201, 203, 205, 208, 215, 216, 217, 225, 228, 230, 232

Evans, D. A., 205

Evans, Ifor, 199

Ewbank, Inga-Stina, 230

Fairchild, Hoxie N., 219

Farmer, Richard, 215

Feldman, A. Bronson, 193

Fergusson, Francis, 203, 207, 210, 229

Ffarrington, William, 89, 209

Fisher, P., 198

Fleay, F. G., 198, 199, 200, 202

Fletcher, George, 204

Fletcher, John 184, 226, 232, 233; *The Island Princess*, 184; *The Loyal Subject*, 184; *Philaster*, 184

Foakes, R. A., 191

Freedman, William A., 226

Fripp, E. I., 199

Frost, David L., 233

Frye, Northrop, 4, 8, 189, 194, 227, 231

Furness, H. H., 199, 202

Furnivall, F. J., 197, 223

Gaw, Allison, 192, 202

Generosa, Sister M., 199

Gervinus, G. G., 195, 211

Gilbert, Allan, 207, 233

Gildon, Charles, 205
Giles, Henry, 204, 210, 230
Goddard, Harold C., 191, 195, 196, 198, 203, 204, 211, 213, 217, 218, 226, 230, 232, 233
Goldsmith, Robert H., 216
Gollancz, Israel, 51, 199, 210, 215
Gordon, D. J., 205, 206, 207
Gordon, George, 204
Gorgeous Gallery of Gallant Inventions, A, 51
Greene, Robert, 25, 50, 194, 228; *James IV*, 50; *Pandosto: The Triumph of Time*, 164
Guarini, J. F., 184; *Compendio*, 233; *Il Pastor Fido*, 233
Gulick, Sidney, 190, 204
Gupta, S. K. Sen, 3, 196

Hall, Lawrence Sargent, 223
Halliwell-Phillips, J. O., 198, 199, 208, 221
Hapgood, Robert, 212, 216, 220
Harbage, Alfred, 3, 202
Harding, D., 226
Harris, B., 191, 192, 197, 198
Harrison, G. B., 195, 197, 199, 200, 204, 212, 229
Hart, Alfred, 212
Hart, Edward L., 218
Hart, H. C., 225
Hart, J., 232
Hartley, Lodwick, 205
Harvey, William, 217
Hathaway, Anne, 221
Hazlitt, William, 200, 207, 217, 222, 224
Henry IV, 1, 2, 62
Herford, C. H., 217
Heywood, John, 6
Heywood, Thomas, 211
Hill, Charles J., 191, 200, 201, 206, 217, 228
Hillberry, Conrad, 233
Hockey, Dorothy C., 206
Hoeniger, F. D., 212, 227
Holland, Norman N., 210, 211, 225
Hollander, John, 210
Holleran, James P., 201
Hosley, Richard, 201
Hotson, Leslie, 210, 216

Howarth, Herbert, 226
Hudson, H. N., 197, 201, 228
Hugo, Francois-Victor, 231
Hunter, G. K., 212, 216, 223
Hunter, Joseph, 210
Hunter, R. G., 4, 190, 205, 209, 218
Huon of Bordeaux, 50
Hyman, Lawrence W., 221

Inchbald, Elizabeth, 204
Island Princess, The (Beaumont and Fletcher), 184

James (king of England), 108, 184, 224, 225
James IV (Greene), 50
James, R. A., 210
Jameson, Anna B., 204, 217, 222, 228, 229
Jenkins, Harold, 208, 209
Johnson, Samuel, 209, 213, 214, 222
Jonson, Ben, 3, 8, 24, 108, 183, 184, 185, 189, 192, 215, 216, 219, 231; *The Devil Is an Ass*, 192; *Poetaster*, 231
Jorgensen, Paul, 206

Kemble, F. A., 231
Kempe, Will, 216
Kermode, Frank, 198, 230, 231, 232
King, W. N., 204, 217
Kittredge, G. L., 209, 232
Knight, Charles, 198
Knight, G. Wilson, 4, 215, 216, 218, 219, 224, 227, 229, 230, 232
"Knight's Tale, The," 50, 51, 52, 54, 59, 199, 200
Knights, L. C., 210, 220
Knollys, William, 89, 210
Knox, Bernard, 232, 233
Kökeritz, Helge, 206
Krapp, G. L., 216
Kreyssig, F., 206, 208
Krieger, Murray, 215, 219
Kuhl, E. P., 231

Laguardia, E., 214
Lamb, Charles, 210
Lang, Andrew, 204, 205, 217
Lascelles, Mary, 224
Latham, Minor White, 200
Law, R. A., 197

Lawlor, John, 189, 228
Lawrence, W. W., 214, 216, 217, 221, 223, 224, 225
Leavis, F. R., 218, 220, 227
Leech, Clifford, 209, 217, 225, 226, 233
Lennox, Charlotte, 222, 228
Lever, J. W., 213, 224, 225
Love's Labour's Lost, 9, 13, 20, 24, *40–46*, 61, 67–68, 205; Boyet and Biron as comic pointers, 45–46; level of the characterization, 42–45; significance of the subplot to the comic perspective, 46–47; structural similarities to *Much Ado about Nothing*, 42; structural similarities to *The Two Gentlemen of Verona*, 41
Love's Labour's Won, 202, 215
Lowell, James Russell, 232
Lowes, John L., 212
Loyal Subject, The (Beaumont and Fletcher), 184
Lyly, John, 4, 25, 194

Mabie, Hamilton, 222
MacCracken, H. N., 205
McGinn, D. J., 220
Mackay, Eileen, 223
Malone, Edmund, 51
Mankind, 192
Mansell, Darrell, 219, 221, 224, 225
Marlowe, Christopher, *Dido, Queen of Carthage*, 50
Marsh, D. R. C., 226
Marston, John, 108, 183
Martin, Helena, 208
Masefield, John, 194, 196, 217
Matthews, Brander, 203, 221
Maxwell, J. C., 220
Meader, W., 205
Measure for Measure, 11, 45, 97, 99, 108, *128–153*, 155, 184, 189, 212, 213, 214, 215, 216 218–226, 232; Angelo as a character of transformation, 128–137, 218, 219; character development in Isabella and Claudio, 137, 222, 223; function of Lucio, 142–145, 220, 221, 224; parodic subplot (Pompey, Mistress Overdone, Elbow), 138–142, 223;

Vincentio as major comic pointer, 146–152, 224, 225, 226; structural flaws, 152–153; thematic and structural similarities to *All's Well That Ends Well*, 99, 137–138, 152–153, 155, 212, 213
Menander, 5; *Dyskolos*, 11
Merchant of Venice, The, 24, 62–65, 74, 81; character development in Antonio, 64–65; character development in Bassanio and Portia, 63–64; multiple strands of plot, 62–63
Merchant, W. Modwyn, 197, 202
Merry Wives of Windsor, The, 3, 24, *61–62;* Falstaff as a comic butt, 61–62; level of the characterization, 61–62
Messiaen, M., 206
Metamorphoses (Ovid), 50
Meuschke, M., 204
Meuschke, P., 204
Mezieres, A., 230
Midsummer-Night's Dream, A, 9, 11, 13, 24, 26, 27, 38, *47–59*, 62, 108, 197–202; "The Knight's Tale" as source, 51–54, 57–59, 199, 200, 201, 202; level of the characterization, 47–50, 197; Shakespeare's major achievement in situation comedy, 47, 198, 199; structure, 50–59, 198, 199
Milton, John, 194, 231; *Comus*, 231; *Paradise Regained*, 231
Mincoff, Marco, 225
Miracle plays, 6, 21
Montaigne, M. E., 197
Montemayor, Jorge de, 51; *Diana*, 51
Morality plays, 6, 190, 220
Morris, E. C., 222
Mouffet, Thomas, *The Silke-Wormes and Their Flies*, 51
Mucedorus, 229
Much Ado about Nothing, 7, 9, 11, 20, 24, 42, *67–81*, 190, 202–208; character development in Benedick and Beatrice, 67–74, 204, 205; function of Dogberry and Verges, 74, 77–78, 207; Leonato, Don Pedro, Claudio, and Hero as minor comic pointers, 74, 78–80, 205, 206; significance of the melodra-

Harvard Paperbacks